John Fullerton is a 33-year-old British journalist who spent two-and-a-half years covering the Afghan conflict from Peshawar in Pakistan. He ventured into Afghanistan several times with the guerillas and contributed regularly to the *Far Eastern Economic Review, The Daily Telegraph, The Economist,* "Voice of America" and the BBC's Eastern Service. He now works for Reuters and lives in Hong Kong.

Published by Far Eastern Economic Review Ltd.,
Centre Point, 181, Gloucester Road, Hong Kong.

Printed by Yee Tin Tong Printing Press Ltd,
Tong Chong Street, Quarry Bay, Hong Kong.

ISBN 962-10-0020-3

This book is dedicated to the memory of Afghans who have died fighting for their faith and country

Contents

Illustrations follow page 112

Cover photograph by courtesy of the United States Information Agency

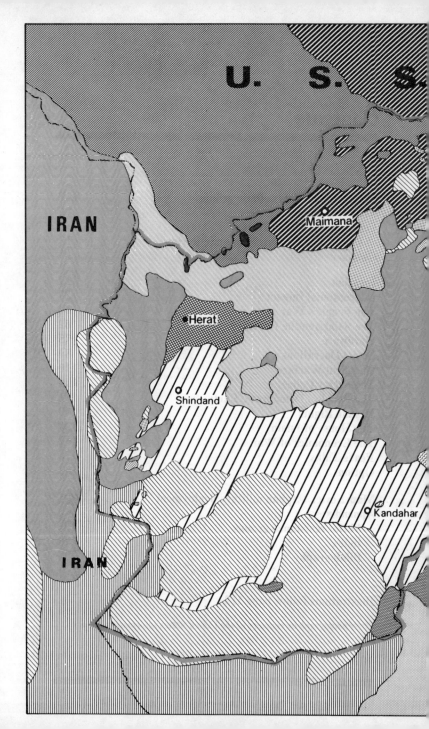

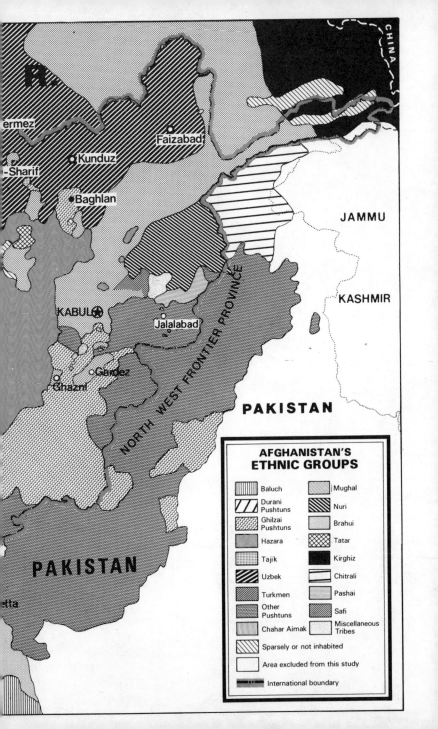

AFGHANISTAN'S
ETHNIC GROUPS

Baluch		Mughal
Durani Pushtuns		Nuri
Ghilzai Pushtuns		Brahui
Hazara		Tatar
Tajik		Kirghiz
Uzbek		Chitrali
Turkmen		Pashai
Other Pushtuns		Safi
Chahar Aimak		Miscellaneous Tribes

Sparsely or not inhabited

Area excluded from this study

International boundary

THE SOVIET OCCUPATION OF
AFGHANISTAN

JOHN FULLERTON

FAR EASTERN ECONOMIC
review

Acknowledgements

I would like to thank spokesmen of the Afghan resistance for their help, including Haji Mangal Hussein of Hezb-i-Islami (Hekmatyar), Sharafat of Hezb-i-Islami (Yunis Khalis), Dr. Najibullah, Engineer Rahim and Massoud Khalili of Jamiat-i-Islami, Hashmatullah Mojadeddi of the Afghan National Liberation Front (ANLF), Dr. Azizullah Lodin of Harakat Inquilab-i-Islami, Dr. Raheen and Hassan Gailani of the National Islamic Front of Afghanistan (NIFA) and Engineer Nawab of the Islamic Alliance.

Syed Fazle Akbar of the Afghan Information and Documentation Centre, Professor Rasul Amin, Abdullah Khan of the North West Frontier Refugee Commission, Azmat Hayat Khan of Peshawar University's Central Asian Studies Centre and Habibullah Karzai, former diplomat and chief of the Popolzais, provided much material.

I would like to express my gratitude to Professor Barhouddin Majrooh, Director of the Afghan Information Centre, without whose monthly Bulletin this book would have been all the poorer. My thanks also to Alain Coat of the UNHCR, David Delapraz of the International Committee of the Red Cross (ICRC), Mr. Sethi of the Press and Information Department in Islamabad, Walli Khan of the banned National Democratic Party (NDP) and to fellow correspondents and colleagues, including Tony Davis, Oliver Roy, Edward Girardet, David Kline, Aernout van Linden, Selig Harrison, Wilhelm Dietl, Ken Guest, Dominique Vergos, Alain Guillo, Peter Jouvenal, Pierre Issot-Sergent and Brian Williams of Reuters.

Derek Davies, editor of the Far Eastern Economic Review, showed remarkable patience and enthusiasm for this project. Douglas and Ellen Davidson of the US Information Service (USIS) provided me with hospitality and sumptuous isolation in which to write the first draft. My wife Romey gave me not only her support but much-needed professional advice and research.

Peshawar 1983.

Foreword

In 1838, Lord Auckland, Governor-General of India, issued a manifesto of intent from Simla, the Himalayan hill station of the British Raj. He stated the British intention of restoring to the throne of Afghanistan the "exiled and rightful" king, Amir Shah Shuja-ul-Mulk, a weak and unpopular monarch deposed three decades previously and since then a pensioned guest of the British in India. The British had determined on this course of action having been wrongly persuaded that the man who had deposed Shah Shuja, Dost Mohammed, was ill fitted for his responsibility and that he and his followers were untrustworthy allies.

In fact the British surmised — almost certainly wrongly — that Dost had thrown in his hand with expansionary imperial Russia, whose empire in Asia was growing (mostly at the expense of China) even faster than Britain's. The Russians were suspected of nursing designs on India in their continuous search not only for new lands but for warm water ports. British suspicions were fed by reports from a motley but courageous collection of agents and spies who played the "Great Game," with the goal of divining the mysterious intentions of the Tsar. Nowhere were these more enigmatic than in Afghanistan and its unfathomable capital, Kabul, lying strategically between India, due to become the brightest star in the British imperial crown, and the British presence (and ambitions) in the Middle East.

Having announced their intention of replacing one ruler with their own unworthy candidate, the British duly set off the following year. About 9,000 mixed troops under British command and 6,000 sepoys of Shah Shuja formed the Army of the Indus, a force accompanied by a monstrous caravan of 38,000 non-combat personnel — wives, families, servants and other camp followers, they and their supplies carried by 30,000 camels. Encountering little resistance, they ceremoniously restored Shah Shuja to his throne in Kabul on August 6, 1839.

All seemed well. Dost himself actually surrendered to the garrison, which admired him as much as it despised the man they had installed in his place. But over the next two years a sense of uneasiness set in; the natives were hardly friendly and the force was very isolated, the escape route back to India lying across forbidding mountainous passes to Jalalabad and on through the Khyber to Peshawar and the plains beyond. Their fears proved all too correct. In November 1841, rioting Afghans stormed the home of the British Resident and hacked him and his companions to pieces. As the British hesitated, what had started as a riot ballooned into general insurrection. The British had lost all stomach for a fight. They negotiated what was for the then triumphant imperialists a humiliating treaty: in return for Dost's return, the British were to be allowed safe, escorted passage back to India.

In the bitter cold of an Afghan January, 16,500 troops and camp followers struggled out of their cantonment and began a terrible nine-day retreat through the high, snow-bound passes. Time after time the Afghan cavalry swept down from the surrounding mountains and wreaked slaughter on the unwieldy columns, which the tribesmen (much better marksmen than the average British infantryman, and armed with long-muzzled *jezails* which easily outranged the British muskets) used for target practice. At the end, only one man survived: no, not Harry Flashman, but an army doctor who miraculously reached the Jalalabad fortress on the back of an exhausted pony.

The British soon returned to exact revenge; Dost returned to the throne, thereafter to prove himself a good friend. The Great Game continued, and the British had to fight another Afghan war 40 years later. But the country of proud and fiercely nationalistic tribesmen never fell completely under the yoke of the Raj. Afghanistan, still enigmatic, still spied upon, still racked with intrigue and internecine tribal wars, continued to provide a buffer between the contending empires.

In the first volume, *Heaven's Command*, of the magnificent trilogy *Pax Britannica*, James (now Jan) Morris tells the above story of the doomed British expedition and describes how, in 1960, he retraced the bloody footsteps of the beleaguered British columns from Kabul to Jalalabad. He found the Afghan feats of arms still fresh in tribesmen's memories as they pointed out scenes of their families' exploits. He asked one patriarch what would happen now, if a foreign army invaded Afghanistan. "The same," he hissed between the last of his teeth.

If history never exactly repeats itself, it is largely true, as Hegel said, "that people and governments never have learned anything from history, or acted on principles deduced from it." For, when the Soviet armies swept into Afghanistan in 1979 on what Christians celebrate as Christmas Eve, their object was the same as that of the Raj before them — to subdue the Afghans and ultimately to impose on them a new ruler — ex-KGB agent Babrak Karmal.

Reportedly some elements of the Soviet hierarchy were against the adventure (notably the KGB itself), just as many British (including the directors of the East India Company and the Duke of Wellington himself) were horrified by news of the 1838 manifesto of intent. Similar hypocrisies accompanied both invasions: the British claimed they would restore Shah Shuja and "support him against foreign interference and factious opposition" and that, once he was "secured in power and the independence and integrity of Afghanistan established," the British Army would be withdrawn. The Russians made similar pledges about withdrawal after Afghan independence (that is, subservience) had been established, claiming that their invasion was a "limited contingent" in response to repeated requests for assistance from Kabul.

Why the Kremlin decided to move, risking and duly receiving grave censure not only from China and the West but from most of the Islamic world, from most of the Non-aligned Movement, from the members of the Association of Southeast Asian Nations (already nervous of Vietnam's growing closeness with Moscow) and from many fellow communists for whom this act of blatant imperialism proved the last straw, is still the subject of conjecture.

In this book, John Fullerton argues that the invasion was not part of any grand design, in no way a natural sequel to Tsarist expansionism. Nor does he believe that it was a deliberate acquisition of a beachhead from which the West's sources of energy could be threatened. He argues that Moscow had convinced itself that it must intervene to prevent a humiliating collapse of the Marxist (but unsatisfactorily subservient) regime of Hafizullah Amin, who had himself overthrown and murdered his revolutionary predecessor, Nur Mohammad Taraki.

Many other theories have been propounded to explain the Soviet action; I accept the Fullerton thesis. Just as they cannot allow Poland to go free today, the Russians could not afford to countenance the loss of a newly-acquired colony of their empire, any more than could the nineteenth-century Raj. I believe also that the Kremlin mistakenly attributed similarly imperialist attitudes to the overly-idealistic administration of Jimmy Carter, however obvious his desire for detente and Salt II. Moscow simply could not believe that Washington would not move into Iran to rescue the hostages then held in the American Embassy in Tehran. Thus, on top of the necessity of preserving the regime in Kabul, the strike was a pre-emptive measure against an expected US move against neighbouring Iran.

For the moment, their ruthlessness has prevailed. They are paying the price in blood, equipment and morale in Afghanistan, as John Fullerton reports so graphically. Triumphantly, however, they have not forfeited the backing of their closest friends, even in the Subcontinent. India has made its displeasure known in the most mealy-mouthed terms, referring to "intervention" and "interference" rather than "invasion" and "occupation" and farcically welcoming the puppets from Kabul as representatives of their nation at the Non-aligned summit in Delhi in March, 1983.

A body of opinion, led by American scholar Selig Harrison and another former *Far Eastern Economic Review* correspondent Lawrence Lifschultz, argues that the chances of a negotiated settlement involving the withdrawal of the Soviet occupation forces are good. Part of this case is based on the original reports that the KGB was against the invasion and that, now the former KGB chief, Andropov, wields power in the Kremlin, the Moscow factions advocating withdrawal are stronger. I suspect that such reports (like those leaked to the Western press that Andropov was no monster, but a liberal, jazz-loving sophisticate) are simply typical pieces of KGB misinformation, designed to weaken the resolve of the Afghans, of Pakistan and of all those who support the Afghans in their war of liberation.

Future historians will answer the speculation about the Kremlin's real motives, and will chart whether the Red Army is doomed to suffer the same humiliating defeat as was suffered by their British predecessors. In the meantime this book, written as a result of the years John Fullerton spent based in Peshawar reporting on Pakistan and Afghanistan for the *Far Eastern Economic Review*, is the best possible account of the latest colonial rape of a proud nation, and of how that nation is fighting back.

Derek Davies,
Editor,
Far Eastern Economic Review.

16

Glossary

AFV	Armoured fighting vehicle
APC	Armoured personnel carrier
ashrar	Gangsters, bandits — the term used by Kabul and Moscow to refer to the Afghan resistance.
Basmachi	Violators, rebels — the name given to the Central Asian uprising against Moscow in the 1920s. While the Soviets still refer to the Basmachi, the pejorative sense has disappeared for most Muslims and it is now synonymous with "freedom fighter."
GRU	Soviet military intelligence.
Hajj	The annual pilgrimage to Mecca, an event of the greatest importance to Muslims.
hezb	Party, hence Hezb-i-Islami or Islamic Party.

Ikhwan	Shorthand for the Ikhwan-i-Muslime or Muslim Brotherhood, an international movement dedicated to the establishment of a revolutionary Islamic order.
jabha	Front, as in battle-front or the Afghan National Liberation Front (ANLF).
jamiat	Society. Hence Jamiat-i-Islami Afghanistan, or Jamaat Islami Pakistan.
jehad	Religious struggle, just war implying a self-sacrifice and submission to God.
jirga	Traditional assembly of elders, the established manner of arriving at a decision by democratic means in tribal society.
kafir	Unbeliever. Communists fall into this category, while Christians are regarded as "people of the Book."
Khad	Acronym for Khidamate Aetilaati Daulati or literally, state information services, but in fact Kabul's security and intelligence service, formerly known as AKSA and before that, as KAM.
Khalq	The "Masses" faction of the ruling People's Democratic Party in Kabul, which is Pushtun, provincial, in the majority but out of favour.
khan	Denotes family or tribal authority among Pushtuns, often inherited or conferred by official patronage.
makaz	Guerilla camp or base, usually of a primitive and improvised nature, such as a shepherd's hut.
Mujehad	A warrior of the *jehad*, but not necessarily someone who bears arms. Literally it means one who struggles or sacrifices himself for his faith. Pl.: *Mujehadeen*.
malik	Tribal elder elected to a position of local responsibility.

mullah	Local parish priest, a conservative figure with little or no formal training and a controversial role in the *jehad*.
MVD	Soviet Internal Affairs (security) troops.
Parcham	The "Flag" faction of the PDPA which is Dari-speaking, pro-Soviet and predominant, but in the minority in the Communist Party.
Pir	Saint, a hereditary title.
Pushtu/Pukhtu	The language of the Pushtun/Pukhtun tribes living in southern and eastern Afghanistan. The "sh" denotes the softer vowels used in the south, the "kh" the northern dialects also spoken in Pakistan's North West Frontier Province.
Pushtunwalli	The Honour Code of the Pushtun tribes: a democratic yet strict code of conduct embracing hospitality, vengeance, courtesy towards women and unarmed guests or travellers, and blood feuds directed mainly against a first cousin, the natural family rival.
Reydoviki	Soviet term for Moscow's equivalent of the US Rangers.
shabnama	Nightletters, or underground literature.
shaheed	Martyred, killed in the *jehad* by the atheist enemy, ensuring the Muslim a special place in heaven.
Shuravi	Afghans' term for Russians.
ulaswal	District, usually used to refer to local government office.
ushr	Islamic tax on agricultural producers.
Vysotniki	Soviet special forces, Moscow's version of Britain's Special Air Service (SAS).
zakat	Islamic tax on income.

mullah — Local parish priest; a conservative figure with little or no formal training and a controversial role in the jehad.

MVD — Soviet Internal Affairs (security) troops

Parcham — The "Flag" faction of the PDPA which, supporting, pro-Soviet and predominant, but in the minority in the Communist Party

Pir — Saint; a hereditary title

Pushtu, Pukhtu — The language of the Pushtun/Pukhtun tribes living in southern and eastern Afghanistan. The "sh" denote the softer vowels used in the south (ie. "sh" in the north and dialect; also spoken in Pakistan - North West Frontier Province.

Pushtunwali — The Human Code of the Pushtun tribes; a democratic yet strict code of conduct embracing hospitality, vengeance, courtesy towards women and unstinted guests or travellers, and blood feuds directed usually against a first cousin, the natural family rival.

revduzil — Soviet term for Moscow's equivalent of the US Rangers

skhanana — Intelligentsia; of underground literature

shaheed — Martyred; killed in the jehad by the atheist enemy; ensuring the Muslim a special place in heaven

shuravi — Afghan; term for Russians

uluswal — District usually used to refer to local government office

ushr — Islamic tax on agricultural products

Tsanduki — Soviet special forces; Moscow's version of Britain's Special Air Service (SAS)

zakat — Islamic tax on income

20

Invasion

S peed and surprise were the essential ingredients of the Soviet military invasion of Afghanistan. On Christmas Eve, 1979, units of the "special assignment" 105th Guards Airborne Division seized Kabul airport in an operation lasting less than five hours. This opened the way for about 280 individual transport aircraft, a massive airlift bringing in the rest of the division as well as paratroopers from the 103rd and 104th Divisions.

As these elite troops in their distinctive blue berets and striped jumpers rushed on the capital, the first of four motorized rifle divisions — the 357th, 66th, 360th and 201st — rolled across the country's northern borders and sped south, covered by several squadrons of Mig-21 and Mig-23 aircraft. A special KGB "hit squad" in Afghan Army uniforms assaulted the city's Darulaman Palace, gunning down the country's communist leader, Hafizullah Amin, and his immediate family.

In military jargon, the Soviets had successfully mounted a "vertical envelopment": the use of paratroopers to seize a bridge-head from the air and to hold it until ground forces link up with them. By January 1, 1980, there were nearly 40,000 Soviet combat troops in the country and less than three weeks later the figure had doubled. The Soviets' 40th Army headquarters was established in the Tajbek Palace in Kabul. It was a fait accompli, or so it seemed at the time. In fact the Soviets were involved in fighting the guerillas even as they sought to establish bases and communications.

Western correspondents were rapidly on hand to report the event. One reporter was handed an automatic rifle by Soviet troops as he joined a supply convoy braving occasional sniper fire on its way down the Salang highway from the Soviet border. Another newsman described the "bizarre" situation: "A journalist in a taxi can be waved on by soldiers, slide around a couple of bends beneath high banks of snow, and in a few minutes be halted by half a dozen

Afghan guerillas . . ."

For Western politicians it was the first time the Red Army had intervened directly outside the "traditional sphere of influence" in Eastern Europe. They dubbed the invasion an extension of the "Brezhnev doctrine," an allusion to the Soviet takeover of Czechoslovakia in 1968.

Surprise was achieved at all levels. The Soviets employed deception to neutralise any possible opposition from the Afghan armed forces. Russian advisers persuaded Afghan commanders to recall their armoured units for technical modifications. Tanks from two key Afghan divisions were immobilised in workshops with their engines in pieces when the invasion began. Other Afghan units were having their vehicles "winterised" and an inventory taken of their anti-tank weapons and ammunition.

Mobilisation procedures were kept to a minimum to give as little warning as possible to the West. But they could hardly have picked a worse time for weather. They experienced great difficulties surmounting the combined obstacles of weather, terrain, blown bridges and local resistance. During the first two weeks of December some 1,500 advisers and specialist troops were quietly slipped into Kabul. These are believed to have included military intelligence (GRU) "diversionary battalions" — units used as pathfinders in the invasion of Czechoslovakia 11 years before.

Politically, the Soviets chose a time in which the immediate costs of invasion would be minimised. While the Americans were distracted by the hostage crisis in Iran and the presence of a Soviet combat brigade in Cuba, the Soviets timed the Afghan invasion to coincide with a new "low" in their relations with both Washington and Peking. NATO countries had agreed in principle to deploy 572 new medium-range missiles in Europe to match Soviet nuclear superiority in the theatre, while President Carter had decided to go ahead with the controversial MX and Trident strategic nuclear systems. Peking had not started to arm Afghan guerillas, but its incursion into Vietnam poured cold water on Moscow's hopes for a normalisation of Sino-Soviet relations. The Russians were also concerned about the American naval build-up in the Eastern Mediterranean following the November 4 seizure of American Embassy staff in Tehran. Moscow tried to keep the hostage crisis on the boil by offering the Ayatollah Khomeini unspecified "support" in the event of American military intervention.

The invasion used lessons learned in Hungary in 1956 and in Czechoslovakia. In the case of Budapest, the Soviets withdrew their divisions to reinforce the impression of a climb-down from confrontation, while in Czechoslovakia in 1968 Warsaw Pact manoeuvres covered invasion preparations. By contrast, world opinion over the Polish crisis removed the element of surprise and the Soviets could not assume that they would not face opposition from Polish military forces in the event of a Soviet assault.

Afghans first heard the voice of their new leader, Babrak Karmal, on pre-recorded tapes broadcast on December 27 from Termez in Soviet Central Asia on Kabul Radio's wavelength. The announcement was followed seven hours later in the early hours of December 28 by Kabul Radio, which announced Amin's death and the names of the regime's new Revolutionary Council. The radio said 15 minutes later that the regime had requested Russia to "render urgently political, moral, military and economic assistance."

As the Indian writer, Kuldip Nayar, pointed out, Moscow later gave December 26 as the date when Kabul made its "request." But no request could have been made by Babrak Karmal on the 26th because even the Soviet broadcasts announced his takeover on the evening of the 27th. Kabul Radio announced his appointment as Secretary-General of the People's Democratic Party of Afghanistan (PDPA) on the morning of the 28th. If he had sought Soviet assistance earlier, his "request" could have had no legal basis, as he held no official mandate.

Had the Western world suffered a major intelligence failure? Professor John Erickson of Edinburgh University, in evidence given to the House of Commons foreign affairs committee, said there were three distinct phases to the Soviet build-up. The first was in March, 1979, when the Soviets produced an operational contingency plan for the area. The second was in April, when half a division of Soviet troops was sent to Afghanistan. Erickson said the third stage was in October when Marshal Pavlovsky, commander-in-chief of Soviet ground forces, went over the ground with 60 of his senior commanders on a full-scale reconnaissance.

"Either the British Government knew what the Russians were planning and kept the information to themselves so they could orchestrate it to fuel their anti-Soviet cause; or they genuinely didn't know, which would be a grave scandal. If the invasion came as a surprise, that has staggering implications for Western Europe. If the British Government could not predict the Soviet invasion of Afghanistan, God help us in Western Europe," he said.

In retrospect, State Department sources in Washington believe there were two parts to the Soviet decision-making process on

Afghanistan. The Politburo's "green light" was probably given in the first two weeks of October as Marshal Pavlovsky was seeing for himself how steadily the Afghan armed forces were disintegrating in the face of a rapidly expanding insurgency. The operational decision — not whether to invade, but when — was taken in the first week of December. As Erickson said, the invasion plan was prepared as early as March.

State Department officials were aware of the introduction of special commando-style Soviet units into Kabul in early December. In the first week of that month one foreign service officer, Eliza Van Hollen, accurately predicted in one of her reports that Hafizullah Amin would be removed by the Russians and replaced with someone more reliable. In fact during the two months preceding the invasion, the Soviets were contacted on five occasions by the Americans, who expressed their growing concern over developments in South Asia.

There seems little doubt now that Western governments did have intelligence of Soviet military preparations. The military *capability* was there, all right. But what did it mean? It is one thing to know what a potential adversary can do, but it is another matter altogether to predict his intentions. Even then, presidents and prime ministers may have other priorities: in this case Iran, arms control and China's "punishment" of Vietnam. The regional power in the area, India, was on the threshold of an election and presumably in no condition to act on what must have been clear signals of an impending invasion by early December.

Soviet intentions towards Kabul could only be interpreted accurately through an understanding of why Moscow should need to invade a country which was already a close ally and which had for many years been the recipient of a considerable amount of Soviet military and economic assistance. The invasion was to break the back of the SALT II agreement and it severely strained Moscow's relations with the Third World. It buried the process of *detente*.

Above all, *why*?

To this day many people, including newspaper editors and politicians, have only the vaguest idea of where Afghanistan is. They generally think of it as a small, unimportant and nasty place tucked into North Africa, the Middle East or perhaps Southeast Asia. At any rate, it seems a long way from anywhere that matters. They may have some notion of turbaned Pathans and mysterious princesses drawn from the fanciful myths of popular fiction.

The Far Pavilions and the dusty recollections of British imperial soldiers are just about the sum of knowledge of the country for most people. The fact that it lies at a crossroads linking Iran, Soviet Central Asia, China and India has, however, never been lost on Moscow.

Part of the answer lies in the very nature of Afghanistan. It is less a country than a highway along which armies, peoples, religions and cultures have moved back and forth, from east to west and vice versa and from north to south. Until ships revolutionised commerce, it was the hub of international trade. When America was merely a gleam in a seafarer's eye and when Europe and Russia were little more than pagan fiefdoms, Afghanistan boasted a literature, science and a well-established, rich culture.

Its borders have contracted and expanded under pressure from competing empires. Successive rulers have enjoyed a tenuous and short-lived authority over the patchwork quilt of tribes and ethnic groups that make up its landlocked population. They have jealously preserved their independence with the tactics of the weak — by using one foreign power against another, a kind of diplomatic judo.

Freedom of action has been considerably curtailed by the lack of access to the sea. Extremes of climate and terrain and the lack of a link to the outside world have ensured that its inhabitants have remained deeply conservative, with each patriarchal community isolated from its neighbour. Despite these innate restrictions it gained considerable prestige internationally as one of the very first independent Muslim states to join the League of Nations.

Twentieth century monarchs, princes and dictators have without exception sought to extend their authority over their fiercely independent subjects both by authoritarian powers and by attempting to reform, modernise and develop the country. From time to time they have sought external diversions to maintain their grip over fractious communities: direct but shortlived support for the Basmachi revolt in Soviet Central Asia, for example, or encouragement for the Pushtun tribes' desire for autonomy on British India's North West Frontier.

Afghans have vigorously and instinctively resisted foreign pressure and interference. They have also used these pressures to their own advantage. As early as 1921 Kabul sought foreign advisers to expand education and built up an embryonic bureaucracy — measures designed to consolidate the rulers' power in the capital and beyond. Very often excessive oppression of minorities or hasty, ill-judged attempts to reorganise society along Western or Eastern lines have thrown the capital into episodes of violent crisis. Assassination, civil strife, coups d'état, rumours of conspiracy and counterplots heavily tinged with suspicion of foreign intrigue have indelibly marked the country's attempts to drag itself into the modern world.

This has helped form the archetypal Afghan character: parochial, proud, fiercely independent, highly conscious of his heritage, extraordinarily individualistic, suspicious of all foreigners and capable of deep and lasting friendship and loyalty. He makes an implacable enemy, but regardless of wealth or education places great emphasis on courtesy, hospitality and personal honour. Bravery — especially physical courage — is prized, but the poet and artist receive a popular respect unequalled anywhere else. He is unpredictable, humorous, inclined to exaggeration, gentle to women and children and cruel to an unspeakable degree to his foes.

The Afghan is ambitious. Democratic out of power, with it he becomes dictatorial and intolerant. Deception, deceit and evasion are his natural camouflage and armour. Yet there is no limit to his generosity. In short he is a creature of extremes — much like the country which he loves with a gut passion long out of fashion in many other nation-states. Perhaps, after all, because he does not have a state in the full meaning of the term. Its sovereignty has always been an elusive, ephemeral affair.

The Afghan does not work for, or under, a foreigner. There is no surer way to turn an Afghan friend and ally into an enemy in a moment than to give him the impression that he is dominated, controlled or in any way possessed. He demands to be treated as an equal. Essentially he is out for himself, be he a communist or an Islamic revolutionary. His natural innocence is matched by an inherent political cunning or *savoir faire*. He may be illiterate and without a penny to his name, unwashed and his clothes in tatters, but he knows he has no betters in this world and his belief in the next is his constant, everyday companion.

The Basmachi or "bandit" revolt against Bolshevism in Central Asia during the 1920s grew out of a Soviet unwillingness to countenance an equal partnership with an autonomous Muslim community at a time when Moscow found itself surrounded by not only Tsarist "White" armies but also Western military contingents from all points of the compass. Kabul exploited the affair, while Lenin in his turn sought to take advantage of the issue by turning the rebels' energies towards the British colonial administration in India.

Afghan leaders flirted with Moscow, too. Afghanistan was the first country to recognise the USSR. Later Kabul leaned towards

Germany, which Afghans saw as a useful — and distant — counterbalance to be used both against the Soviet Union and British India. Both the Soviets and later the Nazis were to cultivate links with the Pushtun tribes living on either side of the Durand Line marking the frontier between Afghanistan and what has subsequently become Pakistan in an effort to tie down British forces. Who was using whom was — and still is — difficult to establish.

Before World War II the Comintern was active in trying to harness both Islamic and nationalist movements in the Middle East and Asia against European and American power. One elderly villager who lives in a village near Nowshera in Pakistan's North West Frontier Province (NWFP) remembers those good old days. A Pushtun nationalist, he visited Moscow and met both Lenin and Stalin.

Another Pushtun, this time an Afghan of the Ghilzai tribal group, worked as a peon for a Bombay millionaire in the 1930s. He was soon caught up in Indian trade union affairs at a time of growing Indian discontent over British rule. The young man was Hafizullah Amin. He was to become a prominent and highly effective organiser of Marxist-Leninist cells back home on his return from India. Many years later he was to help found the People's Democratic Party and to lead the violent coup which brought the first openly pro-Soviet regime to power in Kabul. His own overriding ambition was to be his undoing and he was forcibly removed, shot down and replaced by Babrak Karmal at the behest of the invading Soviets.

The traditional Soviet sense of territorial insecurity, Afghanistan's key geographical position and attempts by Moscow to use nationalist and pan-Islamic movements as a spearhead for the export of communism help explain the fundamental interest of Moscow in the country. The opportunity for embedding Marxist-Leninist seeds in the fabric of Afghan society came with the development almost overnight of an embryonic middle class, a bourgeoisie responsive to an idealistic creed promising rapid economic development, an end to inequality and a rapid transfer of power to ambitious minorities eager for a slice of the cake of foreign largesse.

The tiny urban elite was drawn from the armed forces, the civil service, the rapidly expanding educational system and the wealth generated by innumerable foreign aid projects. Maladministration, the system of patronage reserved for the "old boy network" of leading families of sophisticates with royalist, Mohammadzai connections, ensured that the wealth went to the cities and merchant class rather than to the rural communities. By the 1960s the number of secondary school graduates far exceeded university places, while a newly-trained generation of teachers, doctors, lawyers and agriculturalists found that jobs were simply not available to absorb their skills and ambitions.

For Soviet scholars and orientalists actively cultivating small, clandestine cadres of Afghan communists, this had important side-effects: it aggravated the traditional enmity between town and country, accelerated competition between the Dari-speaking intelligentsia of Kabul and the majority, provincial Pushtuns and finally increased general resentment against King Zaher Shah and his nephew, Prince Daoud. The polarisation watered already fertile ground for revolutionary agitation and organisation. Belated attempts to democratise the country did not relieve the pressure — it simply widened it to a newly-formed parliament and led to the formation of a plethora of politically vociferous newspapers and political parties.

Under steadily increasing pressure from within, the authorities sought to distract public attention and obtain greater control over their subjects through manipulation of the *terra irridenta* of eastern Afghanistan and the Pushtuns living across the 1,400-mile border in northwest Pakistan. At this point in time the Soviets were once again feeling unsure of themselves along their southern borders: the rift with Peking and the formation of what Moscow perceived to be a distinctly unfriendly move in the formation of the American-led CENTO defence pact enforced their sense of need to protect the Eurasian border of the USSR.

Kabul's fomentation of the issue of Pushtun autonomy meant that Washington firmly and repeatedly turned down Afghan requests for military equipment and training. It provided Moscow with a timely reward: Kabul turned to its northern neighbour for military aid from 1954 and by 1970 some 7,000 Afghan armed forces officers had received instruction in the USSR. Many of them would prove to be "sleepers" in readiness for the communist takeover in 1978, when there were already 3,000 Soviet advisers in Afghanistan, roughly half of them military officers. By this time the country had joined that exclusive club of four pro-Soviet states receiving nearly 90 percent of all Soviet foreign aid.

The United States had committed its first error — over Kabul's intentions. Pushtun autonomy was a diversion, not an objective. For an independent Pushtun state incorporating Pakistan's NWFP and

Afghanistan's south-eastern provinces would have looked to the Pushtun politicians in Pakistan, especially Ghaffar Khan and his son, Walli Khan, rather than to the Afghan royal family. A Pushtun state would have been mainly drawn from the Ghilzai branch of tribes, whereas the Kabul rulers were from the rival Durrani branch. Afghanistan's rulers would have had more to lose from a successful Pushtun insurrection than Pakistan, but American officials clearly overestimated the threat.

But why was it necessary to invade?

The Pushtun tribes of Afghanistan form the majority of the country's estimated 15 millions and they live in a rough crescent stretching from the eastern province of Kunar, south along the Pakistan border to the south-west. For some 200 years power in Kabul resided among the Durrani branch centred on the country's second city, Kandahar. By contrast, the young provincial Pushtuns who joined Kabul's championship of the Pushtunistan cause were from the rival, out-of-favour Ghilzai tribes.

"Mirwais" is an Afghan communist now in hiding both from the guerillas opposing the Soviet-backed regime of Babrak Karmal and from his former comrades in the People's Democratic Party of Afghanistan (PDPA). He explained what happened.

"There were two schools founded in Kabul for development of Pushtun nationalism. I went to Rahmanaba, reserved for the sons of Pushtun tribal chiefs inside Afghanistan. The other lycée was Khushal Khattak Khan and it was for the sons of tribal *maliks* living across the border in Pakistan.

"We discovered a new sense of national consciousness there. The schools were attached to the Ministry of Tribes which was involved in the Pushtunistan issue. I remember Hafizullah Amin then — this was between 1952 and 1963. He was a teacher of physics and algebra. He was at the Darulaman Teachers' Training College and he used to come over and teach us free of charge. I was impressed by him. He was a fine orator. He used to bicycle all over the place and there was nothing he wouldn't do to help solve someone's personal problems and difficulties. He was initially a nationalist, too.

"We had no time for the Kabulis who spoke Dari. They were 'city stuff.' We wanted a share of power in Kabul. We wanted our Pushtun language to be officially accepted in the capital. We were after all in the majority, and we didn't see why the Dari-speaking minorities should dominate everything."

Like many other Afghan students, "Mirwais" went overseas to further his studies: "In Frankfurt the first political term I understood was 'anti-imperialism.' It was the time of demonstrations against American involvement in Vietnam. Five out of the 15 Afghans studying in Frankfurt joined the People's Democratic Party after its founding in 1965. We were all members of the Khalq (Masses) faction of the PDPA because we were all Pushtun and both Nur Mohammad Taraki and Hafizullah Amin were our leaders. We were encouraged to link up with the West German Communist Party and told to organise secretly and to be careful of spies from the Afghan Embassy in Bonn. Above all, we were told to read and read. By that time I could read Marx and Engels in German..."

The "city stuff" about whom "Mirwais" was so disparaging had its own leftist champions, of whom Babrak Karmal was one. Typically, he was related by marriage to the royal family and his group — named Parcham or Flag after its newspaper — favoured a gradualist approach to taking power. They could afford to — the Parchamites were to front their leap into the driving seat by using Prince Daoud in his bloodless coup in 1973, carried out when his uncle, Zaher Shah, was out of the country.

Moscow was therefore cultivating, organising and financing a party of Marxist-Leninists who were deeply divided between town and country, Pushtun and Dari speakers, and also divided over tactics. This proved to be a major consideration in the decision to invade.

The underground cells came together to form the PDPA in 1965 and it ventured into the open during a brief constitutional period when the authorities tried to take the steam out of dissent by relaxing political and press controls. But within a year they had split into their respective Flag and Masses factions, each of which was led by a group of distinctive, competitive and self-assertive characters.

The PDPA temporarily overcame its difference in 1976 under Soviet pressure as it prepared the ground for an assault on the last of a long line of Mohammadzai princelings. Daoud was turning his back — somewhat belatedly — on the "progressive forces" which had facilitated his rise to power and his close relations with Moscow.

An arrogant man who overestimated both his power and personal popularity, he lost little time in purging the Islamic revolutionaries who dominated Kabul University campus by 1974, but he delayed moving against the PDPA leadership until it was too late. Daoud panicked into arresting PDPA leaders when they mounted a successful public demonstration. For Moscow, he signed his own death warrant when he began to mend fences with neighbouring

Iran and Pakistan's Prime Minister, Zulfikar Ali Bhutto. He bungled the arrests of Nur Mohammad Taraki and Hafizullah Amin, and the latter managed to give the signal to move to the cells he had so carefully planted in the Soviet-trained officer corps. In fact Amin may have escaped the round-up.

There is at least evidence suggestive of direct Soviet involvement in the 24-hour military operation which placed the Khalq or Masses faction of the PDPA in power. Colonel Mohammad Rafie abruptly left his studies in Moscow — as well as an ill wife — five days before the coup. Rafie and Abdul Qadir, an airforce officer who was to play a central role in the coup, met the Soviet military attaché, who used a wooden model of the presidential palace to plot Daoud's last hours.

The meeting reportedly took place hours after Daoud put out an alert to four of his army divisions: the 4th, 7th, 8th and 15th. Later there were to be reports that Soviet aircrews mounted Afghan fighter missions against the presidential palace and the Rishkor garrison in Kabul which held out until aerial attacks reduced it. There is no doubt that the innumerable Soviet military advisers played an essential role in reporting the reliability or otherwise of military units around the country.

The blow came after breakfast on April 27, 1978. Fighting raged all day and the insurrectionists broadcast their victory that evening from Kabul Radio. Shooting continued throughout the night and sporadically until the following afternoon. The former ambassador and minister, Shamsuddin Majrooh, went out onto the street to see what all the rumpus was about. One of his sons pulled him back into the house and told him not to be a fool. People locked their doors and waited.

Lt. General Naiq Mohammad Azizi was in charge of the 400-bed military hospital in the capital. He received casualties from both sides. They included not only two members of Daoud's family but Daoud's assassin, Eimamuddin, the young lieutenant who received a bullet in the arm from Daoud's pistol. Azizi took telephone calls from the communists' rebel headquarters established at Bagram airbase north of the capital, ordering him to turn away loyalist wounded. From time to time he spoke directly to Daoud who was holed up in his palace where his West German-trained bodyguard put up a stiff but futile resistance. Azizi refused to take Daoud's portrait down from his office wall. He was waiting to see which way the wind would blow, just like everyone else.

Seizure of Bagram airbase and its military communications was an important factor in the success of the coup. It was well planned and implemented, considering that it was brought forward several months and lacked total surprise. Amin was later to make a film of his "heroic" activities, and there is an extraordinary scene in which he appears to be giving orders for the coup to a uniformed officer by telephone *after* his arrest — if he was in fact detained at all.

The Soviets felt obliged to give their support to the Khalq *putsch* because Daoud was moving against communists at home and seeking ties with "reactionary circles" abroad. He had to go. At first all seemed well with Taraki and his new PDPA cabinet, superficially divided evenly between Khalq and Parcham factions. A strange lull followed the violence, as the new regime tried to consolidate its position in the armed forces and the civil service. At first regime propaganda stressed the reformist, nationalist aspect of its character.

"Mirwais" returned from West Germany in November and went home to his tribe in Paktya. He was greeted as a long lost son, as the first educated member of his Zadran tribe. His fellow tribesmen were unaware of the April coup. After all, it was a Kabul affair and what went on in Kabul was almost as alien as whatever went on in New Delhi or Tehran. They had no knowledge of the PDPA, or its Khalq and Parcham factions. "Mirwais" took a number of elders back with him to Kabul, largely to demonstrate his own loyalty to the regime.

"They met Taraki and they were very surprised. They turned to me and exclaimed, 'Why, the man speaks Pushtu. He speaks our language. And what's more, he tells very good jokes!' The Government encouraged them in the belief that they would get what they wanted from the PDPA regime: good roads, medical care, schools for their children and jobs aplenty."

"Mirwais" was appointed secretary-general of a key government ministry and he discovered that several Soviet advisers were already busily working on an overhaul of the entire organisation. "They worked day and night to get the new programme ready. I knew nothing of the work; I was appointed simply on the basis of my loyalty."

His first "embarrassment," as he described it, was his introduction to high-level party and regime meetings. "You see, I had learned the necessity of rational thought and discussion in Germany as a communist. But there was a singular lack of logic to everything in Kabul. 'You have to obey,' was the order of the day. I rationalised this out, telling myself that I had been out of the country for a long time and was therefore not aware of all that was going on. I simply sat there at meetings with a silly smile, gazing at the faces around me, quite bewildered by it all. I fought my own growing feelings of hostility. I told myself there must be something going on I knew nothing about which could explain it all."

"Mirwais" quickly put his finger on the weakness of the PDPA — a weakness which persists today. "You know that in theory we were a communist party which opposed discrimination in any field. In practice, of course, the Khalqis represented the countryside Pushtuns and the Parchamites the city people who spoke Dari. In practice they trusted people from their own tribes and promoted their own people into top positions in the regime."

At first Soviet advisers were courteous towards "Mirwais" and treated the Khalqi as a colleague they respected. That changed. "They became increasingly inclined towards the Parcham faction. At first they'd telephone me and ask for an appointment. Then later they would simply order me to appear before them. I realised my advisers had become my masters."

Within weeks of coming to power, Taraki began to arrest Parchamite rivals within the PDPA. Senior members of the Parcham faction were put out to grass as ambassadors abroad. Babrak Karmal was packed off to Prague. "Enemies" of the April Revolution were rounded up by the thousand — monarchists, conservatives, theologians, social democrats and nationalists. They all disappeared into prison, or worse. Some Parchamites were afforded protection in the Soviet Embassy where the city's "little tsars" directed their operations: KGB *rezident* and minister-counsellor Vassiliy Safronchuk and Ambassador Puzanov.

The population was shocked by the formal unveiling of the new national flag in October, 1978. It was entirely red.

Just as the Khalq had relied on Amin as the prime, full-time organiser of secret Marxist-Leninist cells in the armed forces, so now Amin was Taraki's right-hand man in implementing the purges and executions of the Khalq's suspected opponents. Assadullah Sarwari earned the nickname The Butcher for the personal interest he showed as head of AKSA, the secret police, in his victims' discomfort. He would amuse himself by touring interrogation chambers and urge his inquisitors on to new heights of inventiveness by stubbing out his cigarettes in the eye sockets of political detainees.

The fact that Taraki was not Mohammadzai or even from the Durrani group of Pushtun tribes was not lost on the country's rural population. His Ghilzai origins meant legitimacy had not been preserved. When the PDPA launched its radical educational and agrarian reforms at gunpoint throughout the country, the nation rose in arms. The *jehad* or religious struggle against communism began in earnest. Attempts to reform the traditional system of marriage and to enforce the education of women in the tenets of Marxism-Leninism together with random shootings of local elders left common people in doubt as to the nature of the atheist assault on their customary and Islamic way of life. Their very independence was threatened.

Entire garrisons rose in revolt. The Herat uprising in March, 1979, was a severe shock. Almost every one of the country's 29 provinces was affected by fighting. A sweeping reorganisation was required and Amin seized the opportunity to take over the prime minister's job and to pack his followers into the first echelon of the PDPA apparatus.

Moscow was concerned by Amin's failure in April to crush the resistance in Paktya, and by October the province of Badakshan, situated on the Chinese, Pakistani and Soviet borders, was up in flames. General Sergei Yepishev, head of the Soviet army and navy Main Political Administration (MPA) led a large delegation to Afghanistan ostensibly to investigate the needs of the Afghan armed forces, but in reality he assessed the need for possible Soviet intervention on a large scale.

Soviet anxiety deepened when Amin arrested Taraki and killed him. Despite deteriorating security in Kabul, Taraki visited Havana in September, 1979, to attend the Non-aligned summit. On his way home he stopped over in Moscow for talks with Leonid Brezhnev. There are several versions of what happened, but here is an account provided by "Mirwais":

"Taraki met Babrak Karmal in Moscow. Unfortunately for Taraki, one of his aides, Major Talun, was an informer of Amin. Amin had forewarning of a plot engineered by Taraki and Karmal to remove him. When Amin turned up at Kabul airport to greet Taraki on his return, he took a strong bodyguard with him. Taraki shook Amin coolly by the hand instead of embracing him. They drove off separately.

"That night at a meeting in the presidential palace Amin failed to win support in his attempts to expel four of Taraki's closest supporters from the Politburo. This was the turning point. Taraki summoned Amin, who was assured by Soviet Ambassador Puzanov that he would come to no harm. Amin took a well-armed escort to the Defence Ministry and they refused to be disarmed at the entrance. Shooting broke out between Taraki's men and Amin's guards, and Amin escaped to his car outside which was waiting with its engine running.

"Amin convened the whole of the Central Committee and told the assembled members of Taraki's attempt to kill him. Taraki refused to heed the Central Committee's order for him to appear, and the Central Committee formally expelled him from office. Amin arrested him."

The generally-accepted version is that Moscow connived in Amin's removal, that Amin was not fooled by Soviet assurances and that Taraki was wounded in the shoot-out.

"What made Amin confident was a telegram of congratulations from Brezhnev. He assumed he had Moscow's support. Twenty-three days after Amin detained Taraki, Taraki was killed — some say he was strangled."

"Mirwais" said Taraki's death marked Amin's downfall. "Under Taraki the Khalq faction worked against the Parchamites. But after Taraki was murdered the pro-Taraki group in the Khalq began to make contact with the Parchamites under the guidance of the Soviets. It ended Russia's even-handed approach to the two factions within the ruling PDPA. The Russians became increasingly pro-Parcham. Taraki's men were openly against Amin and he knew it and blamed the Russians.

"Right from the point of Taraki's death, this was a watershed for me as a party member. I was so disillusioned with it all I began to think of ways of escape, "Mirwais" said. "Amin thought of himself as an Asian version of Tito. He started making overtures to the guerilla forces in the country. He wanted to have good relations with the Pakistanis and Iranians and even the Americans. He offered Afghan tribes self-rule and he wanted to build a huge personality cult for himself. Anyone who didn't go along with all this was going to be killed."

The Soviets had tried everything by this stage; coups d'état, advisers, economic aid and political "advice" in the form of hundreds of civilian advisers in the capital. Like Daoud, Amin was more ambitious than he was loyal to Moscow. The armed forces were breaking up and insurgents were steadily taking over provincial areas. Counter-revolution was in the air. There was only one option left: invasion.

For the Soviets it was not only a matter of ideological imperative in seeking to save an ally, but it was also a matter of territorial security. Above all, it was a question of international prestige. To ignore the destruction of a friendly, socialist regime on its doorstep would have an impact on other Soviet allies and friends — and there were few enough of those.

The USSR invaded Afghanistan to prevent the imminent collapse of the Marxist regime and probable expulsion of Soviet influence. This would have been a blow to Soviet prestige and strategic interests which the Kremlin was not prepared to tolerate. Soviet anxiety about the regime's stability deepened as Taraki and then Amin showed themselves incapable of defeating the Muslim insurgency and less and less amenable to Soviet advice and control.

According to a former KGB major, Vladimir Kuzichkin, who defected to the West in June, 1982, the Soviet Politburo's fears also included the possibility that Amin would come to terms with the resistance in the country. When Moscow decided to support the elimination of Amin and to replace him with a more reliable Babrak Karmal, already a KGB agent, according to Kuzichkin, it was assumed that under new leadership and with substantial support the Afghan Army would press home the fight against the resistance and that the latter would correspondingly lose heart.

Afghanistan's sensitive position on the southern border of the Soviet Union, and the considerable economic and military investment in it, complemented and reinforced the ideological motive of preserving communist gains.

There is no reason to suppose that the invasion was part of a "grand strategy" to enable the USSR to threaten Western oil supplies or to secure the oilfields for itself. Nevertheless, the move into Afghanistan clearly brought Moscow what the former Pakistani Foreign Minister, Agha Shahi, called "new strategic options" and it undoubtedly sees this as a valuable gain. Looking eastwards, the Russians could move against Chinese influence in the region. To the south and south-west the Indian Ocean and southern Iran were within reach, while severe pressure could be applied to Pakistan.

Similarly, privileged access to Afghanistan's considerable mineral wealth is an additional bonus. While not a primary factor in the decision to invade in December, 1979, this will, like the strategic factor, have contributed to the long-term Soviet view of the desirability of bringing Afghanistan firmly into the Soviet camp.

International Impact

The Soviet invasion shattered President Jimmy Carter's dream of a new era in that much misunderstood process, detente.

Ratification of the SALT II agreement was already in deep trouble. The Senate Foreign Relations Committee began hearings on the pact on July 9, 1979. In the midst of the deliberations, a Democratic senator pressed the administration's witnesses to comment on rumours that a Soviet combat force had been deployed to Cuba. The administration denied any changes in the Soviet presence on the island. On August 29 Chairman Frank Church told reporters that increased surveillance of Cuba confirmed indications that a Soviet brigade was indeed there.

At the September 5 press conference at which Secretary of State Cyrus Vance said the force numbered some 2,000-3,000 soldiers backed up by some 70 tanks, he indicated that although it was a "very serious" matter, the SALT pact was of "fundamental importance." On October 1 Carter flatly rejected hardliners' demands that SALT II should be subordinated to the general US-USSR political competition. Eight days later the Senate committee finally voted 9-6 to send the treaty up for full Senate consideration. But the Soviet invasion began on Christmas Eve, and on January 3 Carter asked Senate majority leader Byrd to defer the issue. SALT II was the direct casualty of the invasion.

The invasion dismayed US leaders. Carter liked to think that earlier in 1979 relations with Moscow had been on the upswing. Trade between the two superpowers was growing. SALT II had been signed in Vienna. But the airlift of Soviet paratroopers into Kabul delayed — and effectively killed — further action on the all-important barometer of East-West relations, pulled the US out of the 1980 Olympics and halted grain shipments to the USSR. Carter imposed tighter controls on the export of high technology to the Soviet bloc as well.

The grain embargo was imposed on January 4, and it affected all transactions over and above the eight million metric tons provided by the 1975 US-Soviet agreement, thereby blocking a previously approved sale of 14.7 million tons of corn, wheat and soyabeans.

Five days later the International Longshoremen's Union announced a total boycott of Soviet vessels and Russia-bound cargoes in both East and West Coast ports. The United States and its West European allies also suspended a range of economic and cultural contacts with the Soviet Union. Formal contacts by Americans at or above the rank of assistant secretary could only be made with the President's personal approval.

The policy included suspension of plans for a US consulate in Kiev in the Ukraine, and for a Soviet consulate-general in New York. Seven US diplomats preparing to set up shop were abruptly given other duties. Moscow was told to withdraw 17 diplomats from New York. Aeroflot, the state airline which had provided a third of the airlift for the invasion, was ordered to cut down its three US flights a week to two. Scheduled conferences on marine pollution and navigation were cancelled.

Carter said he was shocked by the invasion. On January 23 the President told the Soviets to stay out of the Gulf. He was to sound a note which was to characterise American response to the Afghan issue in the years to come: fears of destabilisation of the Gulf area. "The Soviet effort to dominate Afghanistan has brought Soviet military forces to within 300 miles of the Indian Ocean and close to the Strait of Hormuz — a waterway through which much of the world's oil must flow. The Soviet Union is now attempting to consolidate a strategic position that poses a grave threat to the free movement of Middle East oil." The Soviets called Carter's charge an "absurdity." For once, they may have been right.

When the Soviet ambassador to Britain saw Mrs. Thatcher to explain Moscow's position, the British Prime Minister lost no time in giving the envoy a lecture on Afghanistan. When he argued that the Soviets' "limited contingent" had been requested by Kabul, Mrs. Thatcher reportedly told him not to be "childish." The Foreign Secretary, Lord Carrington, cancelled high-level contacts with the Soviets, ended the preferential commercial credit agreement and agreed to impose tighter controls on the flow of high technology to Soviet bloc states. But the bipartisan approach was somewhat undermined by the British Government's attempts to stop sportsmen from attending the Olympics: the issue of Afghanistan was lost in the Labour opposition's criticism of the Iron Lady's perceived high-handedness. Nevertheless, what turned out to be a partial boycott of the Games must have been a blow to Soviet prestige.

India was the odd man out on the crisis, although this was partly due to the fact that the invasion occurred just before national elections, and although the caretaker Prime Minister, Charan Singh, was critical of the Soviet action, he waited for the new administration to take over. India vacillated. Mrs. Indira Gandhi, still an opposition leader at the time, was ambivalent. "We are against all foreign intervention," she said. "But people have long been interfering in this area one way or another."

New Delhi has had a long and warm relationship with the Soviet Union. The Soviets supported India in its wars with Pakistan — a country Mrs. Gandhi regarded as a Chinese and American proxy. What New Delhi was anxious to avoid was a confrontation between the superpowers in the area. When Lord Carrington later toured Turkey, Oman, Saudi Arabia, Pakistan and India he found a similar theme running through all the capitals. There was certainly a greater sense of insecurity as a result of the invasion, but his hosts ensured that he understood that any Western military capability should remain "over the horizon." No one wanted Washington to take the opportunity to establish bases and a permanent, visible military presence in the region. The Rapid Deployment Force (RDF) was not welcome — and local fears of greater superpower rivalry certainly was to affect Western policy towards the Afghan resistance struggle in the years ahead.

On January 7 Moscow vetoed a Security Council resolution sponsored by the Non-aligned group of states, a resolution which condemned the "armed aggression" in Afghanistan and called for the immediate withdrawal of foreign troops. The Council then voted by 12 votes to two — the Soviets and East Germans opposing — to transfer the issue to the General Assembly. It subsequently adopted four resolutions affirming the Afghans' right to choose their own form of government. The debates turned out to be acrimonious. Afghan Foreign Minister Shah Mohammad Dost said the session was an "open and flagrant intervention in the internal affairs of the Democratic Republic of Afghanistan." Soviet bloc states obediently backed him, but the issue was placed on the agenda nevertheless.

Pakistan's delegation said its country was the one most endangered. India tried to put up a resolution calling for an end to all foreign interference in Afghanistan. Moscow would have been gratified had this succeeded; it would have given international credibility to the Soviet view that the Afghan resistance was the creation of America, Chinese and Islamic "imperalism." But a resolution spearheaded by

Muslim states, calling for the "immediate, unconditional and total withdrawal of foreign troops from Afghanistan," was adopted on January 14 by 104 to 18, with 18 abstentions — a two-thirds majority. The Soviets vetoed it.

What was striking was the unanimity of developing countries' leaders in condemning the Soviet invasion.

Fifty-two members of the Non-aligned Movement had supported the resolution. An Extraordinary Session of the Islamic Conference attended by the foreign ministers of 34 countries was held in Islamabad. The meeting condemned the "Soviet military aggression against the Afghan people" as a "flagrant violation of international laws, covenants and norms" and demanded the immediate, unconditional withdrawal of Soviet troops.

This was repeated the following year, when 38 ministers condemned the "continued Soviet military occupation." The Islamic foreign ministers met again in August, 1982, in Niger, where they reaffirmed the need for an immediate troop withdrawal and on October 12, the organisation's Secretary-General, Habib Chatti of Tunisia, deplored Soviet defiance of international appeals when he addressed a meeting in New York. He again called on the USSR to renounce armed intervention and to allow Afghans to choose their own form of government.

While French President Giscard d'Estaing hesitated to join the robust American and British positions for fear of jeopardising his country's special relationship with Moscow, others closer to the USSR were less restrained. Yugoslavia, for example, criticised the invasion in blunt terms. The five-member Association of Southeast Asian Nations (ASEAN) — the Philippines, Malaysia, Indonesia, Singapore and Thailand — condemned the invasion. Meeting in Manila in June, 1981, ASEAN foreign ministers said in their final communiqué that the situation in Afghanistan and Cambodia had as a common denominator the invasion and occupation of a small independent state by a foreign power in open violation of international law and they repeated their support for the UN, Islamic Conference and Non-aligned resolutions on the subject.

In Venice in June 1980 and in Maastricht in March the following year, representatives of the 10-member European Community called for respect for the sovereignty and territorial integrity of Afghanistan and for an end to external interference. On June 30, 1981, the council proposed a two-stage conference on Afghanistan to work out a peace plan.

African countries expressed their misgivings. President Tolbert of

Liberia said events in Afghanistan endangered world peace, while Kenya demanded the withdrawal of foreign troops and President Kaunda of Zambia condemned the Soviet intervention. President Mobutu of Zaire described the situation as extremely dangerous.

If there were differences in style and emphasis among NATO allies, this was also true of Warsaw Pact countries. Czechoslovakia actually congratulated Moscow, while Hungary and Poland were less enthusiastic in their coverage of the event in their official media. Romania implied criticism and North Korea dissociated itself from a declaration of solidarity with the Kabul regime by 12 communist states' representatives. Predictably, Albania angrily denounced the Soviets.

The Soviet invasion not only weakened the Cubans' pro-Soviet leadership in the Non-aligned Movement, but it had considerable impact on communist parties in Europe. British, Belgian, Italian and Swedish CPs were critical, but those of Denmark, Finland, Luxembourg and Portugal supported Moscow. Prominent individual communists quit after many years' membership of their respective parties.

Saudi Arabia played an important role in the Muslim states' outright condemnation of the invasion. It encouraged Bangladesh to sponsor the idea of a conference and it suggested another Saudi beneficiary, Pakistan, as the venue. Both countries receive considerable aid from Riyadh. Afghanistan, Syria and South Yemen absented themselves, not unnaturally. General Zia ul-Haq, the head of the martial law administration which had for the previous two years been something of an international pariah following the overthrow of the Pakistan People's Party and execution of former Prime Minister Zulfikar Ali Bhutto, took full advantage of the situation. Zia emphasised the anti-Islamic nature of the invasion — partly, no doubt, to establish himself as a bona fide Muslim.

"The Soviet armed intervention was a tragedy to befall the Muslim world," he said in his inaugural speech. The conference was however quite restrained in its language. The Islamic world had plenty of problems of its own to worry about. Above all, it feared the United States would exploit the situation. The Muslim countries blamed Washington for having split Arab ranks by winning over Egypt's Anwar Sadat to a peace accord with Israel. The Saudis had just emerged from a crisis in which religious zealots had stormed the holy Ka'ba in Mecca, while Soviet support for the Palestinian movement was not without significance.

Washington did not ignore the message. Clearly, to involve itself by directly aiding Afghan resistance forces would jeopardise the international trend against the Soviet Union. It would have to be a "hands off" policy, designed to encourage Muslim states to fund and arm the Islamic guerillas. America would have to walk softly on the Afghan issue if it was not to harm the Third World's disillusionment with Moscow.

Kuldip Nayar put this well:

"What Russia did in Afghanistan was reprehensible. But so was what the USA had been doing in the region. Making an enemy of the Soviet Union was not likely to help them. So the Arabs' argument ran. In any case there was little that the Muslim countries could do against Russia. They had only money — and money they did promise to Pakistan to look after the Afghan refugees whose number had risen to nearly half a million by February. . ."

During the course of the next two years India was to show signs of amending its ambivalent stance. The Indians showed they were genuinely concerned about the Soviet military presence in Afghanistan, primarily because they saw it as having brought superpower rivalry closer to home.

Publicly Mrs. Gandhi usually blamed the Afghan crisis on "foreign interference" in general, implying that there have been several sources of interference. On her return to New Delhi in September 1981 she told correspondents: "While India would like to see the Soviets withdraw from Afghanistan, it has to be pointed out that outside interference is still continuing. The problem should be viewed in its totality." But at her Moscow press conference she had repeated this and gone even further by suggesting that the presence of Soviet troops also constituted foreign interference. The reaction was reportedly one of amazement.

The Soviets attach considerable importance to their friendly relationship with India as the regional power and an influential member of the Non-aligned Movement. Even though Mrs. Gandhi has since reverted to her more cautious line on the issue, her Moscow statement could only have added to the Soviet awareness of the damage their Afghan invasion had done to Moscow's standing internationally. This was evident, too, during the course of the 1983 Non-aligned summit in New Delhi when a shift of opinion towards the moderate camp was discernible.

The other crucial power in the region is Iran, which forcefully condemned the action of the "lesser Satan" in Afghanistan. Moscow's dilemma was evident: here was a virulently "anti-imperialist" Islamic regime whose anti-American sentiment could be put to good use. On the other hand Soviet support for Iraq's war against Iran prejudiced hopes of a stable relationship with Iranian revolutionaries. Iran's support for Afghanistan's three million Shia minority and its refusal to participate in the United Nations peace initiative further dampened Soviet hopes of forming a workable relationship with Tehran for the time being.

Together with its West European allies, the new Reagan administration would evolve a four-point policy on Afghanistan: priority would be given to encouragement of a rapprochement between Pakistan and India; military and economic assistance would be given to Pakistan's coterie of ruling generals while not jeopardising the country's Non-aligned, Islamic status; diplomatic pressure in bilateral and mutlilateral contacts with the USSR would be maintained and finally Afghanistan would remain a central foreign policy issue with commensurate attention given to publicising the resistance to the Babrak Karmal regime and the Soviet troops in the country. Vocal noises of support to the UN attempts to thrash out a peaceful political solution would be provided as a matter of course, without any real possibility of significant progress.

In the months immediately following the arrival of Soviet forces in Kabul, defence officials in North America and Western Europe offered a sombre prediction in non-attributable press briefings given for selected correspondents. The guerilla war, they said, would be based on the law of diminishing returns. The superior technical resources of the Soviet superpower would steadily erode the shallow, ill-led and poorly equipped Afghan guerillas.

Their counterparts in foreign ministries were by contrast full of optimism. If the struggle amounted to no more than mild discomfort for Moscow, then "international pressure" from the UN, the Islamic world and Non-aligned countries, the European Community, the Commonwealth, ASEAN and others would serve to encourage an early regional agreement on the issue, based of course on a Soviet military withdrawal.

It was not to be.

43

The People's War

A distant column of dust came into view from the direction of Kabul. The sight raised mild interest among the group of Mujehadeen *sunning themselves on the edge of Logar's broad, stony plain. Their endless chatter stopped momentarily as they idly watched small dots grow in number and size and take the form of tanks, armoured fighting vehicles (AFVs) and armoured personnel carriers (APCs). Two predatory "Hind" Mi-24 helicopter gunships rushed back and forth over their charges. The vehicles, their desert camouflage paint clearly visible now, turned towards the slight rise where we sat and at a range of several hundred metres opened fire.*

On failing to see the shot fall, I looked around and found myself alone. The guerillas had fled down the slope and milled about an ancient yet bright red bus standing in the village. They jumped aboard all at once and I flung myself after them. We trundled through the maze of alleys and high walls, with Afghans hanging from the doors and windows, gazing at the sky and yelling contradictory orders to the thoroughly perplexed driver. The Pushtun emphasis on democratic debate, I reflected, invariably asserts itself in times of stress. In an area entirely bereft of natural cover, the driver jammed on the brakes and after a few moments of further anxious discussion, we piled out and started to run. I followed from the rear, hampered by the fact that my turban — a splendid affair bought in Peshawar's bazaar over the border — was steadily uncoiling and winding itself about my legs. We ran across fields of clover, over irrigation ditches and through plantations of saplings. About 120 of us gathered in a kerez, or well. In pitch darkness the Afghans prayed for their deliverance to the sound of tank tracks squealing and grinding overhead, and the roar of the helicopters' rockets being fired and the short, sharp bursts of their four-barrel Gatling guns.

We emerged after four hours, dripping wet and blinking in the harsh afternoon sunlight. Not for the first time the sense of being alive when others had died brought an irresistible and shameful sense of exhilaration. At the entrance to the village four donkeys lay on their sides, already bloated and their legs stuck out like matchsticks. Their blood mixed with the dust to form black pools of mud. Three men were killed, their faces terribly pale and streaked with blood. A young man described as the local "doctor" tended the wounded, all female. He had no idea what to do and was shaking with fright. He was reluctant to touch the women and simply covered the unpleasant sight of damaged female flesh with dirty sacking. He busied himself in setting up saline drips which seemed unnecessary. One woman had been shot through the breast, but there was no exit wound. She had small lesions all over her head and one hand was shattered by shell fragments. She moaned in a restrained, muffled way. Another sat bolt upright and seemed very calm although the point of her chin had been shot away and she showed me a small, nasty puncture in one arm. A third was senseless; her husband writhed around in a frenzy of grief. No one objected to my amateurish ministrations. The dead were buried quickly and very deep. Then we had tea.

European underground opposition to Nazi occupation in World War II pales into insignificance when compared to the populist armed resistance to the Soviet occupation of Afghanistan. The unanimity of active protest and irregular warfare is all the more remarkable for the splintered, heterogeneous population in terms of race, tribe, language and class. Laurence Laumonier, a French-woman who worked voluntarily as a doctor for many months with the civilians and guerillas, summed up one vital element of the Afghans' extraordinary motivation: "When a man literally believes that if he dies fighting communism he will go straight to heaven as a martyr, it gives him a strength machine-guns and tanks cannot match."

Islam certainly means different things to different Muslims, but it is undoubtedly the single most important factor which all Afghans have in common. It is not merely a cultural phenomenon; it is a daily observance in the form of prayer, fasting, submission to Islamic taxation, pilgrimage and invocation of the brief creed of faith in a single God whose prophet is Mohammad. A vital part of the faith is the *jehad*, conveniently translated in the Western press as "holy war." It is much more than that. It means religious struggle — a self-denial or self-sacrifice for the common good. A businessman working in the Gulf who contributes substantially to the *jehad* is as much a *Mujehad* as the young man in a pair of plastic sandals

45

with an ancient rifle waiting in ambush along an Afghan highway. *Jehad* implies a legitimacy — in the name of God — for the conflict. It is one reason why guerillas object strenuously to the term "rebel" which may suit headlines for its brevity, but which is clearly at odds with a just war. Afghans do very much believe in the justice of what they are doing on the battlefield.

Religious faith is by no means the sole source of opposition to the Soviet occupation forces. Islam is also customary. The lores of family, clan and tribe are inextricably bound up with religion. Pride, personal honour, the laws of hospitality and vengeance all have a religious patina. Love of country and love of God amount to the same thing, in fact. The sense of "country" is synonymous with the independence of the local community; the idea of nationalism is rejected as something alien, the preserve of an urban elite and the root of the progressive, socialist notions which led to the establishment of the ruling PDPA and later Soviet intervention.

Suspicion of nationalism as an ideology is linked to widespread resentment against the urban intelligentsia which is popularly held responsible by the rural classes for having opened the floodgates to communism and the USSR. But after three years and more of Soviet military occupation and counter-insurgency operations, the suffering and casualties endured by virtually all Afghan population groups have produced a relatively new sense of nationhood.

The war started a decade ago, in 1973. It has progressed through three stages: ideological, populist and national. Each represents an intensification in the conflict, a widening of the impact of the fighting and changes in the way in which the war is fought. During late 1982 and early 1983 the conflict entered a fourth stage: a "war of influence" or contest among rival resistance groups which would have a decisive impact on the future. It would be easy to portray these stages as a clear-cut consecutive series; in fact, they overlapped and in some ways have paralleled each other.

The ideological phase was triggered by Prince Daoud's coup in 1973, largely engineered and supported by the Parcham cadres of the PDPA. It is traditional in Afghan society for a nephew to usurp his uncle's position, and Daoud's move against the king was not a shock to most people. He was, after all, an important member of the Mohammadzai tribe's royal line. But it provoked a strong reaction among the Islamic revolutionaries centred on Kabul University, the "fundamentalists" as they are somewhat misleadingly described in the Western press. By 1974 the cause of Islamic resurgence dominated campus life and Daoud felt compelled to turn against what he saw as a threat from the Right to his reforms and consolidation of personal power.

Prominent figures in the Islamic movement included Professors Niazi, Burhannudin Rabbani, Rasul Saiaf and the obscure second-year engineering student, Gulbaddin Hekmatyar. Islamic "fundamentalism" was very much an international phenomenon. The writings of Ali Shariati of Iran, Mohammad Qotub of Egypt and Abdul Maududi of Pakistan provided much of the inspiration for groups of Islamic scholars and their students throughout the world. They sought a return to the essential teachings of the Koran and the installation of Islamic law or the Shariat, as sovereign as other nations might have assemblies, parliaments, constitutions or monarchs.

It was an idealistic philosophy and a strong reaction against the two great materialist ideologies of East and West: communism and capitalism. It did not reject industrialisation, technological innovation or scientific learning; on the contrary, it sought the very best the rest of the world has to offer, but sublimated these advances to the law of God. It was a daring, simplistic and attractive movement for young people from lowly backgrounds who had had their first taste of education and urban life. Its followers in Afghanistan were among the very first to forecast that Daoud's coup would be the forerunner of communism and greater Soviet interference in the nation's affairs. Ironically, it drew its support from the very same classes that provided the membership of the PDPA cadres in the country.

The warnings of the Islamic revolutionaries fell on deaf ears. For rural people, what happened in Kabul was Kabul's business, not theirs. As long as central government did not interfere in their lives, they would not concern themselves with the goings-on in the fleshpots of the capital. As for the Russians, nothing much was known about them.

"All I knew of Russians in those days," said a woman from a village in Kunar Province, "was that we had a lot of nice, cheap things in the shops which came from Russia. I could not help thinking at that time that a people who made useful things which were so inexpensive for us must be nice, too."

The Islamic revolutionaries went out and about to spread the gospel. They were often either ignored or turned in to the authorities for their pains. Daoud's purge resulted in hundreds of deaths and many more arrests. Surviving leaders fled to Pakistan where they launched their *jehad.*

47

The Islamic movement suffered from two major shortcomings. First, the leaders were divided in opinion over strategy. Gulbaddin Hekmatyar wanted to take to armed revolt immediately. Others, such as Rabbani, sought to prepare the ground first through mobilising opinion in provincial areas and by developing a coherent organisation capable of concerted action on a national scale. Their differences mirrored those of their opponents in the Marxist-Leninist PDPA — they were divided along ethnic and tribal lines, between Pushtun and non-Pushtun and by the personalities and self-assertiveness of their individual leaders. The Islamic movement was urban and middle class, for it was to Islam what the PDPA was to Marxism-Leninism. While both rightists and leftists in the tiny urban elite reflected the intrinsic divisions within Afghan society as a whole, each side had failed to maintain links with its rural, traditional origins.

Their Peshawar-based movement quickly split up into rival factions. Gulbaddin Hekmatyar's men received arms and training and carried out cross-border raids, attempting an insurrection — which failed — in the Panjsher Valley. Pakistan's Prime Minister, Zulfikar Ali Bhutto, employed Gulbaddin's Hezb-i-Islami as a counter to Daoud's encouragement of Pushtun separatism among the tribes of Pakistan's North West Frontier Province. Men like Rabbani preferred to concentrate on political agitation to prepare the way.

These leaders soon made contact with similar revolutionary Muslim societies abroad. Some were to link up with the International Muslim Brotherhood, with its extensive and well-funded international contacts. Others, like Rabbani, made good use of their reputations in the Gulf as Islamic scholars, commentators and poets. Gulbaddin accepted funds from Libya, and he mimicked the revolutionary zeal of the new Islamic republic in Iran to gain the ayatollahs' support.

Premature though this ideological stage may have been, and carried on by people who could not claim to have the allegiance of the Afghan public at large at this time, it nevertheless served to wake the country from its centuries-long slumber. The Islamic movement provided a ready focus for resistance to the PDPA coup which followed in April, 1978.

Just as "Mirwais," a provincial Pushtun, had gravitated towards the Khalq faction of the PDPA in the 1960s, so too Abdul Haq spontaneously began his *jehad* at the age of 15.

"Just after Daoud came to power I remember we had a teacher at our school in Jalalabad who tried to introduce socialist ideas into the

48

class. I objected to this. His job was to educate, not indoctrinate. We formed a delegation to protest to the headmaster and we had a demonstration outside the school. My family was not rich, but we had a few acres of land and so I had a little money to spend on making posters and placards. I was arrested."

Abdul Haq had no further formal education. Classroom politics started him off on a career of dangerous clandestine work. He is now 26 years old and commands 4,000 men in Kabul Province. He has been twice wounded — quite badly — and he is now one of the foremost and truly *guerilla* commanders in the war.

In the months following the PDPA coup in 1978, what had been a limited, Islamic *jehad* projected largely from Iran and Pakistan became a popular war pitting common folk against a clearly pro-Soviet regime. There were two reasons why, by the summer of 1979, not a province was left untouched by the war and why thousands of tribesmen launched often suicidal, mass attacks on army positions, with entire garrisons and even divisions in revolt.

First, Taraki was not of the Mohammadzai royal line. He was not even from the Durrani branch of Pushtun tribes. He was Ghilzai. Legitimacy and continuity had not been preserved. It marked a break with tradition. More important, however much tribal communities in south-eastern Afghanistan may have liked his jokes, the PDPA lost little time in attempting to do what no other ruler had dared to try: to impose its authority and its radical policies right through the country in a forcible, hasty manner never before attempted on such a massive scale.

The ideological warriors of the Islamic movement in Peshawar were soon joined by other leaders with a hereditary religious or traditional political following. Pir (Saint) Syed Ahmad Al-Gailani and Sibghatullah Mojaddedi were two outstanding examples of families with considerable followings which took up arms, formed political parties in exile and declared their *jehad*. Maulavi Nabi Mohammadi's Harakat Inquilab-i-Islami was one of the largest and most widespread resistance organisations, representing parish priests or *mullahs*, landlords and their peasants as well as intellectuals from Kabul with a Western education and democratic ideas. The "populist" stage had begun, and when the Soviets introduced their occupation forces it assumed a national character, an instinctive reaction against a foreign invader. It could no longer be described as a civil war, pitting Afghans against Afghans — the Soviet presence was an unmistakable focus for opposition, even within the PDPA.

Terrain and climate were always the masters in warfare and

especially so in Afghanistan. The nature and shape of the guerilla war was largely dictated by these two elements. Only six percent of Afghanistan is cultivated, mainly the fertile uplands irrigated by the country's four major rivers and their tributaries. This is where the bulk of the population lived, and it was able to pose a direct threat to the cities lying athwart ancient trading routes, to the sparse communications linking these market towns and at the same time able to withdraw when threatened by the security forces into the massive ranges of the Hindu Kush or the vast morass of hills in the central region, the Hazarajat.

The Hindu Kush runs down almost the entire length of the Durand Line before it turns west through Baluchistan. At once an impenetrable barrier to security forces seeking to destroy resistance strongholds (it should be born in mind that a "stronghold" may simply consist of a cave or two, or a cluster of hovels), the mountains also provided a natural refuge and a means of escaping to the safety of Pakistan's sparsely populated and lightly-governed tribal agencies. The Hazarajat is virtually inaccessible as far as conventional forces are concerned, yet its central position within the "ring road" of highways has permitted guerillas based there to sally forth and cut roads, ambush supply convoys, harass military columns and attack military posts.

Kabul was not in a good defensive position. Its main road — Soviet-built — leading northwards to the Soviet border was threatened by natural cover, both in terms of rugged mountain ravines and cliffs, and the orchards of Parwan and Paghman. The 6,000 ft Salang Tunnel inaugurated by the late Leonid Brezhnev was to be the scene of a major disaster for Soviet troops. One stretch of the highway was dubbed "death mile" by Soviet military drivers.

Other roads leading out of Kabul, to Jalalabad on the Pakistan border to the south-east; to Asadabad via Jalalabad; to Khost in Paktya and to Gardez and Kandahar were subject to unfavourable ground. The security forces had to provide increasingly intensive route security for traffic as the months went by. The northern cities of Mazar-i-Sharif and Faisabad were also subject to sorties mounted by guerillas based in nearby mountain hideouts. Herat in the extreme north-west, close to the Iranian and Soviet borders, and Kandahar in the extreme south were sited in relatively open ground where the terrain was more conducive to effective movement by the security forces' armoured vehicles. The guerillas adapted to some extent by using darkness and off-road travel to facilitate rapid movement.

The guerillas concentrated initially on the nearest and softest targets: the local *ulaswalli* or remote district government offices and their handfuls of paramilitary personnel who were easily disposed of or persuaded to defect with their weapons. Throughout 1978, 1979 and 1980 literally hundreds of these centres were overrun; their party members were slaughtered, the buildings gutted or taken over and the local people assimilated into the guerilla movement.

The guerillas *were* the people, warts and all. They made their own decisions, appointed their own leaders, organised their own attacks and their own defence. It was a highly localised, spontaneous and instinctive conflict, but one in which foreign radio broadcasts, particularly those of the BBC World Service in Persian and later Pushtu, brought home to isolated, parochial communities the universal nature of what they were doing. But it was very much a local affair; all too often the guerillas were perfectly satisfied if they could simply remove the government presence from their area and cared little for what happened over the next hill or across the valley. For Pushtuns, the notion of organisation and co-ordination was alien; something which played into the regime's hands.

"There were seven or eight of us in the beginning," recalls a tribal elder and *Mujehad* from Uruzgan Province. "We had a shotgun, a musket and some swords and our knives. We rode out on our horses and made camp in the mountains. We sat there and waited, listening to the BBC and wondering why on earth it was the radio had not broadcast the start of our *jehad* in Uruzgan." Their first military action involved removing all traces of government in their area. Their numbers steadily grew and in common with so many other groups they experienced that age-old Afghan sense of elation at having "liberated" the country. It was to give rise to the repeated but plainly misleading claim by resistance spokesmen in Peshawar to the effect that the *Mujehadeen* had "liberated" or now "controlled" 80 percent of the countryside. Western diplomatic briefings were to echo this theme — to the detriment of an accurate understanding of what the war was about.

The truth was, however, that the Soviet occupation forces *chose* not to occupy or "pacify" the country as a whole. Invasion forces, which brought in all the paraphernalia of a conventional army designed for a European war, were designed to shore up the loyal PDPA cadres under the leadership of Babrak Karmal and his fellow Parchamites, not to take on the "bandits" considered wrongly in 1980 to be merely a nuisance and who originated in foreign, "reactionary" states. Although Soviet forces were compelled to take on a steadily increasingly burden of the responsibility for security operations the following year, they suffered from both political constraints imposed by Moscow and from severe disadvantages in terms of logistics supply and inadequate training for the type of warfare appropriate for dealing with an elusive, ubiquitous enemy in rough terrain.

The presence of the Russians in large numbers, both military and civil, mobilised Afghan society. Academics, intellectuals and professional men and women of a centrist or left-of-centre persuasion had vainly sought to find a middle ground in Kabul between the Marxist-Leninists of the PDPA on the one end of the spectrum and the Islamic revolutionaries on the other. But the invasion and subsequent moves to "Sovietise" society finally convinced them that collaboration or compromise were impracticable. Men such as Professor Barhouddin Majrooh and Rasul Amin formed an underground group of intellectuals in Kabul to try to preserve what remained of Afghan free thought and expression. But arrests of their members forced those still at liberty into exile. There was no middle ground left.

A provincial doctor put it this way: "It was as if we in Afghanistan had been living a wonderful dream for all those years. Life was so tranquil in the 1950s and 1960s. What happened in Kabul was Kabul's affair and was simply more of the same. But the arrival of Soviet forces shattered our sleep. We found ourselves in the 20th century."

Once local areas had been freed from official administration, guerillas concentrated on mounting hit-and-run attacks on the enemy's supply routes. The lack of "run" was often their undoing — in their desire for loot and ammunition, they would hang about the scene of a successful ambush and find themselves caught in the open by helicopter gunships, of which the number available to the security forces was being rapidly increased during the course of 1980.

Guerillas hijacked civilian traffic, seizing cargoes and giving the drivers receipts which the Kabul regime accepted as proof that the drivers were worthy of further employment despite the mounting losses of goods and vehicles. Military posts and garrisons required frequent supplies of rations, cash, ammunition and fuel and the quick-reaction forces in major garrisons seldom bothered to respond to minor crises — and the plight of beleaguered Afghan Army units was considered "minor" in most instances. But by 1981 the authorities were forced to widen the roads and flatten everything which might provide natural cover for ambush parties in an attempt to deter the raids being mounted with increasing frequency and effectiveness as guerillas obtained more weapons and put more men into the field. By April 1983 even Prime Minister Sultan Ali Keshtmand blamed the guerillas for the destruction of 14 percent of the country's transport, 75 percent of its communications and half its hospitals and schools.

During the course of 1980 the Peshawar and Iranian-based resistance parties in exile began to exert their authority inside the country, by virtue of quantities of Egyptian and Chinese weapons weapons they were able to acquire from abroad and smuggle into Pakistan. Each of these parties represented a specific political, social, regional or religious "constituency" in the country; none could, however, claim to represent the internal resistance as a whole — though that did not stop them from trying.

Tribal leaders in Pushtun tribal areas desperately clung to their traditional authority in the face of this challenge. A single tribal chief might send groups of elders as deputations representing his tribe to different parties, swearing allegiance and begging for arms and ammunition. It was not uncommon for a guerilla commander or *malik* to have to wait months in Peshawar, kicking his heels as he waited for a few rifles and land mines. The chief would of course be credited by his people with having obtained the weapons, and by ensuring that no single resistance organisation dominated his tribe, he could maintain his prestige by playing one group off against another in the time-honoured Pushtun manner. In that sense the role of the exiled party offices was negative. It helped ensure that opposition to the security forces remained localised and it militated against the development of talented military commanders. Instead it reinforced the leadership of the Old Guard — the *maliks, khans* and elders — most of whom were ill-suited to the leadership and management of guerilla warfare.

The reverse was true of parties such as Gulbaddin Hekmatyar's Hezb-i-Islami. Hekmatyar had no real base inside Afghanistan, save for his home town of Kunduz. These organisations would try to build up a following by promising lavish supplies of money and weapons. Their guerillas were roving bands with little grass roots support among the civilians. Their tactics were often counterproductive; they would in some instances extort *zakat* or *ushr*, the Islamic taxes, at gunpoint. This aroused considerable hostility, much in the same way as the Khalq's radical and brutal reforms provoked a storm of opposition.

The "common man" in Afghanistan was illiterate and deeply

superstitious. He revered shrines and their guardians, or holy men, who specialised in curing one ailment or another. When the Soviets bombed the shrine of Mir Abdal in Logar, for example, the reaction of ordinary local people was, "We must have displeased the shrine or it would not have allowed the *Shuravi* to bomb it. It would have struck the aircraft out of the sky." Many people thought that the shrines and their keepers were spiritually asleep, and that at some point they would awake and use a secret, religious energy to force the Russians out.

Trying to organise such people into an effective military force was clearly a formidable task. Pir Syed Ahmad Al-Gailani and Sibghatullah Mojaddedi did not try; instead they simply handed over their very limited military resources to tribal elders directly, and were surprised when some of these scarce weapons turned up on the local black market. Later, Gailani tried to form a military command structure, with disastrous results. He tried to introduce military ranks among the Tani tribe, for instance. The tribesmen had no idea of what a rank was, but they fell about trying to get the highest ones for themselves.

Alternatively these resistance groups with traditional followings would make the mistake of appointing several commanders of equal status throughout a particular region or province, each of whom would be directly responsible to the Pakistan-based headquarters. It would not only clog up the parties' burgeoning bureaucracies, but would plunge the party leadership into a vipers' nest of feuds and quarrels as the commanders would employ the traditional *Pushtun-walli* or Honour Code of Pushtuns to score points off their rivals in the area.

Jamiat-i-Islami and the Hezb-i-Islami faction led by Yunis Khalis fared better. They did not have the Western publicity accorded to the Gailani and Mojaddedi families, nor did they have the funds made available by the Gulf to the Islamic revolutionaries. They had little to offer in material terms to the putative membership inside Afghanistan. These two parties had to get things right in terms of organisation at the outset. Commanders were chosen with great care. People who showed promise on the battlefield were promoted according to their abilities, not their tribal seniority or their expertise in Koranic recitation. A single overall commander would be appointed to a specific region. He alone would be directly responsible to the party headquarters. He would appoint subordinate commanders and form an embryonic alternative administration in the vacuum left by the departed regime officials. His word was law, the official party stamp on his written orders could not be questioned. He would discipline or remove — and even execute — his guerillas who were guilty of misconduct. It was a simple, decentralised system based on individuals' capacity for leadership and administration. It was flexible, for it made allowances for local social conditions. Yet the chain of command was clear and could not be questioned, at least in theory.

If during the first year following the invasion, localised commands could effectively launch small-scale operations and mount effective defence lasting a matter of hours, the increasing role of Soviet forces in counter-insurgency operations inevitably meant that actions became increasingly protracted and intense. The use of artillery strikes and multiple 122mm rocket launchers, persistent aerial bombardment and the deployment of fast and well-armed armoured fighting vehicles (AFVs), produced something of a crisis in several areas in 1981. Guerillas were obliged to fight defensive, almost conventional battles lasting several days. Good organisation, careful expenditure of ammunition and the ability of commanders to demonstrate leadership and initiative in unfavourable conditions were at a premium. The guerillas learned the hard way; they could simply not afford to fail to coordinate their actions. If they failed to do so — as they often did — the authorities' increasingly effective intelligence and subversive effort meant the resistance paid heavily in blood for the sins of military omission.

There was a price for success, too: the more able, young guerilla commanders led from the front in action.

"Sometimes it is very dangerous and the enemy is strong," explained one commander from the Yunis Khalis organisation. "We have to get close and my men are frightened. But I go in front, because then they have to follow me. If they don't, and I am killed, what will they say to people afterwards? They have to follow.

"When I go to an area where I am only known by name, the local people tell me not to attack a particular target. They will say it is too dangerous and that if I am killed, they will be dishonoured by the death of such a famous man, etc., etc. What they are really looking for is an excuse not to attack themselves. They can say, well, so-and-so didn't do it, why should we?

"But when I take a handful of men down to the road and we destroy three APCs and the local people can see the bodies and the black smoke pouring from the wrecks, they are very pleased and beg me to stay.

"Having begged me not to attack because of the fear of helicopter

55

gunships coming in and destroying their homes in the inevitable reprisal, they will now beg me to take them with me on another attack. Then they don't care about what happens to their homes. Once they see a commander can really hurt the communists, the people want to fight. But when a commander is no good, no one wants trouble. It's not worth it to them then."

But all this means that promising young combat leaders are killed off at a rate out of all proportion to their numbers. Youngsters in their teens and twenties leading in groups of 50 or 150 men fall much in the same way as subalterns were killed off in the trench warfare of World War II. The sedentary, elderly and ineffectual guerilla commanders live to a ripe old age and perpetuate the failings in their respective organisations.

Fighting has been seasonal. Cold weather and in many areas heavy snow slowed down operations for combatants on both sides. Early spring saw the resistance-in-exile preparing itself for the summer offensives. New shipments of arms would start to move in-country. What was striking was the relative ease with which *Mujehadeen* were able to transit the borders and their traditional communications routes inside Afghanistan. Lines of men and animals could be seen by Western correspondents as far as the eye could see, moving in broad daylight (marching, in fact, over mountains for 16 hours a day very often) to the "front." Roving reconnaissance aircraft and pairs of helicopter gunships shuttling to and fro from operations would force these groups to take momentary cover; after a few minutes the columns would tramp on. The guerillas seldom took precautions for route security — in most cases they did not need to. The fact was that the security forces were singularly unable to make serious inroads on guerilla communications, although from time to time sectarian clashes between Sunnis and Shias or among rival tribes living athwart the Durand Line would hamper movement for a period of days and sometimes weeks.

The small, annual supplies of arms from external sources and the bout of summer defections from the Afghan armed forces each year ensured that the guerillas steadily increased the numbers of armed men available on the battlefield. In 1983 there were estimated to be 150,000 to 200,000 armed guerillas on active service at any one point in time inside Afghanistan. This gave the resistance as a whole one-and-a-half to two fighters for every member of the security forces. By contrast, in the Malayan counter-insurgency campaign the British authorities reached a stage where they could deploy 30 security forces' personnel for every guerilla, or Communist Terrorist as the insurgents were called. But it was evident that the steady stream of Afghan civilians out of the country into Iranian and Pakistani refugee camps ensured that the resistance as a whole was to have to rely more and more on these reservoirs of manpower as a proportion of their fighting strength.

It was a positive factor in the sense that these "sanctuaries" provided able-bodied men with periods of rest, and an opportunity to place their women and children in conditions of relative security. On the other hand it increased the political and military role in the war of the resistance groups or parties in exile and hence the influence both the Iranian and Pakistani authorities were able to wield over the conduct of the war. It also provided a source of Soviet pressure on these two neighbouring countries. Of the total active strength of the guerilla forces in 1982/83, as much as a quarter was drawn directly from these "sanctuaries."

This emphasised the conflict between the more traditional Afghan resistance groups which predominated in terms of numbers of men inside Afghanistan and the "ideological" leadership backed by Iran and Pakistan which concentrated its superior resources on attracting members in the refugee camps, much to the disquiet of the United Nations High Commissioner for Refugees (UNHCR).

By late 1982 a full-scale "war of influence" seemed imminent in northern and central areas of the country. Simplified, the conflict was between Islamic revolutionaries with Iranian, Libyan and Muslim Brotherhood connections and the more traditional Muslim guerilla groups. The Iranian-backed Shia revolutionary groups in central and western areas appeared to have formed an informal alliance with Gulbaddin Hekmatyar's men, for Hekmatyar maintained close ties with Iran, had had financial support from the Libyans and was backed strongly by the radical, rightist Jamaat Islami Pakistan, which dominated key posts of the Pakistani federal and provincial authorities.

The conflict mirrored the internecine violence in ruling PDPA circles in Kabul. As Moscow sought to exploit and control the divisions on linguistic, ethnic, personal and ideological lines within the ranks of its communist clientele in the capital, so too both Pakistan and Iran sought to control and exploit the natural enmities within the resistance movement. But for both Moscow and the two Muslim states, their interference appeared to be counter-productive in terms of trying to adopt a war-winning strategy for either side.

The guerillas' internal conflict, exacerbated by Kabul's moves to turn one commander or leader against his fellows, widened the gulf between the *Mujehadeen* actively prosecuting the war against Soviet and regime forces inside Afghanistan and their brethren proselytising on their behalf, but not always in their interest, outside the country. During the course of 1982 several prominent guerilla commanders threatened to go it alone, and to sever their links with their nominal superiors in Peshawar. But this would have meant going without the cash and weapons these leaders were able to provide from time to time. Saiaf, for example, who speaks Arabic, has been a considerable hit with Gulf leaders and he is spending lavish sums of money on building his followers modern bungalows near Nowshera in what is now called Saiaf Colony. It may be apocryphal, but the story goes to the effect that he tried to make his "colony" look like any other mud village by covering the concrete walls around these homes with mud plaster, but when the monsoon rains came in April 1983 they washed the mud away to everyone's delight. This was one of several episodes which hardly endeared the Peshawar leaders to the guerillas risking their lives in battle.

Despite these disturbing trends, the resistance inside Afghanistan appeared to be making slow but perceptible progress towards tentative military unity, especially in northern areas where regionally distinct, homogeneous ethnic peoples seemed more receptive to the need to organise fighting and civil infrastructure.

Herat, dominated by Ismael Khan and Alauddin, had become the administrative and military control point for a guerilla system extending over three provinces in the north-west of the country. Herat guerillas maintained loose contact with Zabiullah of Mazar-i-Sharif city, another regional commander who had established a workable judicial, military, educational and social alternative to the regime in the area. He in turn maintained links with Abdul Hai, commander of *Mujehadeen* at Nahrin and with the celebrated Massoud Ahmadshah, commander of guerilla forces in the natural redoubt of the Panjsher Valley, north-east of Kabul. In other words, Jamiat-i-Islami and Harakat Inquilab-i-Islami formed a coherent "northern tier" stretching along the Soviet border from Iran in the west to China in the east, and embracing Tajik, Uzbek, Turkomen and Hazara groups.

During 1981 and 1982 the security forces mounted no less than six major operations designed to subdue resistance in Panjsher. Interest in subjugating the residents of the area rested upon its role as a springboard for guerilla operations directed against the Salang highway, Bagram airbase, the area immediately north of the capital, the town of Paghman, which stubbornly remained in insurgent hands, and the capital itself. The Soviets appeared to aim for a neutralisation of Panjsher, but the Kabul regime sought to re-establish a government presence in the valley. This took the form of a beleaguered post at Rokha, but this toehold was gained at considerable cost not only in terms of lives and military resources, but the exacerbation of Khalq-Parcham enmity, for it was the Khalq faction which bore the brunt of the regime's use of party activists and troops to staff the town. This created considerable resentment on the part of the Khalqis, who felt that their fellow Parchamis were granted a privileged exemption from the dangers involved in "volunteering" for duty in Panjsher.

Massoud's command grew in size in fact, despite the considerable economic damage wrought by the security forces and the impact on civilians, many of whom suffered from acute food shortages. The 1978 civilian populace of the valley was around 80,000, a figure which was halved by the winter of 1982/83. Kabul approached Massoud indirectly on three occasions with the offer of a truce, backed up by promises of non-interference and large sums of cash. There were reports that Massoud accepted a six-month ceasefire in December 1982.

It might well simply have been a question of "live and let live" on the part of both sides, as Massoud rebuilt his forces and the regime redeployed its security forces to south-eastern border areas in anticipation for the summer's fighting season. Zabiullah was also one of the major commanders approached by the regime with offers of money and a kind of mutual non-aggression pact. Much of this campaign could be attributed to Kabul's need to "pacify" the country for the forthcoming UN talks in Geneva, and to relieve its overstretched armed forces for duties in border provinces where troops would try and block, deter or at the very least delay the movement of men and supplies moving in-country for the new season of guerilla operations. Abdul Haq of Kabul Province refused an offer of 27 million Afghanis from Kabul in return for an assurance from him that he would refrain from his attacks on Kabul's power plants and transmission lines which had during the course of December 1982 plunged the capital into darkness for weeks at a time.

The "southern tier" of Pushtun province was weaker than the north in guerilla terms. The tribal Pushtuns were by nature highly localised and competitive. They clung strongly to their traditional way of life and yet, oddly enough, were more deeply affected by the authority of the "ideological" resistance parties just across the border in Peshawar and Quetta. The prominence of Khalq cadres in the ruling PDPA's armed forces and the Ministry of Tribes and Nationalities gave the authorities an opportunity to try to "atomise" Pushtun tribal society, by promising arms and cash to tribal leaders if they would lead their respective families, clans and tribes against their traditional rivals in the region. They tried to turn Kunar's Safi tribe against the Nuristanis, for example, and Wazirs against the Zadranis in Paktya.

The Pushtun manner of warfare is a form of sport, no less. All able-bodied men, by virtue of the extraordinarily democratic nature of their society, will gather at a pre-arranged spot to fire off scarce ammunition at a distant militia or army post. The "battle" may rage for hours with no decisive result in most cases. Honour is satisfied, the tribe concerned has avoided taking an unacceptable level of casualties (weapons are often fired at a range which ensures neither side really loses out) and everyone returns home to live to "fight" another day.

A good example is Paktya Province where the resistance claims to have liberated most of the countryside as well as the road leading from Khost across the border to Miramshah. In fact the road is quite open with trade flourising almost as normal. Guerillas use it, and so does the local regime presence, for the acquisition of food and the despatch of its agents to Pakistan to stir up trouble. Government posts fall to the guerillas now and again, but new ones are soon established. The level of warfare is stable; the Soviets should be quite happy with a situation in which thousands of guerillas who should be better led and organised are tied down by second-rate Afghan army conscripts, an unreliable militia and a few hundred party activists in the major towns of Khost and Gardez. The guerillas are quite satisfied too, as long as Paktya is open to columns of men and arms moving further afield from their base camps in the mountains.

There are exceptions among the Pushtuns. Able young commanders do emerge who are not *mullahs*, revolutionary brigands or tribal *maliks*. One example is Abdul Haq, who mounted a series of a dozen coordinated attacks against targets in the capital itself over a 24-hour period to mark the third anniversary of the Soviet invasion. Abdul encourages initiative among his subordinate commanders. He tries to rotate his men in the firing line and he tries to develop special skills — such as demolition work — suitable for the greater efforts several guerila leaders were by 1982 devoting to urban warfare.

Ironically, for the Afghan resistance to become decisive in military operations the guerillas must destroy the very thing they have been instinctively fighting for — a traditional tribal order intensely individualistic, parochial and above all, independent. The very weight of conflict over several years or generations has to produce far-reaching changes in the way Afghans regard themselves, and their place in society. To evolve politically in the struggle, many young Muslim fighters believe that independent sources of arms and training will be necessary if they are to free themselves from the inhibiting interests of neighbouring states.

The revolutionary fervour and ideologies of the ruling PDPA and, at the other extreme, of the Muslim Brotherhood seem equally unsuited to engaging the loyalty of the rural Afghan population groups. Only the new generation of promising young guerilla commanders now in their 20s and 30s with a decade of combat experience seem to offer a way to break through this impasse. They admit that whether they prevail militarily and politically or not is largely conditional on their power and prestige being enhanced sufficiently to produce a viable, self-sustaining resistance structure on a national or at least regional scale, and one which depends for its survival neither on Kabul's bribes and offers of "self-government" on the one hand, nor on the weapons and cash thrown at the problem by the unrepresentative resistance-in-exile groups supported by Iran, Pakistan and other foreign sources.

There is a sense of urgency among the more enlightened, politically-conscious guerilla leaders in the field. They know at first hand the ravaging of inflation and food scarcities on their ability to conduct offensive operations. They fear that growing pressure on Pakistan's military rulers will persuade Islamabad — and possibly, Iran after the Ayatollah Khomeini's death — to come to terms with Kabul through the offices of the UN. They believe there is limited time in which to build a coherent military and political command capable of raising Soviet costs of continued occupation to a level at which Moscow must review its policy. During 1981 and 1982 the resistance showed signs of developing into a "war of movement," a trend demonstrating the ability of the internal resistance to shift men and weapons across ethnic and political boundaries from one part of the country to another. This, they say, will have to be taken much further to escalate the war sufficiently to make Moscow reconsider. These young commanders look increasingly to the West for material help. Would Western governments ignore these Muslim versions of Che Guevara and Ho Chi Minh?

The Saint and the Engineer

Commando Zikria never hurt anyone. His victims were journalists and diplomats and all they lost was valuable time. He did not look like a commando. He was overweight and wore tight-fitting Western sports clothes. He would lurk in the overgrown gardens of the dilapidated Deans Hotel in Peshawar and waylay foreigners. He wore a wristwatch of which he was particularly proud. At the press of a button the instrument would play a metallic rendering of *Yankee Doodle Dandy*. Commando Zikria let it be known that it had been a gift for unspecified but clearly patriotic services. He would rummage through his briefcase and produce an advertisement clipped from an American newspaper. It sought linguists for the CIA, and with a nudge and a wink Zikria would indicate that this was where his special talents lay. The naive or courteous would listen to his incoherent monologue on derring-do in the *jehad* until the "commando" leaped to his feet, waved his arms about and shouted excitedly: "I am ready! Ready for anything!" Few of his victims were impressed, and even fewer responded as Zikria would have liked. An American consul remained unmoved by Zikria's offer of a case full of lapis lazuli in return for a visa for the United States.

Peshawar, capital of Pakistan's North West Frontier Province and situated within a couple of hours' drive from the border post of Torkham, had more than its fair share of Zikrias in the months immediately following the Soviet invasion. It attracted Western adventurers, war groupies and mercenaries, too. If Western visitors found the Afghans they met somewhat puzzling, the sense of bewilderment and incomprehension was mutual.

For example, there was the faded blonde highschool teacher in long white gloves nicknamed "Aeroplane Annie" who managed to import a number of large, radio-controlled model aircraft built by her Scottish boyfriend, said to be an aeronautics engineer. The couple sought to sell these craft to Afghan resistance leaders in the city because, they claimed, the models could be directed to fly over the Bagram airbase near Kabul and bomb the fighters and helicopters parked there. Little came of it; the local Special Branch were not amused by this improbable scheme and in any event, Annie's boyfriend disappeared. Although he had been known to suffer from bouts of amnesia in the past, Annie was convinced to the last that he had been abducted. Unable to pay her hotel bills, Annie was compelled to hand over all but one of her model planes to the management as security, until at last her husband arrived and they flew home.

Mercenaries surfaced in 1981. They were mainly British "veterans" of the Congo, Angola and other notorious campaigns. One group stayed at the conspicuous Khyber Intercontinental Hotel from time to time. They registered under their own names and described themselves in the hotel register as "aircrew." They ran "extraction operations." In other words, they crossed the Durand Line into Afghanistan and tried to bring back exotic items of Soviet military equipment. They were particularly interested in the Soviet Mi-24 "Hind" helicopter gunship's armour plating and electronic equipment. It was widely assumed that this amateurish affair was initiated by the Pentagon. The portly Englishman in a business suit who looked after their interests in Peshawar was well liked by the hotel staff. They thought him very distinguished. It was rumoured he was related — distantly — to both Lord Snowdon and Kim Philby.

The operation was "blown" when other freelance mercenaries trickled into Pakistan, eager to muscle in on the war. They managed without difficulty to get drunk in diplomats' clubs in Islamabad and began to boast to foreign correspondents of their previous exploits. The Pakistani authorities promptly expelled several of them.

One elderly American mercenary was unable to find work and he would drift into the local American Centre nearly every day to scan the papers in the hope of finding a market for his skills. He was eventually taken on by South African interests in Namibia. Arms dealers were quickly disappointed. One demolitions expert lent a detailed map of Afghanistan to one major resistance group and when the guerillas failed to return it he loudly threatened to blow them and their headquarters sky-high. A personable Belgian dealer and veteran of the Indochina war offered silent mortars, miniature incendiary grenades and other specialised weapons for urban guerilla warfare, but there were no takers.

Peshawar is still a London waiting for its de Gaulle, as one French pundit described it. Adventurers aside, it is the centre for literally dozens of Afghan resistance groups and political parties, from eccentric royalists to secretive Maoists. If one includes Quetta, capital of Baluchistan Province, and the border towns of eastern Iran, there are more than 40 externally-represented groups. Today there are two main alliances embracing seven major organisations recognised by the Pakistan Government as representing the resistance as a whole. They are distinguished primarily from one another by the personalities of their leaders, their ideologies, their ethnic or tribal origins, and finally by their effectiveness — or lack of it.

The relationship between the alliances and parties in exile and the *Mujehadeen* fighting inside Afghanistan is in general terms tenuous. The exiled leaders have two roles to play: they provide credibility to the resistance in international terms and more important, they provide arms and funds for the guerillas. But the constant rivalry and in-fighting among the Peshawar leaders are increasingly resented by the men at the front. The latter may well carry membership cards of one exiled party or another, but their loyalty can be measured in direct proportion to the patronage they receive from Peshawar, nothing more. No one leader in Peshawar and no combination of leaders can be said to truly represent the resistance as a whole. Each party — and to some extent each of the two alliances — does reflect a particular "constituency" of the Afghan peoples. As yet there is no firm indication that any one leader is likely to emerge as the overall national figurehead able to command a significant degree of allegiance across ethnic and political boundaries.

Initially, observers maintained that these divisions were healthy; a multi-faceted resistance meant that Soviet and Afghan security forces would be unable to neutralise the leadership at a stroke. The sheer chaos of resistance activity was in itself seen as an advantage. More recently, however, the divisions have been assumed by reporters and diplomatic observers to be a distinct drawback in attempts by guerillas to escalate the war. Much of the effort and limited resources have been devoted to intra-resistance competition, and the Kabul authorities have been able to make gains in playing one group off against another.

Opinion still varies considerably on this point, but it is interesting to note that since the formation of the two broad alliances — exercises, it must be said, on paper rather than in practical terms — some field commanders complain that the resulting bureaucracy in Peshawar has meant delays in the distribution of arms, ammunition and cash as well as decision-making — a loss of a sense of direction, in other words. The larger the alliance, the more people there are to be satisfied and it is increasingly difficult for the exiled leaders to concentrate resources, say, on one province or city rather than another for strategic reasons. Everyone wants to have his say, and each "constituency" must be appeased, with a commensurate loss in effective military planning.

The exiled party organisations have evolved during the past three years. Almost constant contact at various levels with a variety of foreigners representing refugee relief agencies, newspapers, television organisations and foreign embassies has helped develop a rudimentary but nonetheless fresh awareness of the outside world and international politics especially. Afghan leaders and spokesmen have travelled throughout the Muslim world and further abroad, to Western Europe and North America. The whole process has undoubtedly helped the resistance-in-exile to polish its efforts to gain credibility and support. While suspicion, innate hostility and simple ignorance ensure the retention of a conspiratorial view of world affairs, Afghans in Peshawar have learned to press the argument that what is happening in Afghanistan is not a localised affair, but one which must be seen in the global context.

Coming from the mouths of largely uneducated and hitherto insular Afghans, this is remarkable. Contact with the outside world has reinforced their sense of correctness in their struggle. It has helped give them a sense of importance, a feeling of not being entirely alone. The resistance-in-exile can take much of the credit for that.

A factor common to all the groups is a feeling of bitterness over the West's apparent lack of material military support. There is an obvious contradiction here. While complaining that the West has failed to provide the guerillas with sophisticated anti-aircraft weapons, for example, a party spokesman or leader-in-exile will in the same breath denounce the West for trying to use Afghanistan for its own anti-Soviet propaganda purposes. "It's our war — not something between Americans and Russians," is a common remark. "You (the West) are quite happy for the war to go on as long as we continue to bleed to death for your propaganda," is another comment often heard here. The issue is exploited by the Afghan security and intelligence organisation, the Khad, in despatching agents across the border into the refugee camps. One agent was told to emphasise the point that the war was one between superpowers and that ordinary folk should simply stay out of it.

Obviously the guerillas cannot have it both ways. Afghans suffer from an odd duality in their response to their political crises: they at once blame outsiders for the problem and at the same time search around for a foreign power to champion — and finance — their cause.

A matter of weeks before Egyptian President Anwar Sadat's assassination at the hands of a group of Muslim Brothers, one "fundamentalist" resistance leader, Rasul Saiaf, held a press conference in Islamabad in which he denounced Sadat for having stated publicly that Egyptian weapons were being supplied to the Afghans, which of course they are still. Saiaf's own men, in fact, are armed with Chinese and Egyptian weapons of Soviet design — the markings are plain enough. It is no wonder then that Western governments — if they are helping — choose to do so at arm's length.

One leader, Pir (Saint) Syed Ahmad Al-Gailani, still commands considerable respect in Washington and London, largely by virtue of his Westernised background and the fact that so many of his entourage live in the West and maintain contacts with Western governments. But Gailani's traditionalist following is dwindling. He can no longer claim to be one of the top half-dozen resistance leaders. His authority is based on his hereditary, spiritual leadership of the Sufi Qadirrya sect which has pockets of adherents throughout the Middle East. He still commands considerable respect among the Pushtuns, but despite the reverence with which he is regarded, he is not an impressive figure. While party posters depict him in traditional dress, he reportedly prefers Gucci loafers and Liberty scarves. Otiose, sedentary, sleepy-eyed and boastful, he worked as a Peugeot car dealer in Kabul. This does not qualify him for the demanding task of forming a politico-military organisation. Family members still dominate key posts in his National Islamic Front for the Liberation of Afghanistan (NIFA).

Gailani has no disciplined, distinct military command worth consideration. His nationalist, moderate and democratic philosophy may appeal to Londoners and Parisians, but it is far from attractive to the bulk of Afghanistan's rural Muslims. Gailani maintains respect for — some claim contact with — the exiled king, Zahir Shah. Royalty is unpopular in Afghanistan today; dedicated guerilla commanders in many instances launched the *jehad* against the king's first cousin and son-in-law, Prince Daoud, and they regard Zahir Shah as the man who let the Russians in through the back door.

If the Pir is out of step with the rest of the resistance movement, it is also true that he has received the least support in terms of arms shipped secretly through Pakistan to the guerilla groups' headquarters. Both in quality and quantity, NIFA has remained at the bottom of the list for military aid as far as Pakistan is concerned. It goes without saying that Jamaat Islami Pakistan — a banned rightist political party in Pakistan which has played an important role in bankrolling some "fundamentalist"Afghan leaders — has not patronised NIFA. The party's supporters say the poor performance of Gailani's men is a direct result of this discrimination; others believe that it is Gailani's poor capability which has caused a loss of confidence among potential benefactors.

The Gailani family following has joined up with Sibghatullah Mojaddedi, leader of the Afghan National Liberation Front (ANLF). Mojaddedi hails from the "king-maker" Shor Bazaar sect in Kabul and is of considerable traditional importance, but he also demonstrates a singular lack of natural force of character or administrative skill. His following is also primarily Pushtun, and ANLF policy is very similar to that of Gailani's NIFA.

His followers are essentially tribal and the party has failed to develop an effective military line of command. A sense of accountability is lacking, and there have been unconfirmed but frequent reports of officials selling off weapons on the local black market for their own financial benefit. ANLF has had little external support in the form of cash or weapons, however, and it has steadily lost ground to the better-organised, better-led and frankly more vigorous "fundamentalist" guerillas.

The third element in the "traditionalist" alliance is Harakat Inquilab Islami Afghanistan led by Maulavi Nabi Mohammadi. He is the odd man out in this tripartite alliance, which has set up a huge bureaucracy — a veritable paper factory — in a large office block on the outskirts of Peshawar. Harakat is truly national: it has its members throughout Afghanistan. Its weakness and its strength is that it has managed to combine both Westernised or modernist Afghan intellectuals with a strongly traditional religious following. The party is huge, but it is also very badly organised. The strains within the organisation have threatened more than once to tear it apart at the seams. Three factions have broken away to the "fundamentalists," but Harakat has survived. It stands on the middle ground of resistance politics, straddling nationalist and Islamic trends. Mohammadi is an impressive man; few people have a bad word to say of him. Harakat has received less external support than its "fundamentalist" rivals, but it has certainly done better than either NIFA or ANLF and the traditionalist alliance of the three parties does very much depend on Harakat for its survival as a credible entity.

At the opposite end of the political spectrum from Gailani is "Engineer" Gulbaddin Hekmatyar, leader of the revolutionary Hezb-i-Islami Afghanistan. The 36-year-old, slightly built and fastidious leader is the centre of considerable controversy and arouses very strong feelings in Peshawar both among Afghans and local Pakistani politicians. He is well guarded and takes extraordinary precautions for his own safety, which is hardly surprising. His opponents — and there are many — believe the young autocrat is working for the Soviets.

His party office is in Fakiribad, a dusty and crowded part of town. Visitors are thoroughly frisked and questioned before they are allowed inside. But they are treated with considerable courtesy and apart from an obligatory and irritatingly superficial lecture on the nature of Islam, the fanaticism with which Hekmatyar's party is associated is absent from the public relations office, where excellent English is spoken. The office is usually busy and there is an air of effective administration. Party spokesmen have a fairly accurate idea of what journalists and television crews want. This contributes to the impression held by some American diplomats in 1980/81 that Hezb was the most effective fighting organisation inside Afghanistan itself. That impression was reinforced by Pakistani officials who insisted that Hekmatyar was the only guerilla leader of national stature. But it takes more than PR and the remarks of Pakistanis who follow the "fundamentalist" Jamaat Islami Pakistan party line to make a guerilla movement.

Hekmatyar comes from the northern city of Kunduz, but he is of the Pushtun tribe of Kharut — an anomaly, in other words. His critics claim he was a youthful member of the Parcham faction of the communist People's Democratic Party before turning to Islam when he entered the engineering faculty of Kabul University, dominated at that time by the "fundamentalist" Islamic movement opposed to the socialist policies of Daoud. He was for a time a cadet at the Military Academy, and his opponents say he was expelled for personal misconduct. Defamation of this kind is common among exiled Afghans, but in Hekmatyar's case the stories are pervasive. Together with Islamic theological students and teachers, Hekmatyar launched clandestine agitation against Daoud in the early 1970s and barely survived the prince's purges of what is generally called the Ikhwan or Muslim Brotherhood on campus. He escaped with the survivors to Pakistan and launched his *jehad* with military backing from the executed Pakistani Prime Minister, Zulfikar Ali Bhutto, in 1974.

Bhutto's support for Hekmatyar was prompted by fears of a resurgence of separatism among Pushtuns in Pakistan's North West Frontier Province, encouraged by Kabul. Hekmatyar's men received training in a special military camp and were infiltrated back across the border to carry out sabotage. Hekmatyar was certainly one of the first to launch the *jehad* and has been Pakistan's protégé for many years: a strategic asset.

On the face of it, Hekmatyar's political philosophy parallels that of other leaders in the so-called fundamentalist alliance. He wants to install a truly Islamic state in Afghanistan but his party apes the revolutionary fervour of Iran's Ayatollah Khomeini, whose portrait dominates many Hezb posters. An anti-American stance is prevalent during political gatherings.

At one such meeting in an Afghan school run by the party in Peshawar, Hekmatyar's speech was punctuated with his followers' cries of "Death to Brezhnev, death to Reagan!" Considering the history of superpower rivalry in South Asia, a distrust of Washington is not unusual, unnatural or even undesirable, but it is particularly marked in Hezb-i-Islami. And there is little doubt that for Hekmatyar an Islamic government in Kabul is synonymous with personal power.

A decade and more of guerilla warfare has hardened Hezb-i-Islami in terms of military and ideological discipline. The commanders receive the largest cut of the small and irregular shipments of Chinese and Egyptian weapons. Hezb-i-Islami's underground organisation in Kabul was for a time without equal. But during the past 18 months the party's guerillas have clashed in several provinces with rival partisans. Initially the target was Harakat. Occasional battles in Helmand Province reportedly resulted in more than 700 casualties.

During the course of 1982 Hezb-i-Islami turned its weapons on Jamiat-i-Islami groups. Takhar, Baghlan and Badakshan were among northern provinces affected by internecine conflict. During the winter of 1982/83 the Jamiat-i-Islami stronghold of Panjsher Valley was all but isolated, primarily by Hezb men blocking the Andarab route of access. Two Western journalists who returned from four-month trips through northern areas reported in December 1982 not only fighting between the two organisations, but they gained the impression that Hekmatyar's fighting groups were more vulnerable to enemy subversion and penetration than others.

A written order, stamped and signed, which found its way to Pakistan in September last year was eagerly seized upon by Hekmatyar's numerous rivals as evidence of his collaboration with the Soviets. Admittedly, it could easily have been forged. Forgery is a flourishing activity in Afghanistan. Passports, military exemption papers and other documents are all readily available for those seeking to escape the attentions of the PDPA.

Whoever was responsible for the document bearing Hezb-i-Islami's crest and Hekmatyar's signature had an unerringly accurate sense of the way in which the Hezb guerillas behave on the front line. The order instructed Hekmatyar's commanders to harass rival groups, to take their weapons and stocks of food wherever possible, to drive them from key areas and to encourage other guerilla units to take first place in the firing line to keep Hezb casualties to a minimum. What was noteworthy was the fact that other Peshawar-based resistance leaders — even those participating in the Islamic alliance along with Hekmatyar — were prepared to display copies of the "order" to Western reporters; a sign of the increasingly open hostility felt towards Hekmatyar and his followers.

It is probable, in fact, that Hekmatyar prematurely launched a series of operations against his rivals to place himself at the forefront of the Islamic alliance and in a pre-eminent position in the field. It is also likely that a number of his groups have been bought out or "turned" by the Khad. In fact, a combination of the two is said to have provoked the inevitable local disputes and differences which exist throughout Afghan society. And while Hekmatyar is painted as the rogue in all this, there is no doubt that his rivals are not entirely innocent, either.

There is no doubt that Hekmatyar is now losing ground both in Peshawar and inside Afghanistan. Until very recently he received most of the funding and weapons available. That may have changed. In an interview in February 1983, Professor Ghafoor Ahmad of Jamaat Islami Pakistan admitted in Karachi that Jamaat had channelled money to individual Peshawar parties and to Hekmatyar in particular. He said that the policy had changed, however. From now on, funds would go to the Islamic alliance as a whole and would not go through the banned political party.

That may be one reason for the rumours that Hekmatyar has been considering a transfer to Iran. But he still has powerful friends in Pakistan, including Abdullah Khan, a Jamaat Islami Pakistan supporter who is the North West Frontier Province Refugee

Commissioner and hence someone well placed to help Hekmatyar increase his influence in the refugee camps. Reliable sources say the cream of international aid was siphoned off for Gulbaddin Hekmatyar's refugees. Even in the camps Hezb has been losing support; many Afghans arriving from Afghanistan now speak of having two enemies — the Soviets and Hezb-i-Islami.

This last issue is important, for Hekmatyar concentrated much of his energies and resources in consolidating his party's hold over many of the refugees. Abdullah helped by trying to persuade newcomers to register as Hezb-i-Islami. The impression in 1981 was that Hekmatyar was systematically building up his power in Pakistan rather than Afghanistan as a sort of reserve, ready for the day when the Soviets finally withdrew. To the considerable annoyance of the leftward-leaning banned political parties in NWFP, Hekmatyar publicly involved himself in local politics in speaking out against such figures as Walli Khan.

It made sense, in a crude manner. Jamaat Islami Pakistan has never been as strong among North West Frontier Pushtuns as it has been in the Punjab or in Sind Province. The NWFP remains very much the preserve of the banned Pakistan People's Party (PPP) and the National Democratic Party (NDP) which still seek provincial autonomy and closer ties with Kabul. Hekmatyar was initially a useful weapon in the hands of Jamaat Islami Pakistan in its semi-covert and sometimes violent battle against leftist opposition groups in Pakistan. But Hekmatyar's recent loss in prestige may in part be attributed to Jamaat's realisation that he had gone too far in provoking local Pakistani opinion against him, and secondly to the federal government's concern that it has given Jamaat Islami Pakistan too much leeway in national politics generally. Hekmatyar's fall from grace in Pakistan may have something to do with the fact that Pakistan desires to be seen to be flexible in the UN-sponsored proximity talks with Kabul in search of a possible political solution to the conflict. Someone somewhere has begun to pull the "fundamentalist" carpet from under Hekmatyar's feet in Peshawar's minaret politics.

Publicly at least, one of Hekmatyar's allies in the Islamic alliance is Rasul Saiaf, who has ample funds at his disposal but lacks a personal power base in Afghanistan itself. He has tried to make up for this deficiency by arming guerillas in Paghman Province and he has been encouraged to act as a figurehead for the alliance in Saudi Arabia and the Middle East generally.

Saiaf, like Hekmatyar, is a Kharuti and is related by marriage to the former PDPA leader, Hafizullah Amin — a point rubbed in by his critics. It is speculated that Saiaf may replace Hekmatyar as Jamaat Islami Pakistan's champion of the Afghan resistance. When guerillas launched a series of operations against major targets to mark the third anniversary of the Soviet invasion, three of Saiaf's commanders claimed to have used 122mm 64kg rockets for the first time — the weapon used by the Vietcong against American and South Vietnamese troops.

Also in the Islamic alliance is another party called Hezb-i-Islami led by Maulavi Yunis Khalis, in visual terms the most impressive resistance leader. In his late 60s, Khalis sports an impressive beard and his large stomach, 7.62mm pistol, turban perched rakishly on the back of his bald head, his ready sense of humour and the fact that he occasionally ventures into Afghanistan to fight alongside his men, make a lasting impression. He holds court in the party offices seated in a broken armchair surrounded by his lieutenants, rough, determined men of lowly origin. The visitor may be surprised to find himself virtually ignored; what the journalist may not realise as he sips tea watching the proceedings is that he is being quietly but very effectively assessed. Communication is intuitive and instinctive and Yunis Khalis is no mean judge of character.

The Khalis group is based primarily on the south-eastern provinces of Nangahar and Paktya. But it is has steadily expanded into other areas, including the non-Pushtun north. This is partly a result of the acquisition of weapons but is also due to good organisation and the relatively careful selection of military commanders. It seeks good relations with other parties, although it has clashed with the other Hezb from time to time. The party has what one American diplomat called a "high tooth to tail ratio," meaning that it is less a political bureaucracy than a fighting organisation, pure and simple. It is "fundamentalist" in so far as Islam is its central political theme — but it embraces the traditional, tribal Pushtun society without the revolutionary and frankly repressive zeal of Hekmatyar's men.

Khalis presides over a coalition of commanders; he holds the balance of power by consensus. He lacks sophistication certainly, but on the battlefield his commanders are more professional than most. The party headquarters exudes cheerfulness. It concentrates on Kabul and is largely responsible for the steady increase of pressure on the capital. Khalis is particularly hostile towards Saiaf; he simply does not trust the man. But he would have no truck with the Gailani and Mojaddedi families because of their royalist, nationalist views. Several of his commanders began their fight in the early 1970s against Daoud and they have no intention of handing the country over to a compromise regime resembling the status quo before the 1978 communist coup.

The third major component of the Islamic alliance is Jamiat-i-Islami Afghanistan led by Professor Burhanuddin Rabbani, an Islamic theologian of some considerable repute. He is from Badakshan and the basis of his organisation is therefore Tajik. Like other non-Pushtun groups, they do not suffer from the restrictive customs of tribesmen — they enjoy a degree of homogeneity and are better able to organise and specialise on the battlefield. Jamiat-i-Islami has in the past three years come to dominate the northern areas of the country, but it also has important fighting groups in the west and the south. While Rabbani seeks to install an Islamic political and social order in Afghanistan, the tone of the party's ideology cannot be described as strident or immoderate. Rabbani could be criticised for underestimating his own influence, in fact.

A softly-spoken man with an academic air, he seems too mild to head one of the largest and most effective guerilla organisations. But appearances are deceptive; Rabbani enjoys considerable personal stature in the Gulf and he has managed to keep his expanding following together despite the cross-pressures on his party from Jamaat Islami Pakistan, Hekmatyar's Hezb-i-Islami and his own field commanders, several of whom opposed the formation of the Islamic alliance which includes Hekmatyar. The party apparatus in Peshawar has a considerable body of intellectual talent at its disposal and it manages to resolve the contradiction felt in other groups between urban sophistication and rural traditions.

Jamiat, like Yunis Khalis' following, is growing in Afghanistan, but relations with Gulbaddin Hekmatyar are badly strained. Jamiat feels itself to be discriminated against for its non-Pushtun character. To some extent this may be justified, but non-Pushtuns do have a chip on their shoulders and have always felt that they have been denied their rightful share of power in national terms by the more numerous Pushtuns.

In early 1983 talks were under way among some of the Peshawar-based leaders with a view to uniting all the parties, with the exception of Hekmatyar's Hezb-i-Islami which has shown itself of late to be divided within its own ranks, a division, that is, between Hekmatyar and his second-in-command, Qazi Mohammad. The talks have not made much progress; Rabbani hesitates as he is clearly anxious not to forgo the funds and arms reaching the

Islamic alliance, while Gailani predictably drags his feet over join-ing an enlarged alliance in which his role would be correspondingly smaller. Many Afghans believe that the Pakistani authorities and Jamaat Islami Pakistan (they believe, somewhat simplistically, that the two amount to the same thing) do not want a unified Afghan resistance. Some foreign observers tend to agree.

One Western ambassador raised the topic in 1982 with Pakistan's President Zia ul-Haq. The general indicated that he did not think further unification was feasible, and the ambassador came away with the impression that Zia's rejoinder implied that Western powers should not try to encourage the process. Similar remarks are known to have been made by the Governor of North West Frontier Province, Lt. Gen. Fazle Haq, in conversation with prominent visitors. Professor Ghafoor of Jamaat Islami Pakistan said he thought the alliances were as much as could be expected.

This approach certainly reflects Pakistanis' accurate assessment of the divided, heterogeneous nature of Afghan society. It may also reflect Pakistan's good reasons for opposing — or at least not actively encouraging — a general unification of the resistance-in-exile. Such a phenomenon would arguably lead to the formation of an Afghan government-in-exile on Pakistan's territory. That would lead to political difficulties in NWFP and in terms of Islamabad's relations with the Soviet Union and, to a lesser extent, with Iran and India. Furthermore, such a development would reduce Pakistan's influence over the resistance and the shape of a future, independent Afghan regime.

There are signs that some guerilla commanders have started an *internal* unification. By maintaining contact with each other, sharing intelligence and resources, they may eventually bypass Peshawar. But that leaves the question of weapons and financial support: Afghanistan is landlocked and its only window on the world — and its only safe haven — lies in the ramshackle party offices in Peshawar and Iran. For the time being, with minor variations, the two alliances — the one Islamic, the other traditional — will have to get along as best they can on existing lines. Without the ability to provide a limited quantity of weapons and cash, they would have little to offer. Even in terms of publicity, regular visitors to Peshawar increasingly make contact with guerilla commanders themselves or their representatives to avoid the proselytising official party spokesmen slowly choking themselves to obscurity on red tape.

Hardware

A fghan and Soviet media insist that foreign powers are responsible for arming the guerilla forces. In one sense they are correct; the primary source of weapons deployed by the *Mujehadeen* is the Soviet Union itself. At the height of each summer the annual rash of defections from the Afghan Army ensures that the resistance receives thousands of small arms and hundreds of mortars, mines and occasionally artillery pieces and armoured vehicles all of Soviet manufacture. The new high-velocity AK-74 5.45mm high velocity assault rifle issued to Soviet troops only is now the most sought-after weapon and the fact that large numbers may now be seen in guerilla hands, particularly in northern areas, suggests that captured arms play an important part in expanding the guerillas' arsenal.

The single most important factor contributing to the ability of the Afghan guerillas to maintain the momentum of their opposition has been the steady increase in the number and variety of weapons since the Soviet invasion at the end of 1979. The concern of the Soviet command over the flow of arms to the opposition is reflected in the fact that Afghan troops, including party cadres, no longer are equipped with RPG-7 anti-tank grenade launchers, weapons which are now the mainstay of the guerillas' capability to ambush security force columns.

Afghan Army conscripts are in many military garrisons and posts obliged to hand in their weapons at night or when not on active duties. Security forces moving out of a base for counter-insurgency operations maintain a careful watch on their troops for fear they will desert — as they so often do — taking with them their personal arms and ammunition as a kind of "passport" to present to the first guerillas they come across. Defectors with weapons and ammunition — or useful intelligence — are welcome. Those who are empty-handed, less so.

In early 1980 the traditionally-favoured bolt-action .303 was still ubiquitous — and respected for its range and accuracy. But by the following year it had been largely replaced by the Kalashnikov family of assault rifles of Soviet design as the common currency of guerilla warfare in Afghanistan. Rocket launchers, once very rare, were also common. A year after the Soviet invasion the number of guerillas who knew how to use an RPG with the simple iron sight were few and far between. That at least has changed; the guerillas have learned through trial and error to use the RPG effectively and they have overcome their initial inability to understand how the more effective optical sights work — which considerably extends the effective but still limited range of the weapon.

Egypt and China appear to provide the bulk of the externally-supplied weapons. The proportion of Chinese and Egyptian weapons of Soviet design in the guerilla inventory is difficult to estimate, for it varies from one area to another. In some northern and western areas even now the guerillas must depend almost entirely on what they can capture or seize from defectors. Obviously Pushtun provinces close to Pakistan are able to exert greater influence on the resistance-in-exile by virtue of their proximity and because they are Pushtun — as is most of the resistance leadership in Peshawar. Certainly weapons smuggled in through Pakistan and Iran are important, if not in quantity then it terms of type.

Egyptian and Chinese versions of the Kalashnikov rifle are common. Recoilless rifles — the Chinese 82mm B-10 and 75mm Type 56 in particular — were first reported in guerilla possession in early 1981. The guerillas use captured Soviet 82mm mortars and Chinese 60mm Type 63 mortars. British-made two-inch mortars probably supplied by Gulf sources have also been seen. Light anti-aircraft weapons, such as the Chinese copy of the Soviet ZPU-2 — a twin-barrelled 14.5mm heavy machine-gun — have been seen, but in small numbers and all too often deployed for reasons of prestige in the wrong area. They are the mainstay of the guerillas' wholly inadequate air defence capability — inadequate both in terms of numbers and the lack of skill with which they are used.

Resistance groups say they have captured the occasional 76mm mountain howitzer and 122mm field gun, although whether the *Mujehadeen* could use these guns properly is another matter. Reporters are invited to inspect captured BTR-60 armoured personnel carriers (APCs) and even one or two of the highly-manoeuvrable BMP-1 armoured fighting vehicles (AFVs). Tanks have also been taken in working order, as veteran war film-maker Nick Downey recorded in a controversial television documentary in 1981. By and large these weapons were of little use at this stage of the conflict and although they could conceivably have been used in imaginative deception techniques — and imagination is not something for which the resistance is generally renowned — they are maintained in something akin to working condition and kept out of sight of aerial reconnaissance.

The black market plays an insignificant role in the war. Weapons are for sale — rifles made in Pakistani, Iranian and Indian ordnance factories, for example. The prestige weapon of 1981/82 was the Heckler and Koch G3 of West German design and manufactured under licence in both Pakistan and Iran. The 7.62mm automatic weapons fetch very high prices — currently 23,000 Pakistani rupees, or about US$2,100. Western journalists visiting Pakistan's North West Frontier Province often made much of the gun-running and small arms production in the town of Darra Adam Khel in the tribal belt. Darra may well provide an interesting colour story for the correspondent with an expense account and two days to cover the war, but locally-made weapons are highly unreliable and do not last. Traditionally, the local gunsmiths were licensed by the British colonial administration to provide the tribes living along the frontier with weapons. It was a wise move — it provided for the Pushtuns' love of weapons while at the same time ensuring that they made use of inferior quality weapons rather than the more effective and deadly arms smuggled in from abroad which could have posed a threat to British India.

Mujehadeen do occasionally sell off weapons to raise cash. This is usually not a matter of party policy, but a symptom of the freewheeling and often corrupt side of the Pushtun character. The buyers are not always Afghan, either. Both extremes of the banned opposition parties in Pakistan are known to be arming their members, according to local politicians and security sources. The flow of arms has accelerated in border areas since the Soviet invasion and it is not only the Afghan resistance which benefits. This is clearly a matter of concern to the provincial and federal authorities.

The residents of Peshawar are witnesses to this. On Thursday nights when weddings are celebrated, it is common for fireworks and weapons to be fired. Today the Kalashnikov automatic rifle is the prestige cracker at these celebrations; the sound of automatic fire and the sight of tracers falling gracefully through the night sky are common signs of the nuptials in progress. Most wealthy households in Peshawar and other frontier towns have their own automatic weapons, while tribal feuds no longer involve merely sporting rifles and shotguns, but mortars and other support weapons. The same may be true of Iran.

How do the Egyptian and Chinese-made weapons find their way to the guerillas? As both Moscow and Kabul repeatedly charge Pakistan with responsibility for the flow of arms from "imperialist countries" and "reactionary Arab circles," so Islamabad flatly denies the charge of complicity in aiding Islamic resistance to the Babrak Karmal regime and its Soviet backers. It is clear that the manufacturer of the weapons in question is seldom if ever the supplier. Pakistan does not directly supply arms to the resistance, but like Iran it is a major conduit — the main one, in fact — to Afghanistan. Keeping open the back-door on landlocked Afghanistan is one very good — arguably the only good — reason why the U.S. chose to agree to the US$3.2bn military assistance and economic aid package for Islamabad's military government. It is widely speculated that the outside world might well have done far more in terms of arms supplies had Pakistan not voiced its concern over its own future stability. In other words, it is generally believed that Pakistan has imposed restraints on the nature and degree of external military aid to the resistance to safeguard itself from Soviet hot pursuit raids and a policy of destabilisation which might result from overt Pakistani help for the guerillas.

Whether this is so or not, Islamabad's generals are caught in a pressing dilemma. On the one hand they feel a common cause with their Muslim brothers and sisters in Afghanistan and recognise a duty to respond to calls for help from refugees and guerillas alike. There have been very real political advantages from this, at least in the short term. On the other hand, an unpopular military dictatorship in Pakistan — and it is unpopular — cannot afford to provoke Soviet pressure. Pakistanis readily recognise the dangers of the war spilling over Afghan borders into neighbouring countries.

Foreign-made weapons do find their way to the Afghan resistance with Pakistan's tacit approval and possibly unofficial help. As the snow clears from the high mountain passes before each fighting season, streams of men, pack animals and military equipment flow across the 1,400-mile Durand Line onto the battlefield. Afghan and Soviet forces have tried and failed to close off more than 250 possible routes into Afghanistan from NWFP alone. Random bombing and the dispersal of an estimated million plastic anti-personnel mines designed to maim rather than kill are evidence of Moscow's attention to resupply efforts. Columns were still moving in 1983 by day, and while diversions are often necessary to avoid newly-established security force positions in border areas, they do get through.

The last people to admit foreign military assistance are the Afghan resistance leaders themselves, although they devote considerable energy to acquiring material support from abroad. This is less hypocrisy on their part than a reluctance to view what they regard as an Islamic struggle in terms of a straight East-West confrontation. They also perceive a need to maintain their own rather shaky authority, independent of any particular brand of foreign ideology. They also show concern that Pakistan might become the focus of Soviet attention as the primary source of weapons. Resistance commanders in the field repeatedly maintain that most of the weapons in their possession have been captured from the enemy. That may be true, but without the Chinese, Egyptian and other foreign arms their ability to develop the struggle would be severely constrained.

Weeks before President Sadat of Egypt was assassinated in October 1981, one resistance leader spoke out against the Egyptian head of state for having openly declared that Egyptian arms were being supplied to the *Mujehadeen*. Rasual Saiaf held a press conference in Islamabad specifically in order to denounce Sadat, although in fact the bodyguards around Saiaf's headquarters in Peshawar were armed with both Chinese and Egyptian rifles. To mark the third anniversary of the Soviet invasion, resistance forces launched a series of military operations and during these, three of Saiaf's commanders used five 122mm single-round rockets for the first time in the war. They were obviously supplied from abroad. These weapons, used by guerilla forces against the American forces in Vietnam, are ideal weapons if used properly. During May rocket attacks temporarily disrupted traffic at the airports of Mazar-i-Sharif and Herat.

There appear to be two parallel channels of external support. The first is funding, which has at least until recently been largely the responsibility of the ultra-conservative, Islamic opposition party in Pakistan, the revolutionary Jamaat Islami Pakistan. Jamaat has been the unofficial pipeline for much of the Gulf's finance, official and unofficial, or so it seems, for there is no solid evidence available one way or the other. Jamaat for a very long time heavily favoured the ambitious Gulbaddin Hekmatyar, with the organisations led by Saiaf, Yunis Khalis and Rabbani further down the list. The hardware has also tended to fall mainly into the hands of the "fundamentalists." The subject is kept under wraps, but what is clear is the unequal manner of arms deliveries. In fact the International Muslim Brotherhood came out into the open for the first time in support of the "fundamentalists" in the summer of 1983.

Iranian sources certainly provide some material support for Shia guerilla groups operating in central and eastern Afghanistan, but the inaccessible nature of Iran today makes a detailed assessment of Iranian military backing almost impossible. There is certainly evidence of growing Iranian backing in ideological and political terms for Shia revolutionary groups in Afghanistan, and it is reported that weapons and possibly some training is also provided, which may help explain Gulbaddin Hekmatyar's tendency to mimic the Ayatollah Khomeini's rhetoric.

A theme running throughout Afghan guerillas' discussions with foreigners is the need for effective anti-aircraft weapons. The need certainly exists, but not entirely as some guerillas would have us believe. It is true that the Soviet and Afghan security forces' primary if not only advantage is air support and supply in the mountainous terrain so poorly provided for in communications. Since the Soviet invasion the guerillas have repeatedly asked visiting dignitaries publicly and privately for weapons designed to cope with this threat.

By and large the guerillas must rely on limited numbers of 12.7mm heavy machine-guns and the handful of 14.5mm ZPU-2s. They are effective against all but the armoured Hind Mi-24 gunship. Even then, weapons which can be sited in such a way as to fire down on attacking helicopters from mountain ridges can be effective. Western diplomatic sources say that in the three years of Soviet military occupation, "hundreds" of Soviet and Afghan aircraft, both fixed-wing and helicopters, have been lost — but these must be assumed to include aircraft downed in accidents and through technical failure. Guerillas' military despatches exaggerate the number shot down.

In early 1982 the first confirmed reports of the existence of very small numbers of Soviet-made, shoulder-launched surface-to-air missiles reached Peshawar from Western photographers and reporters. Four SAM-7s were seen in Paktya Province, while another less reliable report mentions nine of the weapons in the north-east of the country. The SAMs in Paktya were all fired to no good effect; the users had simply no idea how to use these relatively simple weapons.

A SAM-7 should be fired along the line of the target's line of departure, that is, it is fired from behind the target and parallel to its tail fin. It should not be fired or aimed near any surface which reflects heat or it may be diverted from its target. The weapon has a battery which has to be turned on so the weapon can be locked onto the target's heat emission. Obviously, if the battery is turned on too soon the limited power life of the battery will run out. And SAM-7s should be fired in salvos, not singly.

While the weapons, if used properly, may have a marked deterrent effect on airmobile operations by driving enemy aircraft up to higher altitudes and making their crews far more cautious in their attacks, nevertheless the 1973 Middle East war and American involvement in Vietnam demonstrated that they are not the ultimate missiles that many Afghans imagine them to be. The guerilla's incompetence in technical matters is only surpassed by his faith in technology to solve his problems for him. Interestingly, though, Soviet and Afghan helicopters have been seen taking precautionary measures by putting out flares when passing over a ridge likely to harbour a missile launcher to divert the heat-seeking device. This seems to reflect Soviet awareness of a threat.

What Afghans do not readily admit — save for a handful of the better, matter-of-fact generation of commanders gradually assuming greater responsibility for the war — is that the main disadvantage is their inability to organise and secondly to use even the most basic weapons effectively. The past three years have shown that military aid to the Afghan resistance is very largely devalued by the failure of the sponsors to accompany it with effective military instruction on the rudimentary tactical skills most Western professional soldiers learn in their first few weeks of basic infantry training. Afghans are *not* natural guerilla fighters, whatever historical romances or American television reporters say. People do not make good soldiers without good training. "When an Afghan points a rifle in the right direction and pulls the trigger it is a major technological breakthrough," is how one commentator put it.

Photographer Peter Jouvenal has watched a mortar crew fire its ammunition off into the blue without first fusing the mortar bombs. The author has watched guerillas fire some 50 rounds of 60mm mortar ammunition from a weapon which was adjusted from time to time by moving the front legs of the mortar rather than by moving the sighting mechanism. The weapon was also fired at maximum range. The net impact was nil — save for the wasting of a considerable amount of ammunition. Afghan guerillas with few exceptions know little of camouflage, withdrawal under fire or how to position their weapons in such a manner as to ensure that one weapon covers another, with all-round defence. The ejection mechanism of a rifle is played with until it breaks — long before it is brought into action. Small-arms may be fired haphazardly — with the firer keeping his eyes firmly shut. Negligent discharges are alarmingly common. Only now are guerillas in Pushtun areas beginning to learn the use of land mines, while these tribesmen are scornful of the notion of demolition work. For them warfare is all too often a highly individualistic ritual. Against clan rivals or even British administrators with some respect for the rule of law such amateurish duelling might have worked up to a point; against Soviet superpower technology it most certainly does not.

Trying to cut a fuel pipeline with an axe and then setting it alight so that the nearby post can see what has happened is not good sense. Allowing untrained young men to "have a go" at firing a heavy machine-gun may be democratic and it may be fun, but it is not war. Trying to break open an unexploded bomb by cracking away at it with a pistol or hammer has obviously unfortunate results.

The list of errors is long and the point clear — without training, further supplies of hardware, particularly sophisticated anti-aircraft weapons, are very nearly pointless. The supporters of the resistance would do better simply to step up supplies of ammunition for existing weapons and to provide sound basic training. If there are training camps, as Moscow claims, then it is time that the standard of training was greatly improved.

The steady increase in the availability of weapons throughout Afghanistan had given rise to a new problem by early 1983: a shortage of ammunition. The more weapons there are in the front line, the more ammunition is needed to maintain them in action, with a commensurate increase in pressure on supply routes and political pressure on guerilla leaders to deliver the goods. Two years ago an engagement in a specific valley or village might have lasted two or three hours. Today the faster reaction times of the security forces and the greater forces involved on both sides means those same *Mujehadeen* must be able to carry out a fighting withdrawal for two or three days. Instead of having three RPGs with 10 rounds apiece, they may have six to nine RPGs but the same quantity of anti-tank rounds available. They run out of ammunition, often at a crucial juncture.

The resistance does have a sound triad of weapons on which to build and evolve further: the lightweight AKM and AKS rifle, which is reliable and simple to use even if it does lack range and penetrability; the RPG-7 anti-tank grenade launcher, which is also very light and is particularly effective against soft-skinned vehicles and APCs, and finally the Chinese-built land mine which may be unglamorous but is probably the most effective of the three if used properly and with imagination. The gap lies in air defence weapons and skills. A dozen trained men with SAMs for each of the country's 29 provinces could change the war quite significantly. So far the steadily increasing quantity of weapons has not only maintained and widened resistance by putting arms into the hands of greater numbers of men anxious to fight, but it has also helped the resistance to evolve in terms of teamwork and embryonic military specialisation.

Soviet Operations

For the Soviet General Staff, the invasion and subsequent occupation of Afghanistan provides the Red Army with an invaluable testing ground for new weapons, tactics and the operational control of substantial forces projected beyond the Soviets' traditional sphere of control and in what has become a very hostile environment.

More than 80 percent of Afghanistan's terrain falls within the Soviet military category of "special operations." Mountain ranges, deserts, extremes of weather and a notable lack of reliable, all-weather communications pose a formidable challenge to the conscript units.

For centuries Russians have fought their most important campaigns on the flat plains of Europe where the only obstacles of note are broad, shallow and sluggish rivers. The 1941-45 Great Patriotic War — today the primary model for Soviet military spending, organisation and training — was largely fought in this region.

Traditional Soviet operational planning involves the orchestrated movement of large bodies of men, armour and artillery at speed across flat ground. The axis of a Soviet advance through Europe would coincide with continental communications, which run East-West and facilitate rapid movement. Soviet tactics and deployment are predictable, well rehearsed — and entirely unsuited to Afghanistan's extremes.

Moscow regards its ground forces as quantitively among the strongest in the world and the most modern — the only army to follow the "true" ideology of Marxism-Leninism. They regard themselves as unbeatable, and their one-sided press makes great efforts to project this image of invincibility at home and abroad. But Afghanistan has taught the Red Army that it is in fact far from perfect. "Nothing is left to chance," one Western writer said of the Soviet armed forces. "Everything is planned." That planning has been the undoing of occupation forces which see themselves as the best-armed, best-trained and best-equipped army of all.

To some extent the Soviets were aware of their shortcomings before the invasion. The rapid introduction of technologically-advanced military equipment into Warsaw pact arsenals paralleled the evolution of a "combined arms" concept in which the ability of relatively junior commanders to fight a multi-dimensional battle without constant reference to their superiors would only work, the Soviet military press argued, if it was to be matched by a commensurate flexibility in command and control at divisional, army and corps level.

Mountain warfare requires close air support to make up for the lack of artillery supporting fire, for example. Afghanistan has helped persuade the Red Army to improve ground-to-air coordination. The use of aircraft for casualty evacuation is also something the Soviets have had to improve. Reconnaissance is a prerequisite for survival in difficult terrain where the ubiquitous opponent lacks a front, flank or rear. Afghanistan demands a physical fitness and mental stamina few conscripts are capable of providing to satisfaction. The burden is particularly heavy on junior officers who must assess the situation for themselves and act accordingly — without recourse to the textbook or a senior officer hundreds of miles away.

One eye-witness reported these shortcomings on the ground during 1981: "The Soviets stayed with their vehicles when they were ambushed. They went down and took cover as best they could, but they did not try and attack. If an officer or NCO were hit, they tried to run and were cut down. It was only when helicopter gunships arrived and we ran short of ammunition and had to withdraw that they moved forward. They are not good soldiers."

In fact the performance of Soviet conscripts under fire was initially the source of amusement mixed with contempt on the part of guerilla commanders. Initially, 40 per cent of the forces which moved into Afghanistan were reservists from three Soviet military districts in the Southern Theatre; they came primarily from Turkestan and Central Asian MDs and naturally enough were composed very largely of Asians of Muslim origin. Their hearts were not in it. Many fraternised with Afghan Army personnel and even with the guerilla forces. Later, conscripts replaced the reservists and these units were more representative of the ethnic "mix" in the Red Army; nevertheless a form of social "apartheid" persisted, with the minority groups discriminated against and clearly not trusted by the predominantly Russian officers.

The vast majority of Soviet troops receive no special training for fighting in mountainous terrain, and only two or three military colleges have substantial courses for NCOs and officers included in their training curricula. However, those reservist units based in mountainous military districts do much of their training in mountain warfare techniques as a matter of course. The MDs are the Transcaucasian, the North Caucasian, Central Asian, Carpathian, Siberian and Turkestan. In other words the reservists who should know most about it are the least "reliable" politically in Afghanistan: a singular dilemma.

It is necessary at this point to bury a popular Western myth about the invasion. The Soviets did not use Muslim reservists because they thought these troops would more easily deal with the insurgency. In fact the invasion forces, which arrived with their full, standard range of equipment, were charged primarily with shoring up the ruling regime and pre-empting any possible opposition from the Afghan conventional armed forces.

The core of the Soviet military presence in Afghanistan took the form of elite Guards Airborne regiments — elements of the 103rd, 105th (which is under KGB control) and the 104th. The paratroopers played a key role in establishing the bridgehead around Bagram airbase in December 1979 and they are currently established in the major cities of Kabul and Kandahar, where their priority mission seems to have been protection of the PDPA regime's leaders, stabilisation of urban areas and to mount special operations against guerilla strongpoints.

Soviet paratroopers are certainly elite and a cut above the motorised rifle divisions. They wear a distinctive blue beret, striped shirt and camouflage smock and enjoy a certain élan or flair. But they should not be compared with their NATO counterparts. The Soviets lack a "light infantry" concept: their paratroopers have their own armour and would go into battle much as other, more conventional units would. The British emphasis on individual training, toughness and independence of action does not have a Soviet equivalent.

But the GRU (military intelligence) diversionary units which helped to seize Prague airport in 1968 are believed to have carried out special missions in Afghanistan prior to the first airlift. *Reydoviki* units — the Soviet version of US Rangers — were used in commando-style operations against guerillas in Panjsher Valley in early 1982. Afghan sources in Kabul described them as "partisan" units.

It is not yet known whether *Vysotniki* — designed for deep

penetration, reconnaissance and intelligence operations — are being used to any great extent in Afghanistan. It can be assumed that this is so or will be, once they have had time to prepare themselves. They are Russia's version of Britain's Special Air Service (SAS) and they operate in very small teams, some of which are trained in HALO (high altitude, low opening) parachute drops. It is known, however, that one Soviet special forces regiment was transferred from East Germany to the Central Asian MD in late 1981, and later carried out training in mountainous conditions. In early 1983 a guerilla source provided a detailed report of Soviet commando-style operations from Shindand airbase. The account bore the hallmarks of a *Vysotniki*-style campaign.

In June 1980 the Soviets publicised the withdrawal of about 5,000 troops in Afghanistan — in fact these were reservists unsuited to conditions and they were quickly replaced by other units. Soviet forces remained stable at around 85,000 throughout 1980 and 1981. At the end of that year a further 5,000 Soviets arrived and several thousand more entered Afghanistan in January 1982. Many of these reinforcements are believed to have been Internal Security (MVD) and KGB troops — designed to improve security in urban areas while releasing combat units for operational tasks. This reflected the slow but steady assumption by the Soviets of a greater role in the war against the guerillas.

In other words, the Soviets have established the basis for a counter-insurgency effort, combining special forces, paratroopers and KGB and GRU deception and intelligence techniques. It is a slow process and difficult to identify, but Kabul must become to Soviet career officers what Fort Bragg is to American commanders. Just as American career officers sought to "punch their cards" in Vietnam, so too Afghanistan will provide their Soviet counterparts with a useful stepping-stone in a career to the top.

The Soviet occupation troops arrived with their normal equipment, much of it highly unsuitable for the war in which they were to become progressively involved. They established anti-aircraft missile batteries around Bagram airbase. Their military convoys contained ZSU-23 automatic anti-aircraft cannon — although there are no signs that the Afghan guerillas have mastered the technique of flying. Soviet troops dropped by helicopter to seize the high ground around Panjsher Valley brought with them man-portable SAM-7Bs — which the guerillas managed to capture in some instances. Companies, battalions and divisions had their normal complement of chemical warfare troops, an issue of considerable controversy in the

West.

Deployment was rigid. Ed Girardet of the *Christian Science Monitor* said the Soviet move into Panjsher in 1982 looked like a Warsaw Pact peacetime exercise, with tanks, BM-21 multiple rocket launchers and artillery lined up as if on a parade ground. Infantry carried anti-tank weapons into action against the poorly-armed guerillas. On one occasion Soviet forces launched a major attack on the wrong place altogether; while captured Soviet documents show a very high standard of large-scale map making, their map *reading* evidently left much to be desired.

Since the 1979 invasion the Soviets have introduced a large number of new weapons into their units and many have been seen for the first time in Afghanistan. Some of them, at least, were designed specifically for counter-insurgency operations over difficult ground. The SU-25, for example, code-named "Frogfoot" by NATO, is a modern equivalent of the World War II *Shturmovik* fighter; heavily armed and well protected with armour plating, it can loiter slow and low over the battlefield to give support to ground forces. Reports of its deployment in Afghanistan came from guerillas during the course of 1982. The Afghans described it as an aircraft which could not be heard until it was directly overhead (a factor, no doubt, of its low altitude approach), that it stayed around a long time and was accurate in directing its rockets onto guerilla firing points. It is the Soviet version of the American A-10 "tank-buster" and is designed to complement the "Hind" Mi-24 gunship in offensive operations in the European theatre. But Frogfoot is obviously a useful aircraft to have in Afghanistan.

"Butterfly" mines, made of plastic and shaped like butterflies or sycamore seeds, with a "wing" to allow them to spin to earth slowly, have been deployed by literally hundreds of thousands to hinder guerilla passage from Pakistan and Iran and from one safe haven or stronghold in Afghanistan to another. The weapons appear to have been designed specifically for use in Afghanistan. They are green or brown and blend in very well with the stony and sandy terrain. These weapons, which will blow off a foot and hand, maim rather than kill — although the lack of medical facilities and long distances which have to be traversed on foot to reach a hospital ensure that the victims die of blood loss, gangrene or simply shock. Their use contravenes — well, almost — a Geneva convention signed but not ratified by several countries, including the USSR.

The convention specifically bans the deployment of mines which cannot be detected by normal means (i.e. by X-ray) and which have an unlimited lifespan. The ban is only effective once 26 countries have signed it, but it is an interesting example of how the Soviets regard arms control. By signing it they escape public censure, but they know it will be some time before they can be accused of breaking the agreement and have little compunction in going against the spirit if not the letter of international law. The mines certainly last years; the guerilla walking ahead of this correspondent stopped to wash his hands in an irrigation ditch in Kunar in 1981 and blew a hand off and much of his face. It was nine months since the last mine-laying operation had been carried out in that area. There is little doubt the mines can last a decade and are a threat to children and livestock especially.

Another weapon which may have been designed specifically for use in Afghanistan is a new, automatic 81mm mortar capable not only of rapid and continuous fire but also of throwing mortar bombs at a target by means of a high trajectory (in a conventional battle, a high trajectory is not an advantage as the opponent can spot the round by means of special mortar locating radars) which is useful in mountain conditions where conventional artillery is unable to support infantry.

Another new support weapon first spotted in Afghanistan is the AGS-17, an automatic grenade launcher, which is designed to suppress enemy infantry fire and movement. It can be used by two men, or mounted on a vehicle. It fires 30mm grenades from a drum magazine containing 30 rounds. It can also be used from helicopters. The guerillas have captured a number of the weapons.

"Flechette" rounds — small slivers of steel, razor sharp, contained in 152mm artillery shells — are another development first seen in this war. These weapons burst in a cloud of lacerating metal and are designed to catch enemy personnel — in this instance, the *Mujehadeen* — in the open. They create particularly nasty wounds.

The Soviets' new high-velocity rifle, the AK-74 of 5.45mm calibre, is issued to Soviet troops only, together with its light machine-gun equivalent, the RPK-74. In appearance and design very much like the standard AK-47 rifle, the new weapon and LMG is a high-velocity weapon with a well-designed bullet with a hollow core which allows the round to "tumble" and create considerably more damage to human tissue. The lighter ammunition provides savings for the overall Soviet logistics effort involved in keeping men equipped in the field. It is the Soviet equivalent of the American M-16.

The new rifle has an image-intensifier sight which helps troops fight in poor visibility. It was captured by guerillas in 1982 and this was the first time it had been seen. The Soviets have also introduced a new anti-tank weapon, the RPG-16, with range and accuracy improved over its predecessor, the RPG-7. The RPO flamethrower in Afghanistan is a new type. Rather than projecting a stream of flaming liquid towards the target, this seems to be a tube which discharges a projectile like a rocket which bursts into a ball of flame on contact. It is portable, but presumably can be mounted on armoured personnel carriers.

The Soviets have introduced a modified version of the standard BTR-60 armoured personnel carrier, the vulnerable "workhorse" of Soviet and Afghan motorised units. The new vehicle has improved hatches for safer exit by infantry. The BMP-2 is a new variant of the armoured fighting vehicle, the BMP-1, and the new model is armed with a 30mm cannon which effectively outguns its Western equivalents. Soviet troops in Afghanistan are equipped with the RPG-18, a 60mm calibre disposable anti-tank weapon. It appears to be simply a direct copy of the American M-72 Light Anti-tank Weapon (LAW). The Soviets, lacking tanks for targets, use these weapons to blast their way through walls while conducting search-and-destroy operations in villages or urban areas. The Afghans use the discarded cases as drain-pipes or simply decoration.

With the emphasis on airmobile operations, the Soviets have concentrated on improving their aircraft. A new transport helicopter, the Mi-26, has been seen in Afghanistan. The "E" version of the Mi-24 gunship fires AT-6 missiles from its pylons. The helicopter gunship is the Soviets' key advantage in this war and there are currently several versions in Afghanistan. According to a State Department report, Soviet gunships quadrupled in number to around 240 by the end of the first year of occupation. The Mi-8 "Hip" helicopters serving in Afghanistan have been refitted in some cases with a 20mm cannon or machine-gun in the rear hatch position.

The overwhelming physical weakness of the Soviets has been logistical. This was demonstrated when on November 2, 1982, several hundred Soviet troops were killed and injured in the Salang tunnel north of the capital. It appears that a civilian truck collided with a military fuel tanker which burst into flames in the tunnel. Soviet troops reportedly panicked, mistook the incident for a guerilla attack and promptly closed the tunnel at both ends. Burning fuel, combined with panic among the several hundred civilians and Soviet troops caught inside, caused very heavy casualties. While figures have to be treated with caution, especially in the Afghan context, as many as 700 Soviets and Afghans were said to have died.

Although the casualties were not comparable, the avalanche which may have been deliberately set off by *Mujehadeen* in late March 1983 destroyed the Olang bridge, damaged a military post and swept military vehicles off the highway just north of the tunnel. Guerilla spokesmen said they used dynamite to blow the bridge. That may be true, but the avalanche certainly contributed to the two-week halt in traffic. Kabul was seriously affected, and the interruption of normal communications may well have impinged on deployments to provincial areas at the start of the summer offensive. The Soviets and their Afghan military comrades live and fight at the end of a very long supply line which, despite the use of fixed-wing aircraft and helicopters, is vulnerable to guerilla attacks.

The major Soviet garrisons were usually attached to or situated very near major airbases, permitting a rapid response to reinforce military supply convoys on the few good roads. In an effort to protect columns, construction troops widened the verges on either side — cutting down vegetation, levelling walls and homes and removing natural cover which might be used by guerillas. Soviet helicopters would ride "shotgun" over ground forces, while the major oil and gas pipelines were protected by military posts at regular intervals. A major Soviet transit base was established at the northern plain of Kilagai. There were two major Soviet headquarters, at Kunduz in the north and at Kabul's Tajbeg Palace, while intelligence operations were reportedlly run from the Soviet Embassy behind its high and very thick walls.

The Soviets held the major cities, although by the summer of 1982 the effect of the guerillas' deliberate attention to urban areas was reflected in growing numbers of incidents in these towns in daylight and by night. Regime personnel were simply not safe. "Held" is probably the wrong term; by virtue of their proximity to urban areas, the Soviets were able to exert their influence from their own garrisons in the form of patrols, control of Afghan troops and supervision of security and intelligence personnel.

Soviet forces would venture out from time to time to suppress guerilla activity in one area when it assumed the proportions of an intolerable threat. By the end of 1980 it seemed that Moscow's "limited contingent" was obliged to take on a progressively greater burden for the overall military effort than Moscow had originally planned. Not only was opposition fiercer than ever before, but the reliability of the Afghan armed forces had been grossly overestimated. The mere presence of Soviet troops in the country not merely failed to provide the extra backbone to indigenous communist forces, it actually exacerbated the divisions among PDPA cadres in the officer corps and accelerated the defections.

Initially Soviet counter-insurgency operations, normally combined with Afghan Army units and local militia forces, were very large and ponderous. Planning, deployment and implementation took an extraordinarily long time. Staff plans of what was going on normally passed into the hands of the guerillas well in advance of the first engagements. The Soviets' own intelligence was poor during the first year; they seldom came to grips with the elusive resistance — or at least not where they expected the guerillas to be. The civilians seemed to melt away into the hills and fields. It must have seemed an exhausting, time-consuming and frustrating business.

The Soviet weakness was supply. Small units fared no better than large ones. "I learned to divide my group into three," said a Hazara guerilla commander. "One with the machine-gun, another with rifles and the third with our only rocket launcher. My rifle group would open fire and draw the enemy towards their position. On firing, they would slip out of sight and change their position. Meanwhile the other two groups would move parallel to the advancing unit. Then the second group — the one with the machine-gun — would open fire on the flank and the enemy would change direction to deal with it.

"Of course, by this time the machine-gun had been moved onto the flank again, while the enemy's movements, which were by now confused, enabled the rocket launcher to be placed behind the enemy, or close to the rear. That was what we wanted. We would use the rocket launcher to destroy the patrol's petrol tanker and the communications jeep which usually followed the armoured cars and tanks. If the tanks and other vehicles tried to stay there the night, we would go close and try and destroy one or two. That was more than sufficient for us."

The Soviets wisely have not tried to "occupy" the whole country. First, it was never their aim to do so. Second, they lacked the men to do it. Third, resupply was an obviously major constraint. Fourth, their largely conscript forces lacked the morale, the leadership and the training to cope. The young men had been told very little about Afghanistan; simply that they were going to "defend socialism" against "bandits" led by Pakistanis, Americans, Chinese and other "reactionaries." They saw little of socialism and found their enemies were the common people. They found themselves shot at by civilians in the countryside and spat at by civilians in the cities. The Soviets mounted what was essentially a holding operation, and they used indigenous communist forces as best they could.

A characteristic order of battle was evident by the end of 1981 in major anti-guerilla sweeps. Militia forces were the first rank, closely followed by Afghan Army units, while the Soviets brought up the rear. The Afghan militiamen and soldiers were used to draw guerilla fire. If the Afghan conscripts tried to desert — which they did frequently — they found their Soviet "comrades" were not reluctant to shoot them down from the back. Soviet forces were used in *support* of the Afghan Army and Soviet troops only emerged into the open to fight on foot once the ground had been thoroughly prepared with artillery and close support from the air.

By December 1982 — the third anniversary of the invasion — Soviet air losses ran into several hundreds, according to intelligence sources. Although these were in many cases aircraft damaged on the ground, or lost through technical and pilot error, resistance forces had managed to shoot down substantial numbers of helicopters, a high proportion of which were of the more vulnerable, transport type. There were a few instances in which gunships were downed, by guerillas firing from above, at short range and when the helicopter concerned was moving slowly or hovering.

Thousands of thin-skinned and lightly-armoured military vehicles were disabled or destroyed, too. It was noticeable that greater efforts were made during 1982 to recover damaged military equipment in the forms of APCs, armoured cars, AFVs and tanks. No doubt this was partly because the Kabul regime has to pay for its Soviet military supplies; they are not free. The Soviets had previously been known to return to the scene of an action to destroy damaged equipment — whether this was a desire to deny the guerillas the use of the hardware, much of which was of no use to them anyway, or to deny the West useful intelligence is not known. Certainly they would make every effort to recover their dead — the wounded were invariably despatched promptly by the resistance.

Soviet casualties were assessed by Western sources at between 12,000 and 15,000 killed and wounded during the previous three years. These are low figures. The higher number was recorded in the first year. It contrasts greatly with the resistance claim of 40,000 Soviets killed, a figure obviously exaggerated and reflecting the guerillas' inability to assess the military situation in the country with anything approaching clarity or precision. However, the number of deaths as a proportion of the total is probably higher than would normally be the case in a conventional war between two industrialised nations; the guerillas until recently lacked area weapons — killing is done at a relatively short range with weapons which only function when they are used accurately. The number of "clean kills" is impressive, in fact. It should also be remembered that the Soviets did not invade Afghanistan in order to win a war against insurgents; they invaded to bolster the shaky PDPA regime, remove Amin and replace the leadership with one they imagined could provide a reliable and credible force. They were wrong, but they did not invade to get to grips with the resistance. Hence the low casualties.

Six times the estimated number of Soviet battlefield casualties have been hospitalised for serious illnesses, a fact related both to the extreme environment and the poor conditions in which Soviet conscripts are expected to live. The failure to provide adequate medical services resulted in epidemics of infectious hepatitis, too. But it is not the only reason.

The Red Army does not share with its potential Western adversaries the code of conduct normally observed by officers towards their men, for example. Soviet officers verbally and physically abuse their subordinates to an extent which would be totally unacceptable in a democratic state's volunteer forces. Such behaviour in British or American units would signal the collapse of authority, discipline and morale. Instead, Soviet conscripts are slapped, punched, kicked and from time to time systematically beaten by groups of officers. These "disciplinary problems" have accounted for the vast majority of defections from Soviet ranks to the resistance.

Precisely how many conscripts have joined the guerillas is not clear, but they number dozens. The line between what is a defector and a prisoner is not always obvious. A prisoner may seek to curry favour with the *Mujehadeen* by declaring himself to be a Muslim or willing to become one if it seems that this will secure better treatment, stay of execution and greater freedom of movement. But there have been several genuine defectors, and a number now live and fight with their hosts against their former comrades. Most are from the ethnic and national minorities of the Soviet Union and in some cases have developed quite considerable reputations as leaders of their own groups of Afghan guerillas.

For those Soviet prisoners who are communists, or who are willing to demonstrate that they are loyal to their homeland, death is the usual outcome. In one region, though, Soviet captives are being kept alive. The trend towards keeping POWs alive and well has followed Red Cross attempts to gain access to them and have them interned in Switzerland before possible repatriation. The resistance has gone along with this because the Red Cross promised to do all it could to track down and save the lives of resistance members held in regime prisons. No progress had been made by 1983, and the guerillas were beginning to rethink their policy, especially following a Soviet commando raid mounted on Mazar-i-Sharif to rescue 11 Soviet civil advisers seized in a guerilla raid on a bus.

The most striking aspect of eight interviews conducted by the author with prisoners and defectors has been the extraordinary lack of awareness among Soviet troops as to why the USSR maintains a military presence in Afghanistan. The level of political consciousness among conscript riflemen and even NCOs is nil.

Early on the fate of captured Soviets was often gruesome. One group was killed, skinned and hung up in a butcher's shop. One captive found himself the centre of attraction in a game of *buzkashi,* that rough and tumble form of Afghan polo in which a headless goat is usually the ball. The captive was used instead. Alive. He was literally torn to pieces. Russians who display no interest in or knowledge of religion are regarded as infidels, unbelievers. According to the custom of *badal* or revenge, their deaths may properly be demanded by the locals, many of whom will be involved in feuds with the Soviets through the loss of relatives in the war. When Afghans have reached Soviet corpses before the security forces arrive to intervene, the common practice is mutilation. This has had a demoralising impact among Soviet troops and among relatives back home in the USSR. From time to time the Soviets have mutilated Afghan corpses.

The sheer tedium of barracks life, the imposition of a wilful authority by force rather than by shared devotion to the cause or a sense of *esprit de corps,* inadequate rations (the Soviet troops are always hungry, it seems), the lack of alcohol for other ranks and the sense of isolation have all contributed to a general air of apathy and misery. It is possible for conscripts to pass their standard six months' duty in Afghanistan without any involvement in action. For those who do enter the firing line, their letters home — often taken from their bodies afterwards — speak with remarkable frankness of the "muck and bullets" and casualties they endure with something less than phlegm.

There have been several hearsay accounts of Soviet advisers, officers and other ranks sympathising with the resistance. Many of those involved have not unnaturally been of Asian or Muslim cultural origin. There are reports that communists from other Soviet bloc countries have replaced Soviet Central Asians to work as translators, interpreters and in other administrative tasks. But the stories are almost all second-hand. The following is taken from an interview with an Afghan brigadier, trained in the USSR and Eastern Europe, who defected to Pakistan in early 1982.

"I knew the Soviet political affairs officer in Mazar-i-Sharif named Bayatov. One day when he was pretty drunk he turned to me and asked why it was that Afghans did not defend their own country themselves. I had a similar reaction from Major Halik, a Soviet officer I met on a number of occasions. He asked: 'Why are we in Afghanistan?' Soviet soldiers in Kabul seemed similarly perplexed by the situation. One looked me up and down and said, 'Why, you Afghan officers can look as smart as you like in your pretty uniforms. Just wait, you'll see, you will be as miserable as we are one of these days.' "

The presence of Warsaw Pact and Cuban personnel is also reported from time to time, mainly by guerillas. One described the Cubans in a firefight: "They are big and black and shout very loudly when they fight. Unlike the Russians they are not afraid to attack us in the open."

An Afghan officer who defected to Pakistan in October 1982 said he had himself seen both Cuban and Bulgarian troops. He saw Bulgarians arrive by air at Khwaja Ruwash, Kabul's airport, the previous year. He said the Bulgarians normally wore Afghan Army uniforms. He claimed to have seen Cubans in the vicinity of Kabul's Rishknor garrison in 1980. He said he knew they were Cubans because of their distinctive, thigh-length jackets.

Guerilla sources say a Bulgarian military base has been established in southern Mazar-i-Sharif and that the Bulgarians' role is to provide protection for a fuel pipeline to Shibergan. In fact, despite the appearance of literally hundreds of Soviet military identity papers and Communist Party cards in resistance headquarters, there is no sign of an East European or Cuban. It may well be that Warsaw Pact and Cuban personnel do not carry their normal ID papers, but until their presence is positively proved, the reports remain speculative.

An eye-witness of a battle in March 1983 at Sharafat Koh in western Afghanistan close to the Iranian border said Cuban troops, flanked by militiamen on the one side and Soviet troops on the other, attacked guerilla positions and were caught in a crossfire as they entered a gorge. Surat Khan said the local guerilla command already had one Cuban prisoner who had been converted to Islam, circumcised and set to work as a shepherd. But he was unable to say how he *knew* the captive was Cuban. He admitted that the man spoke a strange language no one understood, but that he didn't talk very much at all as he had been frequently beaten by his captors in the first weeks of his imprisonment.

Soviet troops in Afghanistan have sold their personal equipment for hashish and opium. They have traded parts of their vehicles for cash or goods to take home. A thriving black market in military equipment and even ammunition exists in Kabul. Looting by the Soviets is frequent, both in Kabul itself and especially during counter-insurgency operations in rural areas. Tape-recorders, transistor radios, watches, rugs and even household utensils are stolen. Officers reportedly participate in these affairs, too, and one way for a young conscript to get onto the right side of his platoon commander is to share his ill-gotten gains with his superior.

Too much can be read into all this. Such habits and shortcomings may well be insignificant in terms of the Red Army's ability to mount breakthrough operations against NATO defences in Western Europe; discipline can be maintained over crudely-trained troops when they are used *en masse* under close supervision. But in Afghanistan conditions require a higher standard of individual performance and better self-esteem that is clearly lacking for run-of-the-mill motorised rifle and armoured battalions.

There are strong indications of reappraisals occurring from time to time among the Soviet military staffs. The use of helicopters to drop troops in *desant* operations appears to be on the increase, for it is a tactic which can yield good results where the terrain does not pose too great an obstacle for the attacking forces. In Panjsher the mountains proved to be the heliborne troops' undoing. They came under fire as soon as they disembarked and losses were relatively heavy. But in the flat, open plain of Logar the Soviet troops managed to cut and effectively seal off a large group of guerillas who had taken refuge on high ground. Cold, rain, poor organisation and leadership resulted in many cases of severe frostbite and the guerillas tried to break out; when they did so they found themselves — the hunters — hunted down.

From time to time there have been reports of Soviet troops moving on foot at night into positions surrounding a targeted village. There they stay until just before first light when helicopter gunships and jets pound the village houses. Armoured vehicles then sweep into the area, and the concealed positions come into their own as the surprised *Mujehadeen* stream out of the killing ground into the Soviet troops' field of fire. This was first noted during the course of 1981, but it appeared to be on the increase the following year. Helicopters land not only men, but also their equipment in the form of BMPs, possibly the airborne forces' BMDs and their ASU-57/85 self-propelled guns. During the course of 1982 several small guerilla positions would be surrounded or threatened by helicopter-dropped forces simultaneously, effectively preventing the guerillas from re-grouping or withdrawing, and encouraging a sense of alarm and panic.

One photographer has seen for himself on more than one occasion the effective way in which Soviet crews use their BMP armoured fighting vehicles in a rapid fire-and-movement attack, pinning down the guerillas and in one instance employing helicopter gunships to cut them off from an escape route. He filmed one of these incidents, and focused his camera on panic-stricken guerillas running for their lives as the AFVs sent machine-gun bursts spurting through the dust behind them. The film appeared on television in Britain, but to the film-maker's considerable disgust it was presented as a guerilla *attack*. It is not only the Soviet and Kabul media which distort the truth about this war.

The Soviets' aggressive tactics, though still rare, are particularly noticeable in areas which coincide with the guerillas' traditional communications and supply routes. Here the local *Mujehadeen* lack experience of battle and are susceptible to surprise assaults. By contrast, areas around Soviet garrisons are not characterised by active, aggressive foot patrols by the Russians. Instead, security is maintained by the use of frequent flares and patrols by helicopter gunships to keep the guerillas at bay. The impunity with which the foreign correspondent can approach a base or airfield is surprising and one has the impression that on the whole the Soviets do not relish night work.

Soviet operations in Afghanistan *seem* sensible enough; cautious progress being made towards flexible, aggressive counter-insurgency tactics, while the bulk of the Soviet occupation forces are used to hold onto major strategic points and communications, only ventur-ing out in favourable conditions. They employ the Afghan armed forces as bait — by placing these demoralised allies in exposed posts, they draw the guerillas away from more lucrative targets into fruitless skirmishes in desert scrub which matters to no one.

A great deal can be gauged about Soviet military thought on Afghanistan in the military press, much of which is open and available to the West. In contrast to the United States, where technical material about defence is published with apparent abandon and operational methodology highly classified, the reverse is true of the Kremlin. Virtually everything of a technical nature is secret, including the most basic maps. But methods and doctrine are constantly publicised, partly to keep the 4.7 million Soviets in uniform fully informed of their masters' policies. Ironically, the very restrictions placed on Soviet society by the totalitarian regime in Moscow cause the military to use its press as a kind of sounding board for protracted and ponderous debates to air the views of differing and sometimes opposing "lobbies" in the Red Army.

A distinction must be drawn between the official but supposedly "popular" press and the more serious, specialised journals. Initially, at least, the "popular" communist press in the USSR carefully avoided mentioning Soviet troops in combat situations. By late 1981, however, accounts of individual heroism were published. By early 1983, the press began to reflect on the general situation in Afghanistan and tied in the presence of Soviet troops with combat for the first time.

On January 27, 1983, for example, *Red Star* reported a series of bomb attacks in the Afghan capital. The report not only referred to the "internationalist" duty of officers and men in facing the hazards of continued occupation, but admitted that whole regions of mountainous terrain were under "rebel" control. Television audiences have been shown combat footage, but of Afghan troops in action, not Soviet. While for North American newspapers Afghanistan is an "old story," for Soviet readers it is very fresh. *Komsomolskaya Pravda* daringly published a report of a guerilla raid that killed three Soviet soldiers in a convoy. Tass agency similarly reported how Soviet troops supported a regime offensive against "bandits." *Izvestiya* also said rebels had cut Kabul's power lines.

Pravda showed a greater willingness to publicise the Soviet occupation forces. Moscow published complaints by troops over the failure to provide them with a regular and more frequent postal service. Western observers interpreted the greater and more direct war coverage as evidence that the Soviets wanted to show to the public that there was nothing shameful in maintaining forces in the country. Some argued that Andropov was demonstrating that the war would be a long haul, while others suggested he was laying the foundation for an eventual compromise agreement through the UN peace talks.

More specialised military publications reflect the modifications of the Soviets' initial invasion force which was designed primarily to surprise — and remove — the "unreliable" Hafizullah Amin and prevent "reactionary" elements in the Afghan armed forces from opposing their new champion, Babrak Karmal.

The widespread use of helicopters in Afghanistan is due in part to a close study the Soviet generals made of the American involvement in Southeast Asia. In 1979 a Colonel A. Nikitin pointed out that the Americans limited the use of tanks in Vietnam for urban warfare, convoy protection and fire support. At first the lesson was ignored, and it was not until Soviet armoured formations ran into considerable supply difficulties in Afghanistan that the military press, in 1980, began to carry reports of numerous mechanical failures and inadequate maintenance.

"Tankers should also possess thorough knowledge of the locations of weapons in the enemy's disposition under mountain conditions and their tell-tale signs," wrote one Soviet author, implying criticism of the army's reconnaissance and intelligence capabilities. Tanks have been subsequently de-emphasised. The Soviet military press has also concentrated on the problem of snipers. Others have offered advice on how best to extricate oneself from avalanches precipitated by ambush parties on high ground. Colonel A. Ryzhkov reflected Soviet interest in the American counter-insurgency forces' decentralised methods of command and control in Vietnam: "A certain degree of decentralisation of troops' command and control is a unique feature of mountain combat operations. . ." he said.

Douglas M. Hart, writing in the International Institute of Strategic Studies publication, *Survival,* concludes: "The evolution of Soviet counter-insurgency tactics indicates that she is serious about developing the operational concept and the unit configuration necessary to at least restrict the impact of guerilla operations on her efforts to make Afghanistan safe for socialism. The volume of articles and the level of the debate over tactics and doctrine (the commanders of the Transcaucasus and Far Eastern Military Districts have lent their names to tracts on mountain warfare published since the invasion) serve to underscore the commitment of Soviet men and resources to the struggle. The Soviet military is drawing lessons from the continuing conflict and modifying previous operational concepts in a manner that suggests a long term approach to counter-insurgency warfare.

"If the Soviet leadership were looking for a quick way out of its 'international obligations', the resulting diplomatic activity could not be concealed from the military, and officers would be extremely reticent to become involved, especially in print, with a failing enterprise."

Western diplomatic sources say Soviet operational costs in 1982 were running at about US$2 billion a year, or just under one percent of the overall Soviet defence budget. That is not, they say, an unmanageable figure. As far as lives are concerned, the Soviet military specialist, Christopher Donnelly, has pointed out that it would be rash to assume that the Russians will be deterred by heavy casualties in Afghanistan, or indeed to construe an imbalance of casualties as a defeat.

"The Russians have a long track record of winning not just battles but also wars because of their ability to sustain ten casualties for every one inflicted on the enemy. It may indeed be true that the modern Soviet soldier will not accept this rate of casualties as his father and grandfather did, but then again it may not. We have as yet insufficient evidence on this point to reach any firm conclusions."

What Hart and Donnelly say is fine as far as it goes, but it is not far enough. Despite the low casualty estimates given by Western sources, the mere lack of a reliable, free press in the Soviet Union has undoubtedly given rise to exaggerated public gossip in the USSR on the issue of Afghanistan. It is widely believed, for example, that because of the high number of those killed, the Soviets have stopped flying the dead back home. This may or may not be true. But the perception of high losses seems to exist in the Soviet Union and may explain in part why Soviet press coverage has been cautiously increased.

Nevertheless, the steady improvements being made to Soviet airfields, bases, barracks and roads in Afghanistan, with the construction of new fuel depots, the opening of the Hairatan road bridge in rapid time and plans to construct a railway, all suggest that the Soviets plan a long stay. In fact, as one experienced correspondent, Tony Davis, suggested after two three-month trips to northern Afghanistan, the Soviet effort in Afghanistan is only 30 percent military, while 70 percent of their energies are devoted to subversion, penetration of guerilla organisations and to intelligence operations.

There seems to be considerable truth in this, given that the main problem for the Soviet occupation forces and their commanders appears not to be the destruction of resistance forces, but the consolidation of a dangerously divided and hopelessly disorganised PDPA regime. The credibility and effectiveness of Babrak Karmal's precarious government is judged by the ability of the PDPA's own armed forces to shoulder a major share of responsibility for security. That is the main headache for Moscow's men in Kabul.

What Hart, Donnelly and other writers do not mention is that Soviet commentary on Afghanistan is almost exclusively *military* in the narrow sense of the term. The question of how to train troops to scale cliffs or protect their vehicles in an ambush does not answer the key issue of how to win a guerilla war. The Soviets are fighting a physical war of attrition. Marxism-Leninism is something of a blindfold, for it prohibits the Soviets from coming to terms with the fact that the so-called Afghan "proletariat" is to a man opposed to "progressive socialism."

The Soviet invasion forces arrived in Afghanistan to shore up the Parcham cadres of the PDPA, to suppress opposition from within the indigenous armed forces, to remove Amin by killing him and to introduce a new leadership from within PDPA ranks which would be at once more "reliable" in Moscow's eyes and more conciliatory towards the tribes and ethnic groups in the hope of gaining at least some popular support. They were not brought in to fight a counter-insurgency war.

During 1980/81 for every Soviet battalion involved in operations against the "bandits", there were two Afghan units of similar size. By 1982 the position had reversed itself: there were two Soviet units in action for every Afghan communist unit of comparable strength. The Soviets were being steadily dragged against their own better judgement into a war they had clearly — and largely for ideological reasons — underestimated. If the trend continues, Soviet casualties and financial costs can be expected to grow.

It is true to say, though, that so far the Soviets have not taken off their gloves in the conflict. They have not resorted to strategic bombing of, say, the Panjsher Valley, by using night and day intensive bombing with a mixture of incendiary, high explosive and delayed-fuse weapons to dump thousands of tons of explosive in the area, much in the same way as Americans saturated areas of Vietnam and Cambodia with B-52 bombers. One possible reason is that the more conciliatory policies of the Parcham-dominated PDPA is a sign that the Soviets are still trying to win over "hearts and minds," crude though these attempts may be. Secondly, the fact that the PDPA is composed of Afghans with regional ties must be a restraining factor.

During the Smith regime's war against black nationalists in what is now Zimbabwe, the whites' security and intelligence services hired the expertise of a British academic who specialised in psychological warfare. His audience was clearly put off by the young visitor's manner; he was casually dressed, wore a beard and swore like a trooper. The Rhodesians particularly disliked what he had to say. He told them, in effect, that to win a guerilla war, the security forces must discover what it was that the guerillas — or "terrorists" as they were called then — really wanted. Very often the insurgents would not consciously know themselves. It might be a gut instinct or desire of which they were largely unaware. Once that had been defined, the security forces should proceed to hand it to the enemy on a plate. Of course, what the black nationalist forces wanted above all else was political power. The young academic seemed to be saying that the only way for the white minority in Zimbabwe to hang onto the economic reins of the country and their privileged way of life — which is what *they* were essentially fighting for — was to concede politically. Ian Smith's men did not take their guest seriously. So too in Afghanistan the Soviets and their Marxist-Leninist Afghan cadres could not conceive of giving the guerillas what they want — an Islamic government which refrains from interfering in the lives and affairs of rural, provincial communities.

The war in Afghanistan is a political struggle, but Marxism-Leninism is ill-equipped to cope with that. The Soviets may well improve their tactics, their operational control and the quality of military leadership, but they are unlikely to get to the root of the problem.

Every year it happens. Once the summer fighting season is under way, defections and desertions from Afghan military units develop into a flood of young men crossing over to the resistance. Literally thousands of conscripts, acting individually or as entire platoons and even battalions, bring across much-needed weapons and ammunition — their safe pass to join the guerillas. Every year Kabul authorities react by mounting large-scale operations specifically designed to drag able-bodied men out of their homes or off the streets and into uniform.

On paper the Afghan Army consists of about 80,000 troops organised into 14 — theoretical — divisions, including armour, infantry, mountain warfare and commando units. The divisions are deployed according to an administrative system which divides the country up into "zones"; the northern, central, southern, western and so on. Generally speaking, by late summer the real figure of Afghan servicemen falls to around 30,000 and it is beefed up again through the autumn and winter months by means of forcible conscription. At its peak the indigenous Afghan communist forces probably number around 50,000. That is the maximum, and it is very temporary.

Just how forcible conscription works can be seen by visitors to the small surgical hospital run by the International Committee of the Red Cross (ICRC) in Peshawar over the border. One 45-year-old woman in the paraplegic ward was stretched out on her back, unable to move save for painful and very slight movements of her head. She made herself understood in barely comprehensible grunts. She will never recover. When soldiers had come to her house and tried to take her son away to the army, she held on to him, and the intruders shot her in the back with an automatic rifle. A bullet lodged high up in her spine and she is paralysed completely for the rest of her life from the neck down.

New recruits receive little military training. The officers learn to use the support weapons — the privates are not trusted. If a conscript is lucky, he will fire an automatic rifle once, using not more than a half a dozen rounds, before he is packed off to the front line. The front line is often in the form of a small and isolated military post encircled by hostile forces, and he will stay there until he is killed, captured or defects. At night — even when on the move during operations — he will be expected to hand in his weapon. At least, the official reasoning goes, he will not be able to walk off with a present for the guerillas.

One reluctant draftee, 21-year-old Jamaluddin, was sent in April 1982 with the elite 444th Commando Combat Brigade to replace Soviet units occupying tenuous positions in the southern section of Panjsher Valley. The brigade — famous in Afghanistan — numbered by that stage only 400 men instead of a normal complement of about 1,500-2,000. The 2nd Battalion had only 70 men when it took up its position. Two reservists, Abdur Rahman, aged 40, and Mohammed Yusuf, aged 44, both from Herat, defected with 19 others, including a captain, from Rokha in the Panjsher. They reported that members of the PDPA sent to the valley to symbolise the re-establishment of a regime presence were being airlifted out at the rate of two or three a day for medical treatment. They had allegedly resorted to self-inflicted wounds to get themselves out of the front line. Mohammad Fana, aged 18, was seized in Panjsher's Burjaman village on May 20, 1982 and sent off to Paktya in south-east Afghanistan. Seraj Mohammad, 29, was captured while paying a visit to Mazar-i-Sharif and pressed into military service in the

18th Division. Hashem Dad, a driver's assistant in Kabul, was rounded up for the 21st Division in Faran Province in the west, but he is now fighting with the guerillas. Kwaja Nur, a Kabul baker, was conscripted into Paktya's 25th Division despite his having military exemption papers.

The list seems endless. Many conscripts have served in both the resistance and the armed forces by turns. One young man had been pulled in for military duty on no fewer than three occasions, but each time he defected. Another defected 11 days after being conscripted. Taken in Herat, he was flown to Kabul, driven to Jalalabad and then on to Kunar Province. He defected within a week of arriving at his final destination. The cost of mounting the recruiting drives, feeding, training and arming and finally deploying these unwilling troops must be high indeed. They defect in many cases because they are already *Mujehadeen* — caught by security forces' patrols while on leave to visit relatives or while hiding in their home village during a security forces' attack. They defect because they regard themselves as Muslim, because they know their chances of survival with the guerillas in front of them and with the Soviets behind them are slim. And they display a hatred for officers who are party members. To die for serving communism, as one conscript put it, is to die a "dirty" death. Many of the defectors interviewed during the course of 1981 and 1982 sincerely believed it, too.

Occasionally entire military posts are overrun by guerillas simply by virtue of a mini-rebellion from within. A common sight in Kunar Province in the late summer of 1981 was the loudspeaker or bullhorn carried by local guerilla commanders. During the battle, the commander will call out to the Muslims in the garrison to kill their communist officers and come over. Often the scheme is well prepared in advance, with contacts established with a military post's dissident officer who helps plan a mass defection, co-ordinated with the final guerilla assault. The authorities try to stem the seasonal flood by indoctrinating the conscripts with the notion that they will be butchered by the resistance. Fortunately, these garrisons usually include more than a sprinkling of "old hands" who have been through it all before, and they reassure and often lead the mutinous elements to liberty. Party cadres in the officer corps can expect a less than friendly reception on surrendering. A brisk search, rough questioning and possibly an appearance before a summary tribunal and immediate despatch by means of a ragged firing squad face both Parchamite and Khalqi officers unlucky enough to be taken alive. On occasion PDPA members have got off alive — *sans* ears or nose or both, *pour encourager les autres.*

So serious is the issue for Kabul that on August 2, 1982 Kabul Radio broadcast an announcement of the extension of military service by one year. It also announced new measures to establish law and order against "American imperialism, Chinese chauvinism and Arab reaction." These measures were to prove counter-productive. They drove those eligible under the new regulations either straight into the ranks of the resistance or over the border and into refugee camps. The PDPA decided to increase the length of compulsory service from two to three years, something which was to apply to everyone regardless of educational standards. Reservists discharged before 1977 but not over 36 years of age were called upon to serve a further two years. In due course civil servants, students and others who had been previously exempted turned up together with scores of factory workers in Pakistan. Many joined the resistance.

If that was not enough to reduce the effectiveness of indigenous communist security forces in the PDPA's vain efforts to gain control of the populace, the split in the PDPA regime between Khalq and Parcham factions equalled the issue of defections as a cause of military ineptitude. The officer corps is dominated by members of the majority but out-of-favour Khalq faction, but they are subject to orders from a regime dominated by the pro-Soviet, minority Parcham. There's the rub, for the Khalq will neither forgive nor forget the Parcham for seizing power with Soviet assistance.

The Parchamites in Kabul naturally enough attempt to push forward their own members for senior military appointments, but they are restrained in doing so by the Soviets and by fears that key units and officers will rise against the regime. The Parcham faction is active in pushing Khalq rivals into the front line, while sons of prominent Parchamites receive exemption from military service with relative ease; the "cushy" plum jobs fall on the whole to Parchamites and the Khalq leaders within the PDPA's Central Committee greatly resent this. Consequently relations are not only bad between Afghan military commanders and central headquarters in Kabul, but they are equally poor between the Khalq officer corps and the Soviet advisory teams attached to army and airforce units. For one thing, the Soviet staffs do not in general trust their Afghan comrades — for good reason. But they trust the Khalq even less, while Khalqis are resentful of Soviet excesses directed against the Afghan civilians they encounter. There were three separate incidents reported during the course of 1982 in which clashes broke out between Khalq-dominated Afghan units and Soviet troops, reportedly caused by Khalq officers' violent objections to Soviet looting.

General Mohammad Rafie's fall from grace as defence minister is said by Kabul sources to have been the result of Rafie's insistence on protesting at Politburo level against the abduction and sexual molestation of three Afghan high school girls in Kabul by Soviet officers.

The Parcham-Khalq rift makes itself felt on the battlefield, to the guerillas' advantage. The Panjsher Valley, that natural redoubt of resistance north-east of the capital, threatening Bagram airbase and the Salang highway, has more than once proved to be more than a match for successive attacks by the security forces. But in January 1982 matters went badly wrong. Guerillas, caught unprepared despite their intelligence of an impending assault, were forced to fight what amounted to a defensive battle which lasted a week in the plain below the valley proper. They were subjected to heavy artillery and air strikes while infantry supported by armour wore them down. What could have been a major defeat was narrowly averted because of an innate weakness in the joint Afghan-Soviet offensive: sympathetic army officers ensured the encirclement was never entirely complete and thousands of civilians and guerillas escaped the ring. It was less a matter of sympathy for the guerillas than the Khalq officers' hostility towards their Parchamite and Soviet colleagues.

Relations between the Afghan Army and the Soviets deteriorated sharply during the course of 1981/82. One example was given by a defector to Pakistan, a young but senior Afghan Army officer, fluent in Russian and well acquainted with the USSR.

"I was supervising a football match involving Afghan cadets from the military academy when the incident happened. This was on the field just behind the military club in Kabul which is now an important Soviet intelligence centre. The game was over and the cadets were changing back into their uniforms when a Soviet sentry guarding the gate near the club suddenly started shooting with his Kalashnikov rifle. He fired four times. One shot knocked the cap off the head of one boy. The fourth shot hit a cadet square in the head, spreading his brains all over the grass and killing him outright.

"The Russian just jumped up and down and jeered. His companion simply clapped and laughed. They thought it was a joke. A crowd quickly gathered and when a Soviet officer came out of the club he turned on the people and accused them of selling hashish to the Russian troops. When the cadet's father arrived, the officer tried to give him cash as compensation. The old man threw the money on the ground and said the Russian could not buy his son's blood . . ."

Why does the PDPA regime — and, for that matter, the Soviets — bother with the Afghan Army in such circumstances? What is the use of an army of resentful, mutiny-prone Muslims anxious to join the resistance?

The regime and its Soviet backers take the trouble simply because the ability of the regime to exert control is measured very largely by its retention of indigenous armed forces. It is part and parcel of the illusion of an independent, socialist ally laying claim to international recognition. And the armed forces are an important repository of political power in terms of the tiny PDPA membership. Without the armed forces, the PDPA could be expected to break up rapidly. The Soviets devote considerable energy to the frustrating and ultimately impossible task of trying to mend the rift between the Khalq and Parcham factions. Without the Afghan armed forces that would be a non-starter.

Operationally, the Afghan Army still has some use. In fact some units have improved their offensive capability. It provides the Soviets with a "screen" of military bases established to protect targets of secondary importance to them. Afghan troops provide new military posts, small in size, in vulnerable positions straddling guerilla supply routes.

These bases may well fall and usually do eventually, but in setting them up and replacing them the Soviets know they will draw off guerilla resources and manpower into relatively meaningless engagements. These posts are fortunate if they receive sporadic, inaccurate artillery supporting fire. They seldom get the "quick reaction" air support Soviet troops in a similar position could expect in a critical situation. In other words these Afghan posts allow the Soviets to concentrate their limited resources in Afghanistan on more important tasks.

Afghan Army losses are estimated at approximately twice those of the Soviets. Guerilla sources disagree — they put the Afghan casualty figure at several times the author's "guesstimate." In truth, the losses are relatively light because the bulk of the Afghan conscripts facing guerilla action desert, defect or simply remain passive if they can. "We fired in the air, rolling onto our backs," was one conscript's description of Afghan defensive fire in 1981. However, the losses among officers who are members of PDPA military cadres are much higher. They are targets for their own troops, for one thing. They are seldom taken alive, but are usually killed on the spot by their captors. The fate of those suspected of leftist sympathies hangs in the balance; they are treated as prisoners-of-war and held until their family backgrounds can be investigated by their resistance hosts.

Little is known about the Afghan airforce, which does contribute to airmobile operations in the war, but on a limited scale. Pilots are in short supply and they receive very brief periods of training. They are responsible mainly for transport aircraft and elderly fighters like the Mig-17s still in service, but also Mig-21s and Su-22s. A limited number of the older variants of the Mi-24 helicopter gunships are probably flown by Afghan pilots, but with an escort of Soviet aircraft. Afghan pilots try and defect with their aircraft from time to time; relations between the Afghan and Soviet air staffs and crews are poor. The Soviets frequently carry out investigations and interrogations of their Afghan comrades suspected of being responsible for occasional "accidents" or sabotage on airforce bases. Overall, the airforce capability has improved in three years.

The performance of the Afghan communist forces is characterised by a grievous lack of trained, loyal personnel. No doubt the Soviets are busy trying to develop cadres of reliable, skilled counter-insurgency officers and men. But it is an uphill battle, and likely to remain so for many years to come.

Chemical Warfare

In April 1981 a guerilla commander left his fellow resistance fighters just before first light and walked down one of the innumerable escarpments in Nangahar Province to attend to his ablutions before prayers or *namaz.* He heard a warning shout and he scrambled back up again. As he did so, several helicopters approached, line abreast. Behind them armoured vehicles advanced over open ground.

The fighting continued until four in the afternoon. Commander Yassini was separated from his group. He said he saw the aircraft emit clouds of multi-coloured "smoke." It was a running fight, with isolated pockets of men withdrawing under fire as well as they could to higher ground. Yassini was among them, and they regrouped around a pool at about 4 p.m. where they washed and prayed. They then returned to bury the dead. People from the villages near the town of Kama came out to find any of their relatives who had been *shaheed,* or martyred.

"There was one place where 17 of our brothers had fallen. The local people wanted to take the bodies away and bury them properly, but they were angry they could not do so. You see, when we tried to lift them, the flesh fell away from the bones. The bodies had turned black and the skin was loose. I thought the *Shuravi* had poisoned them or something and we were afraid."

This was one of more than a dozen separate reports brought in by word of mouth, by eye-witnesses or written on the scraps of paper or linen that form the guerillas' despatches which reach Peshawar each week. Much of it was hearsay. Detail was lacking in most cases. On occasion the impression was that the guerillas had been simply perplexed by what had occurred. Others could conceivably have made much of it up to impress the foreigner. But the talk of green, yellow, white and sometimes black smoke and cases of blackened, loose flesh on victims were the lowest common denominators. Refugees reported that sufferers who survived still showed symptoms of nausea, headache, loss of hair and weight loss. Dizziness and affected vision were also reported from time to time. Piecing these reports together produced a rough picture of what usually happened: aircraft dropped markers which emitted smoke to provide indications of the direction and speed of ground winds. The chemical and/ or biological agents were then disseminated by dropping canisters or bombs, or occasionally by pumping the material out from the attacking aircraft, not unlike crop-spraying. Areas heavily affected by concentrations of whatever it was produced rapid death; further away, lighter doses produced unconsciousness or incapacitation. The symptoms continued to be displayed by the locals for days and weeks afterwards.

Yassini's own point in his story was not to demonstrate that chemical weapons had been used; he simply wanted to impress upon his visitor how the security forces contaminated the dead to prevent them being accorded a proper Muslim burial. This obviously caused him considerable grief and anger.

Reports of this kind were widespread, but almost impossible to substantiate. The mysterious attacks were carried out in Badakshan, Fariab, Kandahar, Baghlan and Nangahar in 1981. In May 1982, Soviets were described as having walked up to those incapacitated by gas and shooting them. In June, security forces in Herat Province loaded unconscious men caught by the alleged chemical attack onto trucks and drove them off. In April 1983, Surat Khan and a companion described a counter-insurgency operation in Farah Province the previous month in which yellow-green gas was dispersed by canisters dropped by helicopters. The wind changed direction and no *Mujehadeen* were seriously affected although they said nausea and headaches were experienced by a few locals. They distinguished between a black smoke-screen laid by a "machine" to cover the advance of ground forces and the gas. The former was grey-black and was caused by a "smoke machine on wheels" while the latter came from three-foot canisters which broke open on hitting the ground. One Western traveller through Badakshan Province in 1981 said the local population was used to it. They were surprised by his interest in the subject — for them it had become a matter of course to which they attached no special significance.

In October 1981, the first apparently firm indication that the Soviets were using chemical weapons came from an Afghan Army defector, an artillery officer who refused to allow his name to be used for fear of reprisals against his family still living in Kabul. The officer said he himself had received instruction in the use of four types of gas and a liquid poison which he said was used primarily in western and southern Afghanistan to poison the area's typical wells, the underground waterways known as the *kerez* which guerillas use as hiding places in open terrain. The defecting officer's story backed allegations by U.S. Secretary of State Alexander Haig the previous month that mycotoxins — biochemical warfare agents — were being used in Laos, Cambodia and Afghanistan.

The defector told the *Far Eastern Economic Review* that Soviet-supplied chemical and biological agents were being used by Afghan Army units. He alleged that gas companies of the 18th Division of Mazar-i-Sharif and the 20th at Nahrin were responsible for chemical warfare in the north of the country. Despite the considerable fall in the number of troops available to the regime, the officer said that the armed forces' chemical warfare units were up to full strength.

He said the Soviet effort was directed towards the 234th Gas and Chemical Department in Kabul itself. The chemical warfare staff, he said, totalled 2,250 men. Qal-e-Jangi, near the Soviet residential enclave of Mikrorayon, was the department's headquarters. The officer said that substantial CBW equipment was stored at the centre. He added that a chemical field battalion under the Qal-e-Jangi HQ was based at Husein Khot camp near Bagram airbase, north of the capital. The officer claimed elements of the 234th were involved in joint Soviet-Afghan operations in Parwan Province in August of that year. However, there were no other reports to corroborate the last claim, which is a little surprising because connections between Peshawar and Parwan are generally good. The defector said a number of Afghan military officers and other ranks had been flown to Kabul for CBW training. Chemical warheads for artillery shells were supplied to the Afghan Army as well as helicopter-borne gas canisters and grenades filled with CB agents for infantry use. Afghan troops used gas masks and other protective or decontamination equipment where this type of warfare was being carried out.

The officer's report was convincing, primarily because of the wealth of detail. He named units, places and operations. It was the clearest report to date. There were lacunae in his story, though. Why was it that the numerous defectors from the 18th and 20th Divisions had not mentioned the presence of chemical warfare troops and weapons? And why would a hard-pressed regime maintain what must amount to experimental units of CBW troops at full strength when entire motorised rifle and tank divisions each numbered a mere few hundred men? And finally, it is known that the USSR maintains the tightest possible control over its CBW munitions and chemical warfare troops stationed in Eastern Europe

Villagers warily examine an unexploded bomb, one of thousands littering the countryside.

Hubert Van Es/Photoreporters

Hans-Peter Kruse

David De Voss/Stockhouse

Top and clockwise: January 1980, and Soviet tanks and troops prepare to move into Kabul from the airport; armoured personnel carriers on the road; Soviet division encamped.

Top left and clockwise: Daoud, who seized power in a bloodless coup in 1973 and who was assassinated in the 1978 Khalq *putsch;* Taraki: divisions led to his downfall and death — some say he was strangled — in late 1979; Soviet troops with AGS-17 grenade launchers, used for the first time in Afghanistan; Soviet troops lounge among the remains of a Kabul post office; Amin, who deposed Taraki and was himself removed in the 1979 Soviet-backed coup; Karmal: installed by the Soviets to preserve communist rule in Kabul.

Top left and clockwise: the Soviet presence — a military truck rolls through the streets of Kabul; "Hind-E" Mi-24 gunship; KGB border guard-post on Soviet-Afghan frontier opposite Kaldar district in Balkh province.

Peter Jouvenal/Rex Features

Ken Guest/Rex Features

ВПХР

Top left and clockwise: ground-level weaponry — *Mujehadeen* guerillas with flintlock rifle; SAM-7 anti-aircraft missile launcher; 75mm Chinese recoilless rifle and laying a Chinese-made mine; a captured Soviet biological/chemical decontamination kit; a four-barrelled 14.5mm anti-aircraft gun (typically, not dug-in or camouflaged, reflecting poor military skill).

T.A. Davis

T.A. Davis

Top left and clockwise: Leaders of the *jehad* — Maulavi Yunis Khalis, Hezb-i-Islami faction; Qasi Islamuddin, Uzbek commander of Jamiat-i-Islami forces in Ishkamish district; Basir Khan, commander, Faizabad in Badakshan province, which borders the Soviet Union, China and Pakistan; Ahmadshah Massoud, commander, Panjsher valley, who agreed to a six-month ceasefire with the Soviets in December 1982; Amir Abdul Haiy, commander of Jamiat-i-Islami forces in Baghlan province.

ter Jouvenal

Top left and clockwise: summary justice in the desert for three Afghan bulldozer drivers working for the Soviets and captured by the *Mujehadeen*.

Top left and clockwise: The defectors — Afghan Army deserters are escorted into a *Mujehadeen* camp; Soviet prisoner "Ahmad Zia" (foreground) kneeling in prayer at a *Mujehadeen* camp after being captured in an ambush of a military convoy near the Soviet base at Qilagai, Baghlan province, in mid-1982 and subsequently converting to Islam; Soviet defector Berik Bergibardi, 22, a Kazakh, who fled the Soviet base at Kunduz airport in northern Afghanistan after being beaten by his officers and now an acclaimed *Mujehad* with many "credits" scored against his former masters.

Child of the *Mujehadeen:* education is a lesson in weaponry and religion.

— in much the same way that tactical and theatre nuclear weapons are held under the Politburo's thumb. Yet a communist regime which has to pay — at least on paper — for the Soviet military aid it receives and which is, to say the least, lacking in cohesion and reliability, receives the go-ahead for controversial CB warfare, according to the officer. His report indubitably strengthened the probability of the use of these weapons in Afghanistan. But it was not proof.

Ten months later another Afghan Army officer defected. He was not a PDPA member, but he was well informed and had served as a colonel on the Afghan defence ministry staff. He poured cold water over his colleague's report. Husein Khot was nothing more nor less than a "ruin." There was no 234th Department, but instead a battalion of that designation composed of relatives of prominent PDPA figures. It was a unit of what the British Army would have called "bottlewashers and jamstealers." For they stayed in Kabul and were put to guarding regime property. At one point they mutinied against the extension of military service. But they were privileged soldiers with "cushy" jobs behind the front line.

The young colonel did say, though, that the national Ministry of Defence had created a new department during the course of 1981: the chemical and biological warfare department.

Why would the regime form such an organisation if CB warfare was not being prosecuted? And why would *Mujehadeen* from time to time return from the battlefield with CBW equipment, gas masks, decontamination kits, oxygen bottles from armoured vehicles — but no CBW dispensers or unexploded containers of chemical and/or biological agents?

In the summer of 1981 the defence ministry in Kabul was reorganised under Soviet supervision along the lines of similar establishments in the Soviet Socialist Republics. This tightened the links between Moscow and Kabul and cut down on the staff to release more men for combat or provincial appointments. It reduced the day-to-day power and role of the ministry, which has all the window-dressing of a fully-fledged ministry, but very little of the clout. The new chemical and biological warfare department appears to have emerged during the reorganisation.

Soviet ground forces have an estimated 80,000-strong chemical and biological warfare establishment with specialist chemical defence units attached to divisions, battalions and companies. There are said to be in the region of 1,200 CBW training grounds and courses in the USSR and Moscow takes the whole issue very seriously from both a defensive and offensive point of view. The main role is "defensive" — Soviet CBW teams are trained to recce ground contaminated by chemical/biological weapons, to decontaminate military personnel and their equipment once affected.

It is said that as much as a third of Soviet munitions stockpiled in Eastern Europe and the western USSR are chemical-filled. The aim is to use these weapons — particularly non-persistent nerve gas — to suppress NATO's anti-tank defences to facilitate a rapid breakthrough. The CBW troops have the capability to allow Soviet units to transit zones contaminated by their own weapons.

Soviet forces invaded Afghanistan with a full complement of their normal equipment which was more suitable to European-style operations than a guerilla campaign. While there are signs that some equipment found inappropriate for local conditions is left back at base, and other, more suitable weapons and tactics are employed, nevertheless it appears that Soviet formations in Afghanistan continue to deploy CBW troops. Despite Soviet propaganda, the guerillas pose no chemical or biological warfare threat to the Afghan regime. Why these specialist Soviet troops remain is a matter of speculation.

Interest revived again in September, 1982, when a Soviet conscript announced that the Russians were using chemical/biological weapons in Afghanistan. Anatoly Mikhailovich Sakharov, aged 19, from Saransk in the Moldavian Republic, had run away from his unit and fell into guerilla hands the previous month. Despite obvious nervousness, the chain-smoking soldier in summer uniform was quite adamant. He said three types of agent were used.

While he did not himself take part in CBW operations, he said he saw the weapons stored at both Kabul and Kunduz airbases. He claimed to have spoken to a helicopter crewman who confirmed the use of the weapons against guerillas in northern areas. Sakharov said he was an eye-witness of the return of Soviet personnel from CBW operations who had themselves been affected. One, he said, suffered from eye damage.

The first two agents were said to form a dense, yellowish cloud over a target and choked or asphyxiated their victims. The first he called picrine — possibly a compound including picric acid — and this, he said, caused 20 percent fatalities among those affected. The second Sakharov called "oedoeshayshe"; this is said to have caused three fatalities out of every 10 people affected in the target area. The third agent he called "smirch" which killed everyone it affected. "Smirch" blackened the flesh of its victims.

Sakharov alleged the three agents were stored in liquid form in cylinders marked "propan" and that they created a spray or vapour

114

on being released either by rockets fired from fixed wing aircraft or helicopters. Large metal containers as long as an estimated 21 ft. and fixed to the fuselage of propeller-driven aircraft also sprayed the material over the target. The teenage soldier had received training in CBW in Kabul; whether this was simply part and parcel of normal, standard training for all Soviet conscripts or not is unclear. It is possible that he learned all this from the training. He did say he had read a manual on chemical warfare and had watched a training film.

The interview with Sakharov lasted more than three hours and at times the two correspondents present were aggressive and disbelieving in their questioning, which was repeated several times, but Sakharov stuck firmly to his story. Sakharov's evidence bore close relation to similar accounts from guerilla sources. Again, it is possible — just possible — that his captors tutored him, but that would show a sense of political and media sophistication which the guerillas notably lack. It is also conceivable that Sakharov made up most of it in order to gain the confidence of the *Mujehadeen*. He said he wanted to stay with the guerillas and that he was a defector, not a prisoner.

He eventually obtained an interview with the ICRC delegation in Peshawar and convinced them that he was a bona fide defector. He was seen again several months later with the guerilas in Afghanistan.

The interest in chemical and biological warfare in Afghanistan puzzled and in some cases irritated *Mujehadeen*. "What does it matter how the Soviets kill us? They kill us all the same — with bullets and bombs. They burn our people alive. They torture us. Why are you Westerners only interested in this chemical warfare business? Why aren't you interested in an independent country being steadily destroyed by communism?"

One American, an activist based in Paris, tried to explain: "It's like trying to get Al Capone on a tax evasion clause of the law. But you get him behind bars nonetheless."

The American Government's considerable interest in the subject of CBW in Afghanistan and Southeast Asia is not simply a matter of altruistic humanitarian concern. The speeches and articles written in a tone of moral outrage are in fact designed to show that the USSR is breaking one of the oldest and best-established arms control agreements of all. In other words, catch the Soviets breaking one arms control agreement and you can demonstrate that Moscow is not to be trusted, say, with SALT II or the stalled Mutual Balanced Force Reduction talks. A "technicality" like CBW can therefore deeply affect American policies towards its superpower adversary. It is not, as Moscow would suggest, a propaganda campaign designed to justify American military pressure to resurrect chemical and biological warfare production and deployment in NATO. But it is very much a narrow self-interest, and the Afghan resistance fighters sense it. By and large the guerillas resent what they see as a cynical attempt to use their struggle for domestic political purposes in the US. They instinctively shrink from anything that smacks of superpower rivalry in their struggle.

The fact that one cannot "trust" the USSR should, they say, be self-evident by now. No doubt Americans would retort that a greater political awareness on the part of Afghan critics of US policy would permit them to realise that proof of the use of CBW in Afghanistan might lead to a more realistic appraisal by Washington of Soviet intentions and that, in turn, would indirectly benefit their *jehad.*

Official US action over alleged Soviet-supplied chemical and biological agents began before the 1979 Soviet invasion. In October the previous year Washington called to the attention of the Laotian chargé d'affaires the press reports on the use of poison gas in his country, while Assistant Secretary of State for East Asian and Pacific Affairs Richard Holbrooke travelled to Vientiane and discussed American concern over the H'Mong people, said to have been affected by the CBW attacks. Later the same year embassy personnel in the area were instructed to concentrate their efforts in trying to gather information on the issue.

In January 1979, further démarches were made and in March the US representative to the 35th session of the UN Human Rights Commission expressed American concern over the plight of the H'Mong. In May the State Department sent an official to refugee camps in Thailand to interview the victims. In the late summer a medical team was sent out there by the US Department of Defense, while both the Soviets and the Vietnamese backed official Laotian denials. In February 1980 the US protested directly to Moscow regarding the alleged use of CBW in Laos, Cambodia and Afghanistan, while a few months later America briefed her European allies on the issue. In July another protest was lodged with the Russians and in August the US circulated to UN member states a 125-page compendium of reports and declassified intelligence on the Soviet use of these weapons in the three countries.

The study proved inconclusive and the team's mandate was further extended by a year. The second report was published in November 1982, and the investigators found that two of the charges were "well supported." These included claims by

116

Afghan refugees that "harassing agents" were used against the people. A week later, two State Department officials showed newsmen in Washington a gasmask from Afghanistan said to have been contaminated on its exterior with the fungal toxin T-2, the suspected active ingredient of "yellow rain." Both the UN and a separate Canadian inquiry in Southeast Asia seemed to support the general thesis that the Soviets were using CBW, but there remained differences over the role of the alleged mycotoxin.

At least, as one writer in *Science* magazine concluded, the American pressure worldwide had succeeded in encouraging other countries to take the matter seriously.

The State Department's report listed 12 reported chemical/biological attacks by security forces in Afghanistan during the course of 1982. The report quoted an Afghan airport official as saying that he had seen 200-300 gas containers at Kandahar airbase, while his subordinate reported that the three types of gas in these canisters caused burning of the throat and suffocation; a second that caused blistering and what looked like smallpox, and a third substance that made its victims tired and unable to fight or run. The containers produced a yellow smoke on impact. The report also mentioned the case of a Soviet adviser having said before the invasion that Soviet chemical defence troops would bring in substantial quantities of toxic materials. The adviser, who was inspecting sites for housing Soviet troops, indicated that a proposed garrison in Kabul would be inappropriate for a Soviet chemical defence unit because an accident could devastate the city.

The difficulty is that Afghanistan is a remote and rugged country and sparsely populated. The majority of the people fighting the Soviet and DRA forces are illiterate. And "proof" is not only difficult to obtain but can always be denied, as Moscow has done on several occasions, even by going so far as to suggest the scientifically dubious theory that mycotoxins spread throughout Southeast Asia after the US had seeded the region with elephant grass. People tend to believe what they want to believe and short of the production by the guerillas of a bomb, grenade or other item of hardware containing a poisonous substance deployed by communist forces in Afghanistan, many people will continue to doubt the affair.

But, as the State Department says, the weight of evidence is considerable. Soviet use of chemical/biological weapons is a strong probability. If the security forces' deployment of the plastic anti-personnel "butterfly" mines is any guide, international agreements do not inhibit the Soviets from experimenting with the lives of hundreds of thousand of people.

The last word goes to a young Afghan *Mujehad:* "The trouble with the Western public is that it fears the Russians. Because it fears the Russians, it does not want to face up to what they are doing to us in Afghanistan. It may be the Westerners' turn next — who knows?"

The Secret Police

Central to the authorities' prosecution of the war and above all to Soviet attempts to consolidate the Kabul regime is the Khad, acronym for Khidamate Aetilaati Daulati, literally, the state information service, but in fact the regime's security and intelligence organisation. By early 1983 it was to be found at every level of government, in every ministry, army division, television studio, district government, university faculty, school and trade organisation.

Within a matter of months of the Soviet invasion, Moscow used the KGB to reorganise the service and provided substantial funds for the purpose. East German security specialists took up posts at the police academy, while Khad officers were sent on training courses in the USSR, Bulgaria and Czechoslovakia.

Its "investigations directorate" has been supplied with Soviet-made lie-detectors. A special department for what is assumed to be counter-intelligence has been formed, along the lines of the KGB's Third Directorate. It carries out the Afghan equivalent of "wet jobs." It is called, literally, the Sacrificial Directorate.

Information offices have been established at Kabul University and in the capital's commercial and trading offices, public and private. The "information officers" are in fact Khad staffers. In the country as a whole there are estimated to be between 25,000 and 30,000 career employees and regular collaborators, or agents. Kabul has been divided up into 182 administrative blocks for facilitating control of residents. Each sector is reliably reported to have a network of more than 100 local paid informers.

During 1982 a committee at directorate level was formed to weed out dissidents within party ranks. The predominantly Parchamite Khad has been particularly active in suppressing dissidents in the majority Khalq group. Formation of the committee reflects the sense of urgency the Soviets attach to their overriding problem in Afghanistan: welding together loyal cadres of PDPA members and excluding those who display anti-Soviet sentiments.

The Khad is responsible to the KGB and MVD staff headquarters in Kabul. In theory it is answerable to the Afghan Politburo in the form of the Prime Ministry in the capital. In practice its reports are subject to scrutiny by KGB liaison officers under diplomatic cover at the Soviet Embassy. No fewer than 57 Soviet advisers are attached to the Khad directorates in the city.

Its headquarters are situated behind the military club next to the armed forces' sports field in the capital, having been moved from the Prime Ministry. Electronic equipment installed on the roof eavesdrops on foreign embassies' communications. Other major Khad establishments in the capital are situated at Wazir Akbar Khan where there are two offices, one being the "Number Seven" headquarters and the other being in the former home of Prince Daoud's cousin, Rokai; one is directly behind the Prime Ministry, another in Kart-e-Sau in front of the Soviet Embassy; another in Syedi Raian in Darulaman and one also across the parade ground in Noor Mohammad Shah Maina.

Important out-stations have been established in the eastern border cities of Asadabad, Jalalabad and Khost for intelligence and subversion operations in Pakistan's tribal areas, refugee camps and in Peshawar itself, home of the guerilla leaders-in-exile.

The Khad is the primary instrument used in the Sovietisation of the country, from supervision of ideological courses — which are supposed to be compulsory — at university, the polytechnic and schools, to political instruction in the armed forces and introduction of language courses in Russian for party members in the provinces.

A special educational establishment was set up in September, 1981, for young children of PDPA members and orphans of war victims. From the age of seven these children receive basic political indoctrination and are packed off regularly by the planeload for further training in the USSR. This is the Watan Palanzai, or "place where training is given," and is situated in the Wazir Akbar Khan Maina sector of the capital.

The role of this organisation — headed by the very man who is director-general of the Khad itself, Dr. Najib — is linked to the emphasis evident since early 1982 on recruiting teenagers for militias, particularly in towns adjacent to Pakistan in Pushtun tribal areas. These youngsters — whose families are often associated with local party organisations — are paid for their services, armed for guard duties and in promising cases sent away for intelligence training.

The theme is on youth: on isolating recruits from their traditional, tribal or ethnic backgrounds and on turning them into pro-Soviet PDPA Marxist-Leninists — an Afghan version of *Homus Sovieticus*. So far thousands of children and teenagers have gone through the process. The Khad programme represents Moscow's "long view" on Afghanistan: setting up a reliable power base may be expensive and it may take a generation or two, but the Soviets are apparently willing to be patient.

The PDPA employs Islam in attempts to gain credibility both internally and externally. The Religious Affairs Directorate is funded by the Khad and a special liaison committee, known as "Khad-66," has been established to supervise the progress of religious manipulation. Three Soviet advisers specialise in this work in Kabul. All the directorate's religious tracts are vetted by these advisers, while an association with the Khad is a condition of membership of the Afghans' Supreme Council of Ulema in Kabul. The Khad has also created the Society of Islamic Scholars and the Promotion of Islamic Traditions, headed by Maulavi Abdul Aziz, who was busy agitating in the 1960s in the Khalqis' lycée in Kabul for Pushtun tribesmen's sons, Rahmanaba.

Mohammad Qasim Maftoon and Brigadier Mohammad Ayub Mangal, leader and spokesman respectively of the 35-member official Afghan *Hajj* delegation in 1982, defected to Pakistan in November of that year. They said that 20 members of the Supreme Council of Ulema were required to provide speeches and pamphlets aimed at winning people over to the regime. These pamphlets, or "Opiyam-e-Haq" as they are known, are used extensively by the official media and during PDPA members' tours of the provincial capitals.

The "official" ulema are in turn required to hire mosque staff as informers to report regularly to "Khad-66" the speeches, gossip and activities of Muslim worshippers. The two defectors added that of the 4,206 Afghans given permission to perform *Hajj* in 1982, several hundred were persuaded to provide the security police with useful titbits of intelligence. Khad officers were also included on the pilgrimage to propagate the official line once the delegations reached Saudi Arabia.

Minorities receive special attention from the Khad and its KGB supervisors. The Sikh/Hindu community in Afghanistan is small but well-established in Afghan cities and in Kabul in particular. They are encouraged to turn informer and those who belong to the educated classes are treated in a privileged manner: they are invited to join the armed forces but are not required to undergo political instruction. A special effort has been made to persuade several of their number to join the ruling party and promising members have been sent off to the USSR for intensive Russian language training. Successful candidates who have passed through Khad training schools have been attached to its foreign or external intelligence directorate and assigned to duties in India, according to sources in the secret police.

The Khad recruits informers and agents for internal and external work; it supervises party members and regulates the behaviour of army and airforce officers, interrogates prisoners and assassinates enemies of the regime. But by far its most important role is penetration of guerilla organisations, refugee camps and resistance parties in Iran and Pakistan. Moreover it works among the border tribes both in Afghanistan and Pakistan and it plants teams of spies and saboteurs in Peshawar. A rash of violent incidents in Peshawar in February and March 1983 is assumed to have been the direct or indirect result of Khad infiltration by some local security officials and diplomatic observers. The Khad reportedly cultivates Pushtun and Baluch political opponents of General Zia ul-Haq's military administration and it attempts to encourage hostility towards the refugees on the part of the local communities.

The director-general of the Khad is Dr. Najib Ahmadzai, a medical practitioner by training and a man known for his devotion to his job as the top Afghan spymaster. He is said to be in his early 40s and to have relatively well-developed intellectual abilities for someone in the first echelon of the PDPA.

He is closely involved in the work of the Ministry of Tribes and Nationalities. The two government organs work in close liaison with one another in terms of the development of party controls over the country's tribes and ethnic groups. They share responsibility for the recruitment of frontier militia groups to protect the frontier and to help provide intelligence on guerilla movements.

Afghanistan has been divided into three administrative regions. The first, said to be headed directly by the Tribal Minister, Suleiman Laeq, deals with the regionally-distinct ethnic groups such as the Tajiks, Uzbek and Aimaq. The second belt covers the Pushtun tribes living in a crescent from Nuristan in the east to Kandahar in the south-west. The third division is responsible for the Baluch and Pushtun tribal belt in Pakistan. Najib is in effective control of the last two administrative sectors.

Delegations are organised by the Khad and Ministry of Tribes and Nationalities to visit rural communities. Government and party officials with personal and family ties with their respective tribes and regions are flown to the provincial capital concerned and a local messenger is sent out to tribal elders informing them of the delegation's mission and inviting them to a *jirga*, or traditional assembly.

The first and second attempts to establish a dialogue are invariably refused, but further efforts sometimes succeed. The mission is then accepted — but without weapons or military escort — and proposals and counter-proposals put forward by each side.

The official delegates suggest that if the elders accept the status quo in Kabul, there will be no further sanctions taken against the "rebels"; confiscated land and property will be returned to the rightful owners and damaged houses will be rebuilt at government expense. There have been cases reported in which the government team offers payment to those tribesmen willing to accept arms to defend their homes in return for an assurance that they may run their own affairs without government interference or an official regime presence in their area — a prelude to attempts to set up a local militia. The last variation is applied especially to areas where the civilians have suffered heavily in fighting between guerillas and security forces and where intelligence suggests that a degree of "war weariness" may be setting in because of the rivalries of local guerilla groups.

The tribal elders then submit their counter-proposals: they call for the withdrawal of all Soviet forces from Afghanistan as a precondition of recognition of the status quo; they demand an official proclamation by the Kabul regime of the establishment of an Islamic Republic.

The matter usually ends there. But as observers have noted, even though the official delegation may fail in its declared mission, nevertheless it may succeed in winning over a number of informers by exploiting intrinsic clan or family rivalries among the community the delegation visits. This is possible if the delegation is able to spin out its visit over several days. Informers and collaborators are sometimes left behind, planted in the local community for intelligence or political agitation, or as recruits for an embryonic militia the members of which are offered substantial wages — more than a university professor's salary — for minimal government duties.

In several recorded instances the delegations have failed to meet tribal representatives at all. This is not only because tribal leaders refuse to meet the government people. Failure is attributed to the Parcham-Khalq division. The PDPA in Khost, for example, is largely Khalq, but the delegation from Kabul in 1981 was dominated by the Parcham faction. The local Pushtuns of the PDPA's Khalq faction simply refused to accept the Dari-speaking delegation's credentials and they were put back on the plane or helicopter and sent back to the capital, their mission stillborn.

The Khad does its level best to exploit traditional antagonism among sections of the population. In 1981 the authorities urged the Safi tribe to turn against their neighbours, the Nuristanis. Similarly the Khad urged the Pushtuns of Wardak to turn against their Hazara neighbours. The Khad planted one of its agents, a former colonel, in Nuristan where he established a considerable following as a guerilla leader until his communications with the Khad were intercepted. By offering each tribe and sub-tribe self-government along traditional lines by using the tribal *jirga*, the Khad and the Ministry of Tribes together hope to break the Pushtun belt up into myriad competing fragments which can be more easily dominated from the centre.

In northern areas the plan appears to be that each ethnic group will eventually be offered semi-autonomous, regional self-government not unlike the politico-administrative reforms used by Stalin to subdue, divide and assimilate Soviet Central Asia's Muslims.

The military operations mounted by guerilla forces have severely hampered these pacification plans. Not only is the resistance quick to spot collaborators and to deal with newly-formed militias, but the imperceptibly growing pressure on government installations, administrative centres and communications has meant that the logistics of carrying out an operation of this kind is fraught with difficulties and risk. In some areas — where the Government has had no permanent presence for three years or more, not even a school — the mission is very nearly impossible to initiate.

If the regime uses ties of blood to further the communist cause, so does the resistance. Guerillas' agents inside the Khad and other official agencies still flourish. The deceivers are often deceived. In Ghor Province one guerilla was recruited to the militia along with his followers. Once he had received arms and the promised payment, he simply went back to the resistance, better armed than ever. In Nangahar Province in 1982 guerillas of Hezb-i-Islami agreed to parley with the authorities and promptly ambushed and shot their opponents. Blood is thicker than water and Afghan blood thicker still: relatives keep in contact across ideological and military lines and it is difficult to know who is working for whom at times. It is a game that both sides play, but the authorities are at a distinct disadvantage as long as they espouse a communist philosophy and maintain a Soviet presence in the country.

There appears to have been a reappraisal of the intelligence effort in Kabul on the part of the Khad and its KGB staff. It seems that the intelligence effort was overly ambitious to begin with. At first the authorities launched their attempts to divide and rule without adequate information, and they appeared to lack the kind of organisation capable of collating and coordinating intelligence-gathering before implementing their "Sovietisation" plans.

That has changed. The Khad seems to be concentrating on planting agents — some of whom are reported to be equipped with radios — in key areas. They have stepped up their infiltration of individual guerilla units in the field. Effective commanders — particularly those actively encouraging greater unification and coordination of the resistance inside Afghanistan — are targets for assassination attempts mounted in such a way as to create the impression that the killings are the work of rivals within the resistance movement. The murder of a prominent Kabul commander, Halim, was an example of this. Rival guerilla groups are encouraged to fight each other and there are signs that Kabul is generally improving its field intelligence of guerilla activity and intentions.

This was certainly the impression of journalists who made extensive journeys through northern Afghanistan is 1982. Tony Davis of *Asiaweek* and freelance photographer Pierre Issot-Sergent were both struck by the threat of Soviet/Afghan penetration of resistance forces in northern and north-eastern areas. The author was impressed during his visit to Kandahar in December, 1982, by the presence of informers in guerilla ranks and in the villages on which the resistance relies for support.

The Khad maintains contacts with Pushtun tribes living astride the Durand Line and in areas of importance for guerilla resupply. Afghan radio broadcasts and printed propaganda materials are distributed in Pakistan, championing tribal independence from Islamabad. Tribal elders from South Waziristan, for example, have been welcomed in Kabul and promised arms. Agents are sent across the border from Paktya, Nangahar and Kunar provinces with orders to infiltrate the refugee camps to collect information on the numbers of people in the camps, the presence of guerilla reserves and the resistance leaders. The steady stream of refugees over the frontier makes this relatively easy and it poses a considerable security problem for the Afghan resistance and Pakistani authorities.

The Khad also liaises with the Pakistani dissident group named Al-Zulfikar, named after Zulfikar Ali Bhutto, the former premier executed by General Zia's administration in 1977. Dr. Najib personally provided Khad funds for the two Bhutto sons who ran the group. Several dozen of its members have been intercepted in Pakistan after crossing the border from Afghanistan. It is widely held — but not confirmed — that Al-Zulfikar was given backing by Dr. Najib's organisation in the hijacking of a domestic airliner from Pakistan to Kabul on March 2, 1981. Subsequently there have been reports that the Al-Zulfikar headquarters in Kabul, next door to an Afghan parachute brigade's garrison, was closed down for reasons which are far from clear. The Khad has also been instrumental in the past in funding and training members of the extreme wing of the banned Workers and Peasants Party (Mazdoor Kissan) in Pakistan.

The Khad is believed to support some 400-600 Baluch dissidents. Some Western press reports, possibly instigated by Pakistani sources, have greatly exaggerated the numbers of Baluch nationalists under arms and waiting to strike back across the border from their Afghan training camps. But the Khad's arm is a long one, although its links with regional terrorist and nationalist groups are as limited as they are ambitious.

The organisation is clearly increasingly efficient — and dangerous — in its moves to exploit guerilla rivalries. It arms groups of traditional bandits and thieves, for example, in Kunar Province and encourages them to prey upon local residents in the guise of guerillas to discredit the resistance.

The successes — from Kabul's viewpoint — have been the "turning" of individual guerilla commanders. In March, 1983, Kabul Radio broadcast a meeting of several dozen of these people, three of whom were within a few weeks assassinated by the resistance, proving that that the regime has considerable difficulty in looking after those who decide to collaborate. In some cases these men have commanded a handful of fighters. In exceptional instances the commanders of groups of 200-300 guerillas have changed sides. Few joined their communist opponents for ideological reasons. Love of power, money and a desire for vengeance against a family or tribal enemy are the primary motives. Sometimes the rivalry on the battlefield among guerilla groups has "squeezed" out a guerilla leader, especially if he has proved incompetent, sadistic, corrupt or merely the loser in a tortuous clan feud. Overtures organised by the Khad, employing relatives of the Afghan's extended family, have paid off in these cases.

The Khad may leave a collaborator in place to foment trouble for guerilla groups in adjacent areas and to disrupt military activity. *Mujehadeen* led by Abdul Haq who mounted a series of well-planned attacks on the capital in December, 1982, found their passage hindered by one senior commander affiliated with Gailani's NIFA organisation in Peshawar. This commander had apparently been bought off; paid to do nothing, in effect. The deliberate passivity of his men in a key sector east of Kabul was a considerable obstacle in trying to cut power lines and communications. Guerilla commander Sher Agha of Herat joined the regime with his men, but the net result in fact helped the guerilla movement because the resistance tightened up its organisation and security in the area in response to the betrayal.

During the course of March, 1983, hundreds of civilians left the Deh Sabs area just north of Kabul. On their arrival in Pakistan's refugee camps they complained of the oppressive measures imposed by Malang, a former Hezb-i-Islami commander who had gone over to the regime. Malang now has considerable quantities of arms and cash available and he uses his resources with all the ruthlessness of a convert to the cause. Malang's turning has been attributed to the fact that he was for many months under considerable pressure from a rival Harakat Inquilab-i-Islami commander of Kabul Province who was trying to force Malang to submit to his authority.

"We know why he joined the Government," said one Kabul guerilla. "He was being pressured by Harakat Inquilab-i-Islami which was stronger. But we cannot forgive Malang, even so. If we meet up with him we will kill him."

The Malang incident reflects the Khad's concentration on Kabul. Both the secret police and the conventional security forces have set about trying to create what amount to "free fire zones" around the capital following the upsurge in 1982 of guerilla activity in and around the country's main city. "We don't care where you go," one regime official told some local people. "Just go. We want everyone out of this area."

In trying to win over the guerillas, the Khad employs a gentle, sophisticated approach towards some captives. Instead of the torture routinely meted out to political detainees, the service separates those former guerillas it deems suitable for further development. Several are provided with houses and a way of life considerably better than anything they could normally have hoped for in the resistance.

The PDPA is thought to be keeping these people on ice for the day when a new "national government of reconciliation" is unveiled, composed of "official" religious figures, traditional tribal leaders and former guerillas prepared to front a new-look regime allegedly capable of winning both some internal support from a war-weary populace and external credibility — but still kept firmly under the hand of the ruling party.

The rising level of the war and the seemingly irrevocable split in

PDPA ranks are the two constraints which have severely impeded progress towards this goal — one which may slowly take shape as the United Nations proximity talks on a possible political solution of the protracted crisis make progress in the months and years ahead. In this the Khad plays a key role.

The question of a possible Soviet intention to divide up the country came up in December, 1982, when a senior Khad officer was interviewed by Western correspondents. Gulam Siddiqi Miraki, former commandant of the Khad training academy, situated about three kilometres east of Ghazni, had defected to Pakistan some two months previously. He said that Babrak Karmal had been urged by Moscow to adopt a series of strategies, each of which would come into force if its predecessor failed to have the desired result: substantial progress made towards the subjugation of the resistance.

During discussions with Babrak Karmal, the late Soviet leader Leonid Brezhnev had allegedly urged the Afghan President to seek his PDPA colleagues' approval for the USSR's annexation of eight northern provinces and the formation of the 16th Soviet Socialist Republic of Afghanistan as a homeland for the PDPA and all "progressive forces" in the country. An emasculated, neutralised Pushtunistan would be left as a buffer, presumably, with Pakistan. Miraki said the plan was prematurely leaked and at the March 1982 Party Congress the project was torpedoed by the Khalq faction — quite naturally, as they were mainly Pushtun — and some Parchamites. The President failed to get his "vote of confidence" necessary to carry through the proposed constitutional changes.

The Soviets pressed the Afghan leader to draw up a programme to be introduced step by step. Phase One consisted of a deliberate economic war or "scorched earth" policy in which civilian targets would be systematically and deliberately bombed, with the use of artillery and multiple rocket launchers to complement the aerial destruction of villages and crops. The operation would be designed, Miraki suggested, to intimidate the civilian population into denying succour to the guerillas and into at least passive acceptance of the communist status quo. Phase Two would take the form of coordinated military measures designed to seal the Pakistan-Afghan border and the frontier areas to the west. Routes used by guerillas would be blocked or repeatedly hit by air and ground forces. Should these measures fail to have the desired impact, Babrak Karmal's Government would then formally and publicly request Moscow for more troops. Should this in turn create an uproar internationally and increased Western diplomatic and economic pressure on the Soviet

Union and its allies, the PDPA regime would once again be urged to introduce the constitutional and legal changes necessary to split the country up to form the Soviet Socialist Republic of Afghanistan.

Miraki's message was widely reported, but can it be believed? There is no direct corroboration from other sources. A senior Afghan airforce officer who defected around the same time said to reporters that a deliberate civilian bombing campaign had been launched five months previously — in July, 1982. A KGB defector to the West was reported in *Time* as saying that Brezhnev took the burden of responsibility for the decision to invade. Was Brezhnev, caught up in the throes of a crisis of succession in the Kremlin, hurriedly looking for a quick solution to the Afghan issue?

There undoubtedly has been an emphasis on attacks on civilian targets. The authorities have deliberately cleared key areas of civilians to create "free fire zones" on a small scale. In the spring of 1983 the Afghan and Soviet security forces redeployed some 15,000 troops to border provinces in preparation for the summer offensive. But it is possible to throw doubt on the Miraki thesis.

The circumstances of Miraki's defection are unclear. He had obviously spent several weeks in Pakistan as a guest of either Gulbaddin Hekmatyar's radical Hezb-i-Islami resistance group, or in the custody of Pakistan's security agencies. During the interview itself the West German-trained intelligence officer was reluctant to discuss other matters relating to his duties. He refused to talk about the Khad in general terms. Some of his answers appeared to have been well rehearsed, because they resembled Hekmatyar's "party line." The translator at the interview did not give Miraki's answers in full and on more than one occasion told Miraki he could not reply to certain questions put to him. Was Miraki feeding the West a deliberate tale? Was he still under "control" of some sort? And if so, whose? Was he the conscious or unwitting conduit for Soviet disinformation designed to convince Western policy-makers (a) that Moscow had options on Afghanistan (b) that greater Western pressure would mean a commensurate Soviet response, and (c) that an escalation of the war would inevitably mean the incorporation of part of the Afghan state permanently into the Soviet empire? The notion of a Pushtun buffer state would certainly scare off Pakistan, with its historical fears of Pushtun separatism on its north-west frontier. Could Miraki be simply a way of strengthening Kabul's hand in the UN talks?

Another issue which clouds Miraki's interesting theory is the fact that towards the end of 1982 there were several high-level defectors from the Kabul regime, all claiming in interviews to have been

Hezb-i-Islami agents working underground in Kabul before their network was "blown." Why did Hezb-i-Islami choose to publicise this rash of defections or blown agents at this point in time?

The answers may never be known. But following a year in which Soviet and Afghan security forces have persistently struck out at specific civilian centres of population, communist troops carried out a substantial redeployment in March to the south-eastern provinces of Kunar, Nangahar, Paktya and Kandahar in what was assumed by diplomatic observers and resistance leaders alike to be a prelude to a major drive on resistance supply routes across the border.

Was this the start of Phase Two? Some military observers say the redeployment is simply good sense, albeit on a larger scale than hitherto. If 1982 was marked by selective pressure on civilians, then the latter half of the year and the beginning of 1983 were characterised by greater use of Soviet paratroopers and "partisan units" flown directly in for operations from the USSR. It seemed that steadily improving intelligence capabilities were at last being fused together with a relatively new "special forces" style of counter-insurgency strategy, both of which the Soviet occupation forces for so long clearly lacked in Afghanistan.

The People's Democratic Party

W estern diplomatic reports reaching Pakistan on April 12, 1983 said the ruling People's Democratic Party of Afghanistan (PDPA) was preparing lavish celebrations to mark the fifth anniversary of the Soviet-backed coup d'état which brought the communists to power on April 27, 1978. All foreign commercial enterprises were ordered to participate. It seemed as if the event would be held on a larger scale than hitherto; after a winter of increased guerilla penetration of the beleaguered capital, President Babrak Karmal obviously wanted to demonstrate to Moscow that he was still in control. But in control of what precisely?

During preceding days vacant ambassadorial posts were filled, with appointments made to Cuba, Poland and Czechoslovakia. There were changes in the PDPA hierarchy also. Parchamites were promoted in what appeared to be a consolidation of the minority Parcham faction, loyal to Moscow but outnumbered by the openly hostile, Pushtu-speaking Khalq (Masses) group. The Khalqis held onto their considerable influence in the armed forces, but were unable to prevent the appointment of a Parchamite as the new head of the airforce. The Khalqis to this day retain their Pushtu, provincial chip-on-the-shoulder and they blame their Parcham rivals for bringing in the Soviet occupation forces.

Neither group is cohesive. Each is divided into groups-within-groups. Each is headed by a specific PDPA figure, usually an ambitious personality shuffling, fidgeting and bluffing his way to greater influence, forming and breaking short-lived alliances and enmities with his colleagues with dizzying complexity and speed. Ideology has little to do with it; it is a matter of tribal or regional origin, family relationships and sheer self-assertiveness.

The Parchamites are said to be divided into three; there is one group led by Babrak Karmal, another led by Prime Minister Sultan Ali Keshtmand and probably one led by Suleiman Laeq, the Minister of Tribes and Nationalities. The Khalq is also split into three: Ghulam Dastagir Panjsheri leads one, Zaher Ofuq a second and a third consists of the Taraki supporters, led in theory by Assadullah Sarwari, the former secret police chief who was put out to grass as Ambassador to Mongolia, but in day-to-day matters by Syed Gulabzoy, the Minister of the Interior. Then there are "independents."Some say Zaher Ofuq is trying with Soviet support to blend together loyal Parchamites with acquiescent Khalqis; others name Mohammad Khad Jalala and Syed Afghani. The independents are basically divided into two groups. The first consists of the Fatherland Front as well as tame religious scholars. The second group is said to include active and retired service personnel.

In Kabul's dwindling circle of middle class merchants and professional people there is the common belief that the Soviets actively encourage these divisions as a means to control the assertive Afghan temperament in the PDPA. This appears to be similar to some Third World countries' obsession with American and specifically CIA interference in their affairs. In fact, objective analysis suggests the contrary: the KGB is trying its utmost to pull these groups and factions together and to suppress dissidence in party ranks.

During March 1983 it was noticed that larger than usual numbers of Khalq members were travelling to the USSR for courses of one sort or another. They were accompanied by a sprinkling of their Parchamite comrades. Kabul, as ever, was rife with rumour — little of it well informed. Was Babrak Karmal getting rid of his rivals, under Parchamite supervision? Or were the Soviets putting Khalqis into reserve in preparation for the day when Babrak would be seen as having outlived his usefulness? And why was it that Prime Minister Sultan Ali Keshtmand, the Hazara administrator who has adroitly manoeuvred his own supporters into key positions, spoke out on Kabul Radio on the eve of the UN talks in Geneva? He admitted that the *ashrar* or bandits had destroyed 75 percent of the country's communications and half its schools and hospitals. Was this implied criticism of his fellow Parchamite, Babrak Karmal? The President appeared to respond to the Prime Minister's speech the following night when he spoke glowingly of the PDPA's progress in subduing the resistance and claimed a party membership of 90,000 — a figure which has to be treated with considerable scepticism.

Perhaps the most celebrated rivalry among the communist top brass has been the clash between Dr. Najib, head of the secret police or Khad, and Interior Minister Syed Mohammad Gulabzoy. Najib's dislike of Khalqis is well known. Gulabzoy, on the other hand, is recognised as the unofficial protector of Najib's Khalq opponents.

Frequently, the uniformed police under Gulabzoy's control in the capital have had gun battles with Najib's plainclothes secret policemen. The two men have come to blows with each other from time to time. They are also very different characters. Najib is devoted to his work and is well-versed in Marxism-Leninism in which he evidently believes with considerable passion. Although a doctor by profession, he learned his unpleasant trade in a Bulgarian spy school. By contrast, Gulabzoy is a loud, aggressive character renowned for political cunning, self-promotion and sheer rhetorical audacity in Politburo meetings. Najib recently stole a march on his arch-rival by planting one of his men, Dr. Farouq, in the Interior Ministry where as head of the political directorate he is able to block Gulabzoy's appointments of favoured Khalq subordinates.

With few exceptions, the Afghan communist leadership bears little resemblance to the grey, anonymous *apparatchiks* of the Soviet Union. Babrak Karmal drinks a great deal and when he is thoroughly intoxicated is inclined to alarm his neighbours by beating up his wife. One afternoon two years ago a friend was called in to subdue the hysterical wife — who is related to the royal family — who sported a recently-applied black eye. Karmal had meanwhile passed out on his neighbour's sitting room sofa, whisky glass still in hand. Karmal's favourite lady — but not the only one — is Anahita Ratebzad, a leading Politburo member with whom he has had an affair for a number of years. Another Politburo member trains dogs for fighting and bets heavily on poker. They are larger-than-life characters — save perhaps for the enigmatic Zaher Ofuq, a pro-Soviet PDPA official who was a founder-member of the party but has managed to keep a low profile and who today is said to wield considerable influence.

The Parcham-Khalq split has seriously affected government attempts to win over tribes and national minorities. For one thing, Dr. Najib, who is closely involved in this work, is unable to get along with the Minister of Tribes and Nationalities, Suleiman Laeq. Laeq is not terribly bright; he is a Pushtun first and foremost, a poet second and a politician last. Najib is said to be scathing about Laeq's performance of his official duties. And because the Khalqis tend to dominate the armed forces at battalion and divisional level, the Parcham-dominated delegations sent out to suborn local tribes often receive a rude reaction from local military commanders.

A defecting airforce officer, Brigadier Arbab Khan, reported on the Parcham-Khalq friction in March 1982: "I went to see the

Mazar-i-Sharif airforce commander who had not been seen at work for three days. I found him badly beaten up. He told me he had been to a drinks party one evening to mark the inauguration of the Russian consulate at Balkh. At one point the Parchamite governor, Sakhi Tayer, accused him of disrespect for not having stood up when the governor entered the room. The airforce commander stressed his military status. They had a fist fight, but it was stopped eventually by the Russian consul himself."

In November 1981, the Afghan Information Centre in Peshawar — one of the more reliable of the resistance news services — published the following account of events in Asadabad, provincial capital of Kunar: "The Khalqi police commander held a lively party recently at which several young women were present. The local Khad director, a Parchamite named Azizullah, decided to use the occasion as a pretext to remove his rival. Azizullah descended on the police commander's house together with a raiding party of 130 Khad collaborators and shooting broke out. Several Khad personnel were wounded. Both men are said to have been replaced by the Russians."

A similar incident occurred in Khost, centre of Paktya Province in 1982. It was one of a series of violent clashes within the local PDPA cadres: "Mohammad Ali, the strong Khalqi commander of the army division in Khost, has finally been taken by force to Kabul. Previously the situation in the town had become very confused. The defections of the military had increased and over a period of one month four delegations had come from Kabul to enforce the commander's removal. Mohammad Ali still refused to leave his command. Finally, on January 10, 1982, a Russian delegation came for an investigation. While the commander was under Russian interrogation at army headquarters, some Parchamites put his family on a plane and sent them to Kabul. When he knew he was to be arrested, the commander attempted suicide. This was prevented, and on the following day the Politburo member, Aslam Watanjar, arrived from the capital and persuaded the commander to accompany him to Kabul.

". . . his removal is a victory for the Parcham faction, but the Parchamites still face serious difficulties. For instance, on January 27, during their first battle with the resistance after the departure of the former Khalqi commander, his subordinate officer commanding Bashkhel post who was also a Khalqi established contact with the resistance and surrendered. . . On February 4 a number of Khalqi officers met at the hill of Khoja Mohammad Khan and planned a coup against the Parchamites. The new Parchamite general commander was informed and orders were given to bombard the meeting place. . . fighting broke out, which lasted four hours. Some 17 Khalqi officers at the meeting were killed. . ."

On February 28, 1983 fighting broke out in Kabul between the rival PDPA factions. It happened inside the First Headquarters of the party and the clash was stopped when a Soviet military unit intervened and arrested several members of both groups. Party officials were replaced in some cases, while Gulabzoy raised the issue yet again at a Central Committee meeting when he demanded the reinstatement of the deposed Khalqi party officials.

The previous month a similar incident was reported in party district number five. The district cadre consisted of 117 Khalqis and 97 Parchamites. A Khalqi named Ahmad Jan led an attack on his rivals by throwing a hand grenade into a Parcham party office. Two were said to have been killed and nine others injured. The Parchamites counter-attacked and four Khalqis reportedly died and 11 others were wounded. Fighting stopped when the Soviets intervened.

Khalqis particularly resent what they claim is Parchamite patronage in the form of military exemption for their relatives and friends in the pro-Soviet PDPA faction. For example, during regime attempts to encourage party members to go to Panjsher Valley during the course of 1982 to re-establish government controls at Rokha, the Khalq contingents refused unless they were accompanied by equal numbers of party activists from the Parcham group.

In September, 1982, a defecting police officer, Mohammad Jan, said that before counter-insurgency operations in the valley, the regime sent orders to police officers to report for duty in Panjsher. Many refused. A group of 15 policemen went to the Interior Ministry and declared their unwillingness to comply with the order. The man who heard them out was the implacable Parchamite and friend of Dr. Najib, Dr. Farouq. The 15 were promptly locked up and dismissed from their posts as an example to others.

In the lead-up to party elections in March, 1982, Babrak Karmal made a speech in which he criticised a number of central and provincial party organs for failing to fulfil their responsibilities. "Some provincial authorities have even refused to receive operational teams from Kabul," he declared, in an obvious reference to Khalq faction dissidence in the face of the Parcham-dominated party apparat in Kabul. His speech was reportedly followed by instructions to the effect that no Khalqi with strong anti-Parchamite views should be allowed to be elected.

In fact when the voting for delegates to attend the PDPA general conference took place, there were separate ballot boxes for Parcham

135

and Khalq voters — or a single box, with separate slots for Khalq and Parcham ballot papers. When one party member exercised his right to vote for local delegates in the Sarkano sub-district of Kunar Province he allegedly pretended to be a Khalqi, as the Khalq dominated the provincial party organisation. But he slipped his vote into the Parcham slot and was promptly attacked by Khalqi toughs standing nearby. He was injured and taken to hospital.

The conference itself was held in bizarre circumstances, and it failed to patch up relations between the two factions. It was held in secrecy at the city's polytechnic institute and delegates were advised to take with them sufficient rations to last a week. The conference lasted 30 hours in all and ended on March 15, only to be followed by several violent clashes between the two factions which included a skirmish between elements of the Afghan Army's 7th and 8th divisions.

Karmal's dilemma was to provide sufficient Khalq representation to avoid widening the schism still further; at the same time he could not afford to have his draft "action programme" sabotaged by Khalq dissidents during the proceedings. In one eastern city, four Khalqis who were elected as delegates chose to ignore the affair and did not turn up in Kabul. Guerilla intelligence sources claimed that the speeches during the conference were marked by jeers, shouts and even scuffles between prominent Parchamites and their Khalq opponents.

In ensuing months the PDPA launched a purge of Khalq dissidents, a process in which the eager Dr. Najib played a leading role as inquisitor. This raised a problem of a different kind: the result was that the majority of the administrative staff were not PDPA members at all and several reportedly had active contacts with the resistance in the capital.

A.K. Sarwar, who defected to Pakistan in October 1982, reported that of the 200-strong administrative staff purged of Khalqis at the Prime Ministry, only one was a party member — and a Parchamite, of course.

The shortage of PDPA members was aggravated by the anti-Khalq moves. Instead of consolidating the regime, it appeared to reduce the reliability of the bureaucracy and it reinforced the tendencies of all government ministries to submit all proposals to the appropriate Soviet staffs for approval *before* seeking Politburo signatures. Kabul was fast becoming a flourishing "rubber stamp" industry, with power increasingly moving into the hands of Soviet rather than Afghan authority.

Another defector, A. Bari Jehani, former vice-president of Kabul Television in the capital, said in an interview in May 1982 that the

Soviets controlled all aspects of production and policy for the media. Policy plans he submitted to the Minister of Information had to be referred first to Soviet officials for approval. Of the top echelon of six Afghan officials in the organisation, only one was a PDPA member — a Parchamite.

Dissidence on the part of the Khalqis became a lethal affair, even in the relative backwater of Kabul University. Dr. Azam Gul, a former professor of agronomy, fled to Pakistan in August 1982. He said the university's rector, Aziz ur-Rahman Sayidi, was a Khalqi with strong anti-Parcham views which he made no effort to conceal. He was particularly opposed to the steady Sovietisation of education. When a colleague of his, Salim, was mysteriously assassinated, Sayidi gave an outspoken graveside address in which he pointed the finger at the Parcham faction for the responsibility of Salim's violent end. That very evening Sayidi was killed. His funeral was ignored by the regime, which promptly replaced him with a close associate of Babrak Karmal and a Parchamite, Assadullah Habib, who was later to accelerate the Sovietisation programme with the introduction of new Parchamites into key university posts.

In Moscow, the Parcham-Khalq dispute made itself felt among Afghan students. One student reported that two Khalqis "fell" to their deaths from a window in the Afghan Embassy, while PDPA meetings were held separately: Khalqis met in one room and Parchamites in another at Moscow State University.

Many of these incidents may seem trivial. Many are. But they occur every day of the week in a regime which finds itself in a situation where it is almost entirely restricted to the capital itself. This is not the People's Democratic Republic of Afghanistan, but the Some People's Divided Republic of Kabul. Apart from the security and military agencies, Kabul's representation in the provinces scarcely exists.

Consolidation of the PDPA regime inevitably means the exclusion of a significant proportion of its own membership: the Khalq. What is more, the Khalq is predominantly Pushtun and these Pushtun tribes represent the majority of the country's population, concentrated in the most sensitive areas along the Pakistani frontier. The PDPA needs the Khalqis as much as it needs to be rid of them in another sense.

Efforts to Sovietise education, the armed forces, the media (there are plans to extend Kabul's television network right across the nation) and the bureaucracy inevitably alienate the remaining members of the small urban middle classes. Over the past three years the Soviets have inexorably assumed progressively greater responsibility for Afghan administration and policy-making. Moscow has had to restrain Dr. Najib in his persecution of the Khalq; the armed forces are already in a perilous condition. To reject the majority of party cadres in the army and airforce because they are Khalqi in the face of a steadily increasing guerilla threat would be more than unwise. It would be suicidal. In short, the Soviets who carefully cultivated the PDPA and its forerunners since the 1930s find themselves on the painful horns of a dilemma for which they must take the responsibility of having created in the first place.

At times the Khalq-dominated military units have passively or actively collaborated with the guerillas. The Muslim resistance does not, nor is it likely to, accept Khalq members of the PDPA into its ranks, but an unofficial symbiosis has steadily developed between the two apparently irreconcilable and mutually hostile forces. Simply to survive, Khalq-officered detachments clandestinely ship arms and ammunition to the *Mujehadeen* or offer a pass of safe conduct to transiting guerillas in return for an assurance that they will be left in peace. Many non-party officers remaining in the army are resistance agents. They are used from time to time for communications between the guerillas and dissident Khalqis. In turn these resistance workers in uniform are tolerated by their Khalqi fellow-officers because it guarantees the safety of the garrison. The Khalqis fear the Soviets, the Parchamites and the guerillas. The faction is being squeezed from three directions. It has no place to run to.

The future of the PDPA seems downhill all the way. At its peak membership is unlikely to have exceeded 50,000. Kabul sources say it is around 30,000 currently, but it may be even smaller. Two-thirds may be Khalqis. The heritage of Taraki and especially Amin hangs over it still, for the Khalq is itself irrevocably divided.

That is where Moscow seeks to make gains — by attracting those groups-within-groups to collaborate with the Parchamites. But they are unlikely to accept *any* Khalqi into their inner circle, the Politburo, with a degree of confidence or trust.

These factors may explain above all else why it is that the Soviets cannot contemplate any serious military withdrawal from the country. But it also explains the Soviet need to try and win some limited credibility and legitimacy abroad for the PDPA regime by hinting at Soviet and Afghan "flexibility" and "freshness" in the context of the UN-sponsored talks. Moscow has not stopped trying to resolve the faction-fighting, nor to try and attract non-party people into government to widen its support. The National Fatherland Front (*Pada Watan*) was a classic Marxist-Leninist "front" organisation to attract tribal, traditional leaders, Muslim theologians and members of the urban intelligentsia. Many were tempted. They attended the initial meetings, but quickly faded away when it became apparent that it too was tainted by the Parcham-Khalq internecine warfare. For the Parchamites were unwilling to allow it to become a broad forum for the expression of vaguely socialist ideas and nationalist views — for fear it would become a focus for dissident Khalq power and another challege to Parcham rule.

The PDPA is as "feudal" as the traditional, rural social order it tried to revolutionise and control on coming to power in 1978. Far from achieving what other Afghan rulers have never really tried — the total imposition of central authority over the nation at large — its influence has been steadily on the wane. It is unable even to govern itself. It has been a salutary and costly lesson for the Soviet doctrine of infiltrating and developing cadres of Marxist-Leninists in the embryonic bourgeoisie of a developing country. The class was too small, too isolated from its rural origins to be effective. The PDPA never had more than a minority urban following anyway. Now it appears to be disintegrating, and whether they like it or not the price of survival of communism in Afghanistan seems to be the creeping, *de facto* colonisation of the country. That is, if the resistance does not get there first.

Human Rights

Tobah Hamid would without doubt be most parents' notion of an ideal daughter. Physically frail in appearance, modest by nature and highly intelligent, the 21-year-old second-year student in Kabul University's faculty of letters and humanities does not seem on first acquaintance to be the stuff of which heroines are made. Tobah led a double life, in fact. She attended her classes regularly and carried out all the normal functions required of a young woman belonging to a prominent Pushtun family. But her clandestine work as a distributor of *shabnama* or nightletters among Kabul's dwindling band of dissidents plunged her into an ordeal reminiscent of those unfortunate enough to have fallen into the hands of Stalin's NKVD or Hitler's Gestapo.

Once she found herself under surveillance by the Khad, she must have known it would only be a matter of time before she was picked up. The knock on the door came on the evening of July 12, 1982. She was staying with her aunt at the time, having learned that her own home had been searched a few days previously by secret policemen who found incriminating evidence of her resistance work. Her interrogation at the Khad headquarters started at midnight and together with other female students she was repeatedly asked about her resistance contacts and urged to reveal the names of her associates.

At eight the following morning the interrogation resumed. She refused to answer the questions. She was suspended upside down by her ankles from iron rings in the ceiling. After what seemed to her a lifetime she was roughly let down. Tobah felt ill and disorientated. A woman security official held her while a male colleague slapped her face repeatedly and verbally abused her. She was dragged off to a small, dark cell where she spent the following week in solitary confinement. On her return to the interrogation room she was again asked to confess her "crimes against the Saur Revolution." She refused. Wires were attached to her toes and when the current was

140

switched on her body was thrown involuntarily off the floor in spasms which made her vomit and finally lose consciousness.

For 15 days she was left alone in the dark again. She was given medical treatment — in the form of tablets pushed into her cell together with prison food. Forty-six days after her arrest she was driven off to the huge prison complex on the outskirts of the capital, known as Pol-e-Charkhi. She joined 34 other women in a large cell, including a nine-year-old girl and two female informers. The place was bare save for the constantly burning light bulb and a few blankets the more fortunate inmates had managed to obtain on the all too rare family visits to the jail.

Washing was not permitted. All the women suffered from body sores. Tobah still bears the scars. Most of them were sick most of the time. All had been tortured with varying degrees of severity. They were forbidden to talk to each other. They could not see out of the room and sunlight did not penetrate the small, barred window. The highlight of their existence consisted of a twice-daily visit to the lavatory.

One of Tobah's friends in the cell was Sheila, an engineering student whose father had been summarily executed under the Taraki regime. An enthusiastic poetess, Sheila used to defy regulations and recite her work to her fellow detainees. But she was highly-strung and became increasingly depressed and desperate. One night when the others were asleep Sheila used a nail she had found and secretly sharpened to slash open her own throat. As she lay bleeding to death she dipped the nail in her own blood and scrawled a single word on the wall where she lay. It read: *liberty*.

Tobah was eventually released after a total of five months' imprisonment without trial. Her family fled the country. Her story is not particularly unusual. Other female survivors of Pol-e-Charkhi speak of far worse. But Tobah demonstrates that after four years of Soviet military occupation and more than five years' communist rule, there are still educated young people to be found in the capital who are willing to defy the odds and resist, despite the tens of thousands of professional people who have quite simply disappeared into mass graves since 1978. Women have to take on much of the underground work in Kabul, because for every 10 students attending Kabul University by the end of 1982, eight were female. Males have either been forcibly conscripted into the armed forces, have volunteered to fight with the resistance or else have joined the steadily growing number of refugees.

The terror began when the PDPA's Khalq faction seized power in 1978. Within 18 months an estimated 15,000-30,000 people were

141

executed or died under torture at the hands of the secret police, then known as AKSA. The civil service, the armed forces' officer corps, educational establishments and the police were all ruthlessly purged. One senior Afghan Army officer who defected to Pakistan in October, 1982, recalls that the PDPA demanded the return of nearly 300 Afghan officers studying military subjects in the USSR. In groups of four or five they were brought to Hafizullah Amin's office and briefly questioned by the Khalq leader before he decided their fate, like some latter-day Robespierre.

Of the 12 officers in the defector's group, only three survived. He himself spent some weeks in Pol-e-Charkhi where he was beaten. During his interrogation he overheard the current Minister of Tribes and Nationalities, Suleiman Laeq, crying out under torture. "It's none of my business," Laeq was heard shouting. "It's all Babrak Karmal's fault!"

Most of the victims of the purge came from the small urban intelligentsia. Liberals, monarchists, religious leaders and even socialists went to their deaths, many of them machine-gunned by the hundred. In rural areas the villagers who resented the ill-conceived land reforms were simply bayoneted, shot or beaten to death with staves on the spot. In Kabul the star-shaped, eight-storey Pol-e-Charkhi was still under construction, but it soon contained many more than its expected complement of 5,000 inmates. One group of intellectuals valiantly hung on in the capital, trying to form an underground resistance network of their own. Rasul Amin, now a refugee, still shakes visibly when he recalls his experiences at the hands of the communists. In fact during the first week of April, 1982, the last remaining group of academics who managed to survive this period was broken up. Five non-party professors and tutors at Kabul University were rounded up; they included Dr. Fazle Rabbi Pazhwak, a political scientist working in the law faculty, Dr. Hasan Kakar, an internationally-renowned historian, an economist and a scientist. The rest — or at least those who survived to escape — have scattered throughout the world. Poorly-qualified PDPA members and Soviet advisers now form the bulk of the capital's schoolteachers and university staff.

Pol-e-Charkhi holds some 12-15,000 prisoners. Applications from provincial detention centres requesting Pol-e-Charkhi to accept some of their prisoners to relieve the pressure have been repeatedly turned down. Executions occur on a nightly basis. One former prison officer said in an interview in May, 1982, that in his block alone between 10 and 12 inmates were taken out of their cells each night and killed by firing squad. The officer said there were 5,200 politicals held in blocks one, two and three. On May 25, 1982, an uprising preceded the execution of 50 of the alleged ringleaders. While there are apparently no Soviet troops in the prison, Soviet "advisers" are much in evidence. He said that almost the entire former cabinets of Amin and Taraki were still in prison, contrary to rumours that these early PDPA Khalqis had already been slaughtered. But they were held in solitary.

Their fate was described by a member of this faction of the PDPA who spent 14 months in Pol-e-Charkhi before his release and subsequent defection to Pakistan in April, 1982. He claimed there were 4,000 Khalqis in the prison, many of whom were supporters of the former Khalq leader Hafizullah Amin. This group was broken down into four smaller clans; it seemed that even in Pol-e-Charkhi the PDPA failed to get its act together.

In an interview on March 1, 1983, a former university teacher, Abdul Ahad, said that in his block some 300 prisoners were executed without trial over a nine-month period. In addition to the detainees in Pol-e-Charkhi, he said several thousand more were held in makeshift Khad detention centres throughout the capital. Soviet personnel supervised the interrogation teams. He saw one detainee screaming in agony as he was forced to jump up and down with a heavy stone attached to his testicles with nylon.

Ahad was initially forced to share a cell designed for two with five others. Toilet facilities were not provided, with unpleasant consequences. A degree of sophistication was used to try and turn him into an informer. A suave young man in an office offered him tea and nuts and then showed him piles of banknotes in a wall safe and he was asked to name his price if only he would work for the regime. He refused, and was taken along to watch how it was with his fellow prisoners as they were beaten and electrocuted in the interrogation chambers, with Soviets in plainclothes sitting out of sight in darkened adjoining rooms, for all the world like some Peeping Toms of whom the Marquis de Sade would have been proud. Ahad was eventually tortured and just for fun one inquisitor made him spend the night in the jail's stinking ventilation shaft to "improve his memory."

Ahad said the sound of fighting between the security forces and the *Mujehadeen* could be heard by the prisoners from time to time; it encouraged them to refrain from turning informer and raised morale considerably.

The International Committee of the Red Cross (ICRC) was allowed to visit the prison in August, 1982, after an absence from Kabul of more than two years. They saw 480 inmates, none of whom was a resistance member. All were members of the PDPA who had fallen from grace. Tobah Hamid remembers it was the only time her cell was cleaned. Rugs were put on the floor and pro-regime slogans daubed on the cell door and walls to "prove" to the ICRC officials that the prisoners were pro-communist.

That fleeting ICRC visit was a culmination of Soviet attempts to get *their* prisoners back from the guerillas. It was a process which began in May, 1981, when a Soviet fighter pilot survived the shooting down of his ground-attack aircraft over Tora Bora in Nangahar Province. There are two versions of what happened: some say his parachute snagged in a tree, while others say he was intercepted as he tried to make his way on foot to Jalalabad, pistol in hand. His captors disarmed him and won his confidence by pretending to be members of the locally-raised militia. He soon realised his mistake, and in Geneva Soviet officials approached the Red Cross to ask for their help in gaining access to him. As a party member, he was of some importance. The guerillas spirited him over the border into Pakistan in order to publicise his capture, but the Pakistani authorities discovered the "safe house" where he was hidden and handed him over to the Russians.

In September the same year a senior Soviet Communist Party member was kidnapped on the streets of Kabul in broad daylight. E.R. Okrimyuk, aged 67, with the rank of counsellor at the Soviet Embassy in Kabul, was head of the Soviet geological survey in Afghanistan. He knew the country well — he was one of the "old hands." A personal friend of Soviet Prime Minister Nikolai Tikhonov, he was on his way to Khwaja Ruwash airport in Kabul to meet his wife on an incoming flight when his personal driver, a Tajik, stopped their official vehicle at a pre-arranged spot. *Mujehadeen* of the Yunis Khalis organisation knocked him out and drove the jeep through the capital's military checkpoints and out into the countryside.

Photographs were later produced of the frail official drinking tea and smoking a cigarette in what appeared to be relatively clean and comfortable surroundings. Once again Moscow approached the ICRC to seek their help in trying to locate and repatriate the captive. Considerable diplomatic pressure was put on Pakistan as well. As the months went by, it became clear that Okrimyuk was not in good health. The resistance drew up a list of more than 40 of their members in regime jails whom they wanted exchanged for Okrimyuk. The ICRC said it was not prepared to deal in exchanges of this sort, while the guerillas rejected a somewhat naive Red Cross suggestion that the Russian be handed over into ICRC custody without conditions. Okrimyuk was later executed in circumstances which remain uncertain. The Soviets to this day refuse to accept this. They are convinced he is still alive.

The result was that the resistance-in-exile developed a common policy in respect of Soviet captives. Up until 1981 they had been killed as *kafirs* and on the basis of an eye for an eye. But orders went out to field commanders to keep Soviet prisoners alive where possible and to move them to the borders. The resistance hoped to gain in terms of favourable publicity for recognising the Geneva Convention. "We are not beasts," said one guerilla leader on introducing two POWs to the author. They also believed that by allowing the Red Cross access to their prisoners and in some instances allowing the ICRC to fly the POWs to internment in Switzerland, the Red Cross would be allowed back to Kabul and would eventually save the lives of resistance members and their families incarcerated in regime detention centres.

But the inability of the ICRC to make good the other side of the "bargain" may yet mean that in future the guerillas will revert to the practice of killing their Soviet prisoners.

The issue is by no means clear-cut. Several Soviets have refused an ICRC offer of internment and have convinced the Red Cross delegates based in Peshawar that they are genuine defectors. One, Taj Mohammad, leads a group of 50 guerillas against the Soviet security forces in northern Afghanistan. An Armenian interviewed by the author had converted to Islam and was engaged to an Afghan girl. Others are borderline cases; they do not seem to fully understand their options, are frightened of what their Soviet masters will do to them if they return home one day, and fear the *Mujehadeen*. Others do not have the choice to decide, because they are held beyond the reach of the ICRC.

Others have died. Security forces have launched attacks on the area in question and captives have been killed in the shooting. A group of six Soviet POWs being escorted to Pakistan for an ICRC interview had to be killed by the guerillas when they were attacked by regime troops. The escort, to survive, needed to move quickly up into the hills and they were held back by their charges. To save their own lives the escort killed the Soviet soldiers and escaped the net. A group of 16 Soviet civilian advisers, including two women, were captured by guerillas on a bus near Mazar-i-Sharif. There have been reliable reports to the effect that the Soviets mounted a commando-type operation and succeeded in freeing 11 of them, killing at least two of their guards in the process.

Interviews with captured or defecting Soviets in 1980-83 revealed

145

a good deal about the state of the Red Army. The Armenian, Miko Vavaryan, was certainly unhappy in the Soviet occupation army. After an argument with his superior officer, he ditched his truck in an Afghan river and spent two days wandering about in the mountains of Baghlan Province before hunger drove him into a village. Today Miko has a new name: Mohammad Salaam. He was called up for military service in early 1980 and in Afghanistan worked first on military construction sites. He saw no fighting. After fleeing his unit he met guerillas of Jamiat-i-Islami in Klagai village and he explained his predicament by hand signals. He was given food and clothes and offered the chance to join the *jehad*. A robust and extrovert young man, he said he missed his family — and football — but was reconciled to his new life.

Viktor Vladimirivich Zapodnikov, aged 20, from Sverdlovsk and Hassan Mikhailovich Agazanov, aged 21, from Baku, simply wanted to go home after they were captured by Harakat Inquilab-i-Islami near Kabul and brought to Peshawar to be interviewed by the Red Cross. They were seized during a skirmish and Zapodnikov managed to shoot one guerilla in the neck before he was taken. They did not want to be interviewed or photographed, were clearly nervous and stubbornly declined to answer questions. Both are now interned in Switzerland at Soviet expense and they can expect to stay there two years before they are offered repatriation. A Soviet sergeant, in charge of a BMP armoured fighting vehicle, was very much a prisoner. In fact he was reluctant to discuss the nature of his capture because, as he put it, it was a "mistake" which he regretted and was clearly embarrassed about.

Abdul Khalik, from Soviet Tajikistan, said he ran away from his garrison after a scuffle with his superior officer who had begun to beat him. Khalik had fought back and the Soviet officer drew his pistol. Khalik claimed to be a Muslim and he was allowed to wander about quite freely by the *Mujehadeen*. There were reports later that Khalik disappeared, and subsequently sources close to the Soviet Embassy claimed one Soviet conscript had "escaped" and managed to find his way to Islamabad and finally to the Soviet mission. A more credible explanation was that he was picked up by the Pakistani police as he lacked the proper papers and promptly handed over to the Soviets.

The emphasis on interning Soviet prisoners has meant that the ICRC has not begun to look into the issue of political detainees held by Pakistan's military administration headed by President Zia. To have done so would no doubt have jeopardised the ICRC presence in the country. It is not something that can be postponed indefinitely, though, for the issue does not merely centre on the fate of members of Pakistan's own banned opposition parties, but more specifically on the question of Afghans held in the provinces of Baluchistan and North West Frontier Province.

Pakistan plays host to nearly three million Afghans on territory populated by communities which remain strongly nationalist. Peshawar used to be very much part of the Kingdom of Kabul. To many Pushtuns, Afghan and Pakistanis, it still is. The point was made when the author was driving back to Peshawar from a visit to Islamabad in the company of an Afghan intellectual who has subsequently settled in West Germany. As the car crossed the bridge over the Indus River into NWFP, he simply said with relief: "We've left India behind us now. We're back home." He meant it.

It is not surprising that a predominantly Punjabi military dictatorship living next door to a Soviet occupation army should be nervous about the influx of Afghans into its territory. Similarly, all foreign organisations which have set up shop since the Soviet invasion of neighbouring Afghanistan to deal with humanitarian issues directly related to the war are compelled to take their cue from the provincial and federal authorities. They must, not unnaturally, abide by local laws and are requested not to interfere in Pakistan's political affairs or attempt to move against Pakistan's domestic and foreign police.

The ICRC's role is to look after the interests of people interned directly or indirectly as a result of the conflict — and that includes Afghans who cross the border into Pakistan and are then held without trial either by the resistance or by the many Pakistani security and intelligence agencies. Sometimes it is difficult to tell who is doing the detaining, as the distinction between Pakistan's Special Branch in NWFP and Gulbaddin Hekmatyar's own security organisation blurs. The United Nations High Commissioner for Refugees is also involved in establishing the status of newly-arrived Afghans and in monitoring both the material relief they receive and the rights refugees should enjoy according to a UN protocol.

Hezb-i-Islami maintains its own detention centres in and near Peshawar. So do other resistance groups, such as Jamiat-i-Islami and Harakat Inquilab-i-Islami. Hezb-i-Islami concentrates on what it calls "leftists" and "Western imperialists." Small, independent Afghan resistance groups or political parties are particularly nervous of SAKHAR, acronym for the Organisation for the Service of Islam, in effect Gulbaddin's private security and intelligence body which his critics say has its own surveillance and "hit" squads.

It is certainly true that Afghans have simply disappeared into

147

thin air from Peshawar. One, married to an American citizen, was allegedly last seen alive when entering the Hezb-i-Islami headquarters in Fakiribad. Well-informed political opponents of Gulbaddin Hekmatyar say several Afghans have been shot, sometimes after a mock trial. Others are simply locked up. To their credit, Pakistani police have raided two of these unofficial jails and released the inmates. Gulbaddin has spoken out publicly about "leftists" in NWFP and as far as many Pakistanis are concerned — especially those who support the rightist Jamaat Islami Pakistan — he and his bully-boys are a useful asset.

In the four months ending March, 1983, some nine guerilla commanders had been assassinated in Peshawar in mysterious circumstances. A headless corpse — Afghan — was fished out of the city's canal, while three heads were discovered in the back of a truck on its way from Peshawar to the Afghan border post at Torkham. Shootings and bombings were very much on the increase. Abductions were also reported. One senior Jamiat-i-Islami guerilla managed to escape his kidnappers by calling for help as he was repeatedly struck over the head. He crawled away from his assailants, blood streaming down his face, but he took their vehicle registration. It allegedly belonged to Hezb-i-Islami.

Newly-arrived Afghans are under considerable pressure to join Gulbaddin's organisation by Abdullah Khan, the NWFP Refugee Commissioner who is also an influential Jamaat Islami Pakistan member and someone who uses his considerable power to help Hekmatyar's Hezb-i-Islami build up its strength and numbers locally. There is little doubt that the best of international refugee relief aid finds its way to refugee camps dominated by Hekmatyar's followers.

Abdullah has his own intelligence section which liaises closely with the local Special Branch. Abdullah, as a matter of routine, is reliably said to receive the transcripts of telephone taps on foreign relief offices in the city, much to the refugee agency officials' amusement. In the days preceding the start of the UN negotiations on April 11, Abdullah's officials approached the editors of the five major newspapers run by the refugees and told them to stop publication, or in some cases to apply for official permission to continue. Verbal instructions from the same source were given to the major resistance groups: they should move their political headquarters outside Peshawar. The order was not made on Abdullah's initiative — it came from the federal government, according to a source close to President Zia.

Ostensibly, the clamp-down was based on Pakistan's concern over deteriorating security. Afghans feared, however, that Pakistan was preparing for a compromise in Geneva.

The House of Islam

B y the end of this century there will be some 70 million people of Muslim origin living along the USSR's sensitive southern border. The relative increase in the birthrate and the decline in the number of Russians living among these minorities point to future difficulties for the Soviets, both in terms of political control and in manpower availability.

Tsarist and later Soviet policies aimed at suppressing, uprooting, assimilating and finally "Sovietising" these nationalities have not succeeded in eliminating their languages, customs or their beliefs.

The Russian onslaught against Islam began in the mid-16th century and varied from punitive assaults to liberal tolerance. The development of seaborne trade undermined the commercial strength of the region as a whole, while the Tsarist pact with Iran against Turkey provided Moscow with an opportunity to split Sunni Islam in two in geographical terms.

Tsarist expansionism, employing forms of genocide, non-interference, co-option of the Muslim elite and "Russification" in different places and at different times, paused once it reached the Pamir mountain range in 1900, only to be resumed once again in 1979 with the military invasion of Afghanistan across the Amu Darya (Oxus) and the extension of the Kremlin's military power as far as the Durand Line.

The uprooting of minorities and their transportation to Russia's southern borderlands both under Tsarist and Soviet regimes strengthened the minorities' sense of identity. The militantly religious Chechens and Ungush peoples lost their homelands, but emerged more "fundamentalist" than ever.

During World War II the Soviets singled out five Muslim nationalities for special treatment. They were dubbed traitors to the Soviet cause. Once liberated from Nazi occupation, some 50,000 Muslims from southern Georgia died during enforced transportation to labour camps. In 1954 about 300,000 Muslims were forcibly moved and their homes repopulated by Russians and Ukrainians.

Bolsheviks of Muslim cultural origin were at the outset strongly pan-Islamic. They established a single Muslim Council, a single Muslim Army Board and they wanted a single educational system based on a common Turkic language. But once the Whites were defeated, Stalin lost no time in breaking up his Muslim subjects into five administrative nations and eight smaller national groups. Central Asia was itself divided into several "states": the Uzbek SSR, the Tajik SSR, Kirghiz SSR, Kazakh SSR and the Kwakalpah Autonomous Republic.

The major Soviet offensive started in 1925 with the confiscation of all clerical property. Koranic and customary laws were suppressed. In 1927 all Muslim courts were abolished and the last of 8,000 primary schools and madrassahs shut down by 1928. In a single generation the 26,000 mosques were reduced to 1,312. Purdah and polygamy were abolished too. But the Soviets failed to break down the patriarchal, extended family system — the bedrock of Islamic culture.

A new breed of leaders was cultivated, mainly of peasant stock. But despite their Communist Party membership and the advantages and opportunities which accompanied it, the rites of circumcision, religious marriage and burial continued as they do today.

The Soviets then introduced the "positive" policy of building a new socialist order, aimed at achieving the total assimilation of the Muslims into Marxist-Leninist social, economic and political institutions; they sought to create a *Homus Sovieticus* in Asia. Moscow was cast in official propaganda as a benevolent, all-powerful "Elder Brother." But the two communities did not mix, do not still and the area is reportedly "going native." The Russian settlers are moving out.

There are two psychological aspects which help explain current policies and attitudes. The Russians and Slavs display a marked racialism towards Asiatics and a fear of being swamped by them. The Muslim nationals are referred to as "blacks" and "black bottoms." But the Muslim cultures do not share with other colonial peoples a respect, awe and fear of their oppressors. On the contrary, Central Asian Muslims to this day consider themselves inherently superior. Their richer, older culture, their linguistic influence on the Russian tongue, their religious customs and their cultural and historical ties to the Islamic world give them a pride and self-esteem which has helped to preserve their way of life.

On several occasions armed uprisings took place against Soviet encroachment: among the Chechens from 1920 to 1923, the

Basmachi revolt, aided for a time by Afghanistan, from 1918 to 1928, and once again among the Chechens from 1941 to 1942.

Underground Sufi organisations have proliferated in the USSR since 1945. Despite the mystical, shrine-orientated nature of the Sufi following, the Naqshbaniya and Qadiriya sects have managed to develop a clandestine structure of secret cells which in recent years have spread to industry and urban areas and even among "white" Russians. This "parallel" Islam has been the target for a constant campaign of propaganda and indoctrination. In the North Caucasus region alone there are estimated to be some 250,000 members of secret Sufi orders.

There are indications that even prominent Central Asian communist administrators retain customary Islamic practices. One Azerbiyjan administrator allegedly used his MVD troops to seal off from the public the ceremonial circumcision of his child.

To what extent the "Muslim" in the USSR refers to a sense of national identity and customary practices only, and to what degree the five essential activities of a true Muslim — prayer, fasting, pilgrimage, taxation and invocation of the Islamic creed in a single God whose Prophet is Mohammad — are still observed, is not clear. While the Sufi brotherhoods, or *tariqa*, are certainly militant, xenophobic and observe what they regard as essential rites of their religion, there may be a sense of Western wishful thinking here. Babrak Karmal and his PDPA colleagues are "Muslim" in the cultural sense and they may use "official" Islam to legitimise their rule — but they are not by objective standards true Muslim believers. The fact that a man has his child circumcised does not,nor should it, imply that he is an unwilling servant of the state.

One Muslim revolt in particular, though, is of special relevance to the war in Afghanistan today. The Basmachi uprising in Central Asia is very similar in some ways and helps to explain the flirtation of pan-Islamic forces with Bolshevism, and Soviet leaders' attempts to use Islamic consciousness against "Western imperialism."

The term Basmachi originally meant violators or bandits, for the movement was initiated by highwaymen and thieves called upon by the Muslims of Turkestan to help defend their unity against the Red Army. The movement developed into a coalition of religious preachers and scholars, monarchists, social democrats and communists, but its overriding failure to produce a disciplined cohesive response to Soviet counter-attacks and to implement a long-term and commonly accepted policy ultimately led to its destruction by 1939. It sounds very much like the Afghan resistance at its worst. Violent clashes among its various sects and leaders provided Soviet intelligence and military counter-insurgency with opportunities to split and eventually overcome the movement.

To begin with, the pan-Islamic, pan-Turkic movement for Muslim autonomy on Soviet territory was conciliatory and hesitated to seek a confrontation with post-revolutionary Moscow. But the Congress of Soviets in Tashkent repudiated the Muslims' offer of a compromise with a statement which dazzles by its sheer stupidity: "It is impossible to let the Muslims into the revolutionary government at this time because the attitudes of the local population towards the authority of the Soviets is doubtful . . ." The Bolsheviks were quick to label the Ittifaq-ul Muslim's declaration of Muslim autonomy as "bourgeois and counter-revolutionary."

The inevitable confrontation occurred, and somewhat belatedly Moscow sought to undermine the Basmachis by deception and subversion. M.V. Frunze was noted for his reputation as someone who formed his own "Basmachi groups" to carry out a counter-guerilla strategy. Propaganda was stepped up, and food was distributed to potential collaborators. During the famine of 1923 the Soviets cut off the towns from the countryside, isolating the Muslim fighters. To win over an estimated half million people who were starving, the Soviets imported thousands of tons of wheat and rice. The policy of attracting defectors worked in many cases; by offering Basmachi chiefs an "honourable surrender," several were turned and with the dedication of converts were used to hunt down their brother Muslims on behalf of the Kremlin. In-fighting among the Muslim *Mujehadeen* — because that is what they were — was a major contribution to their eventual eradication. Tribalism, ideological differences and above all, overriding personal ambition won the day in the end for Stalin. A rapprochement between Kabul and Moscow effectively removed Afghan military support, while Western aid was insignificant.

The parallels with the war in Afghanistan today are unmistakable.

The weaknesses of the Basmachi also worked in their favour. The intervention of the Young Turk, Enver Pasha, resulted in the unification of the fractious anti-Bolsheviks and a temporary merging of the pan-Islamic and pan-Turkic groups. Enver Pasha had been reportedly encouraged by Lenin himself to seek the leadership of the divided Basmachi movement to use it as a weapon against British India. Enver Pasha certainly seems to have seen himself as another Alexander the Great, leading a victorious Islamic-Turkic army of liberation through the Khyber Pass and on to New Delhi, but Lenin failed to take into account the Young Turk's own burning ambition:

he eventually became a legendary hero, a true *Mujehad* of international repute long after his death. Instead of helping the Comintern spread its "anti-imperialist" message through South Asia, he turned against Moscow. Another Young Turk, Jemal Pasha, made contact with Pushtun tribes on what was then India's North West Frontier and at Soviet behest made a clandestine trip to the Wazir tribesmen to encourage them to rise up against the British Empire, in much the same way as the Nazis were later to encourage Pushtun Muslims to rally against Britain in World War II, or as Kabul seeks to mobilise the tribes against Islamabad's Pakistani generals today.

The potency of the current revolutionary Islamic threat to the USSR — whether from Iran or Afghanistan's resistance movement — cannot be assessed with confidence or accuracy for some time yet. But the Soviets' hasty and brutal response to pan-Islamic forces in Central Asia fatally damaged the Comintern's attempts to win over Muslim radicals anxious to free their countries from colonial rule in the first half of the 20th century. The honeymoon between Islam and Marxism-Leninism was short-lived.

It did, however, manage to plant the seeds of communism in Afghanistan some 30 years or more before the People's Democratic Party (PDP) came into being in 1965. It is no accident that PDPA leaders received their first lessons in socialism from India, then still under British domination. Here the Comintern was particularly active. One of its recruits was none other than Hafizullah Amin, then an office boy in Bombay. Just as the Communist Party of Great Britain (CPGB) played a key role in the formation of the Indian Communist Party (CPI), so too Moscow charged the CPI with the task of supervising the PDPA's formation.

The Soviets do apparently fear the worldwide Islamic resurgence today. The year 1979 marked a turning point in these matters: the Iranian Revolution had placed a militant, outward-looking Shia theocracy in power while the Soviet military invasion and occupation of neighbouring Afghanistan had a profound impact — yet to be fully assessed — on relations between the Russians and their own Muslims and those abroad.

In 1980 there was a change of emphasis in Soviet Central Asia's official media. The Basmachi were back in the headlines, while the KGB and its own "private army" of border guards came in for particular praise.

The KGB chairman of the Azerbiyjan Soviet Socialist Republic, Major-General Yusife-Zade, said on December 19, 1980: "In view of the situation in Iran and Afghanistan the US special services are trying to exploit the Islamic religion . . . as one factor influencing the political situation in our country." He said Soviet state security organs — the KGB and MVD — "resolutely suppress the enemy's subversive activity," had succeeded in their struggle against "ideological subversion" and had suppressed actions by "reactionary Muslim clergy."

The celebration of the 60th anniversary of the foundation of the Azerbiyjan KGB on December 23, 1980, was chaired by Gaidar Aliev, First Secretary of the Central Committee of Azerbiyjan's Communist Party and a former KGB general. He exalted the "glorious" local KGB and the "glorious Chekist traditions of boundless devotion, courage, moral purity and implacability in the struggle against enemies of the revolution." He was later promoted to Moscow as a new deputy prime minister.

In 1980, 154 anti-religious books and pamphlets were published in the USSR. Of these, 20 or 17.5 percent were devoted to attacking Islam. In 1982, 195 anti-religious tracts were produced, of which 44, or 22.6 percent, were aimed at Islam. In the 1970s, the emphasis of the anti-religious drive against "parallel" Islam focused on the North Caucasus, but academics report that this has since switched to Central Asia.

S.I. Nikishov, presenting Moscow's official view in a 1982 booklet, describes Islam as one of the main weapons of "imperialist subversion." He expresses concern that the United States and China are playing the "Muslim card" and he singles out Iran. Imperialists he accuses of arming "counter-revolutionary gangs and infiltrating them from abroad into Afghanistan." He is imaginative enough to accuse China of funding the Muslim Brotherhood.

N. Ivanov, writing in *Aziia i Afrika Segodnia*, No. 3, 1982, warned that there are trends in Islam today which are opposed to socialism, trends represented by the late Bani Sadr, Mohammad al-Ghazali, Sayyid Qotb and other Muslim Brothers' leaders.

On January 25, 1983, M. Gapurov, First Secretary of the Turkmenistan Communist Party, attacked religion. "We consider that the fanning of the fires of religious prejudice is one of the means that imperialist powers, led by the US, are now using in their exacerbated psychological war against our country . . . they are using religious superstitions which still remain in the consciousness of some people, in order to idealise the feudal-patriarchal past, to spread the ideas of the Islamic revolution, thereby creating the basis for a nationalistic and anti-Soviet atmosphere . . ."

On December 7, 1982, G. Zgerskii, Major-General and Commander of KGB border units of the Central Asian military district, described the roots of the border guards in the "bloody and cruel" struggles with the Basmachi. He accused the US and other Western governments of aiming, through their secret services and anti-Soviet émigré organisations, to subvert the USSR ideologically: ". . . they are trying to send us their emissaries, using any legal or illegal means to smuggle across the border their ideologically subversive materials . . . Our own units guarantee a reliable defence against the attempts to infiltrate terrorists into our country and of smuggling in the means of terrorism and subversion."

The theme of "Leninist friendship" has also changed in Central Asia. The Basmachis' reliance on alleged external support is particularly stressed. According to one Soviet propagandist: "Anglo-American imperialism was the true organiser and inspirer of the Basmachi movement, supplying the bands with weapons, equipment, money and even with uniforms."

One prominent Western analyst of Central Asian affairs notes: "The Soviets are saying: 'We have beaten you before and, if necessary, we will beat you again.' To the Russians the message is somewhat different: 'In the 1920s when Soviet power was still weak and vulnerable, we defeated a powerful and well-organised rebellion supported by strong outside forces. Today, the Soviet Army is the world's strongest and it will crush the Afghan rebellion. The collapse of the Basmachi movement was historically inevitable. So it is for the Afghan rebels.' Increasingly, the problem of the Basmachis is being linked directly to the war in Afghanistan . . ."

Several issues arise from this. One is whether the Soviet increase in anti-religious propaganda directed more now towards border areas will achieve its object — or whether it will be counter-productive and simply concentrate the Muslim mind on the struggle or "subversion"Moscow seeks to suppress. Then there is the question as to whether there has been any *significant* contact between the Afghan guerillas and their fellow Muslims inside the Soviet Union.

There have in fact been several unconfirmed reports from Afghan resistance sources that contacts have been established across the Amu Darya with Muslims on Soviet territory. The contacts have taken the form of distribution of Afghan resistance membership cards, the dissemination in very limited quantities of revolutionary Islamic literature, mine-laying operations on a small scale on the Soviet side of the river, livestock rustling to augment local resistance food stocks, the infiltration of Afghan Islamic revolutionaries into Soviet Central Asia and the holding of meetings and discussions between Afghan guerillas and Muslims in Soviet Central Asia.

156

The Soviets have certainly stepped up their border security, and they have been known to use artillery and multiple rocket-launchers to level villages on the Afghan bank of the Amu Darya in reprisal for cross-border raids.

One French traveller who spent eight months in the company of Afghan guerillas in northern Afghanistan reported in 1982 that there were contacts; that weapons were smuggled across from the Soviet side of the border, strangely enough, and that Soviet troops were well deployed on both sides of the river for security purposes. He was reluctant to go into detail, as he felt premature or exaggerated publicity would prejudice the cause of the *Mujehadeen* in carrying their "holy war" into Soviet Central Asia.

One of the reports of contacts across the border was published by the Peshawar-based Afghan Information Centre in June, 1981. A man calling himself simply Chapandaz or Horseman had arrived in Pakistan after a six-week journey from Maimana, the centre of Fariab Province which shares its northern border with the USSR.

"There are seven resistance groups engaged in clandestine activities in Maimana and other small towns of Fariab," he told the editors of the Centre's monthly *Bulletin.* "I am a member of one of these groups. Since the Soviet invasion we have succeeded in establishing contact with the people of Tajikistan and Uzbekistan. We have received messages from them.

"These messages constantly say, among other things, that: 'We want to assure you that the invasion of your country by Russia is deeply resented by the people here. The signs of this popular resentment are already visible. Please do not stop fighting, do not submit to the Russian domination. If your resistance succeeds in lasting one more year, be sure that the economic difficulties which have already arisen will worsen and there will be social disturbances. Please fight the Russians. We are with you.' "

Soviet conscripts of Muslim cultural origin and other national or ethnic minorities have when interviewed described the "second class citizenship" they enjoy in the armed forces and the quite obvious degree of social "apartheid" in barracks-room life. The consistency and frequency of these reports are convincing evidence of the prevalence of the schism between Russians and Slavs on the one hand and Muslim and other ethnic groups on the other.

Afghan students who were studying in Tashkent since 1978 have interesting reports, too, although once again a degree of exaggeration and wishful thinking has to be taken into account. Barialay Habib, who qualified as a doctor in Tashkent in 1981, said that as an Afghan he was afraid to venture onto the streets of the city at night. He learned to describe himself as Iranian rather than admit to being Afghan. The lack of free, objective news simply fed popular rumour with the result that medical college personnel tried to evade the draft by bribing officials once gossip about casualties and deaths began to filter in from the local military hospitals.

He claimed some Uzbeks openly encouraged and praised the *Mujehadeen*, although Russians were hostile, sometimes violently so. Friends of his were "mugged" one night by locals, and shopkeepers refused to serve him if they realised he was Afghan. It was not clear whether the incidents he described were the result of Soviet — or Russian — xenophobia or a sign of public resentment of relatives' involvement in the military occupation.

The underground Sufi brotherhoods in the USSR do share with Afghanistan a common lineage in the form of the Qadirya Sufi sect, which has pockets of adherents throughout the Middle East. In Afghanistan this movement of Pushtuns in southern and eastern provinces is led by Pir Syed Ahmad Al-Gailani, whose grandfather settled in Afghanistan from Iraq and who claims to be a direct descendant of the Prophet Mohammad. Interestingly, Gailani's grandfather was active in World War I in trying to use his hereditary religious following to raise a revolt against the British administration on the North West Frontier.

Gailani's family dominates his guerilla organisation. He has failed to turn it into an effective, military-political organisation. The grassroots membership is illiterate and superstitious. They wear amulets containing passages from the Koran which they believe will ward off the security forces' bullets. Gailani has no significant following adjacent to the USSR's southern borderlands and Gailani is not likely to be able to promote a far-reaching strategy of subversion inside the USSR over such a distance and without a professional, clandestine and well-oiled guerilla apparatus. Gailani is himself a traditionalist, politically "moderate," wedded to Westernised ideas about nationalism and democracy — frankly unsuited to the *jehad*.

Finally, Gailani's advisers are unlikely to want to take the war to the enemy's lair, for fear of provoking a greater military reaction from Moscow. The Gailani *milieu* would probably seize the chance of a favourable political compromise and solution to the Afghan crisis, and it is unlikely that anything would be undertaken which might jeopardise these hopes, however naive and unrealistic they may seem to others in the resistance movement as a whole.

The most likely candidates in the resistance for promoting an extension of the *jehad* inside the USSR are the predominantly Tajik

Islamic revolutionaries of Jamiat-i-Islami and the forces of Gulbaddin's Hezb-i-Islami. Jamiat dominates northern areas by and large, and it is capable of carrying out relatively long-range plans. It has the advantage not only of geographical proximity, but it shares a common ethnic bond with the people of Soviet Tajikistan.

Gulbaddin Hekmatyar's revolutionary zeal and the support he apparently receives from the Revolutionary Islamic Party in Iran and from the revolutionary Islamic movement known as the Muslim Brotherhood make him an ideal source of subversion and agitation among Soviet-controlled Muslim minority groups. At any rate, one can dismiss the Soviet claim of "Western imperialism" interfering in or sponsoring such a policy; both Hezb-i-Islami and Jamiat-i-Islami avoid Western contamination and reject the West as an evil only marginally less undesirable than Soviet influence in their affairs.

The Afghan "fundamentalists" or Islamic revolutionaries of the resistance movement are strongly backed by similar organisations in Pakistan, Iran and the Gulf linked together in the form of the Brotherhood. Senior members of the Pakistani branch, Jamaat Islami Pakistan, certainly see Afghanistan as less a Soviet springboard to the Persian Gulf than as a springboard for Muslim resurgence in the Soviet Union. "Rolling back communism and taking the war north," was how one leading *Ikwhani* in Pakistan described it. The Soviet Union, as he pointed out, is the fifth largest "Muslim" or "fundamentalist" and it detracts from a better understanding of this formidable movement.

This idealism might seem far-fetched were it not for the energy, organisation, copious funding and secrecy of this little-known and much-maligned international movement, whose activities only hit the Western headlines when one or another of its youthful and dissident factions breaks loose to commit an extreme act of some kind, such as the Al-Jehad assassination of the former Egyptian President, Anwar Sadat. Following the seizure of hostages by Iranian students, Americans tend to see red when they hear the term "Muslim" or "fundamentalist" and it detacts from a better understanding of this formidable movement.

The Brotherhood has an international committee which provides its top decision-making body. Its membership is drawn from the national committees throughout the Islamic world. Membership is restricted and upward movement dependent on Islamic qualifications in terms of both learning and experience. It is as well funded as the Mafia, as influential internationally as the Comintern and thoroughly revolutionary in its commitment to installing truly Islamic states in the place of conservative, monarchist or neocolonial and socialist regimes. It is well established in Egypt, Syria, Tunisia, the Sudan, Pakistan and elsewhere, including the Afghan resistance. Its communications are secure, regular and frequent. Many of its leaders are Western-educated to postgraduate level and have a sophisticated appreciation of international affairs. Its leadership appears to be divided between conservative Sunnis and radical supporters of Iran, though.

The movement is the embodiment of the 20th century resurgence of Islam. It is egalitarian in theory, dictatorial in practice. Its younger members are impatient for change, are not averse to violence and view Islam as a trans-national force to take on and eventually overcome both Western and Soviet superpower blocs. A German authority on the subject, Wilhelm Dietl, described liberation of the Muslims in the USSR as one of the Brotherhood's priorities. "They want to spread their message to Muslims in the Soviet Union. But they are in no hurry. They have time."

The aim is certainly there. Soviet propaganda appears to reflect Moscow's apprehensions, too. But there is no real evidence — or even an indication — to support a popular though improbable assumption among some Western pundits that the Soviet invasion of Afghanistan was partly prompted by Moscow's fears that resurgent Islam on its sensitive southern border would fatally contaminate Central Asia. On the contrary, the invasion forces appear to have failed to take into account both the impact of the military occupation on Muslim conscripts Moscow relied upon very largely for execution of the initial move into Afghanistan, and more importantly, on Soviet-Muslim relations internationally. If anything, the invasion and subsequent widening of the conflict in Afghanistan has severely jeopardised Moscow's attempt to exploit and win over the "anti-imperialist" energies of Islamic countries.

Moscow's policy towards Muslim states and communities can be summed up as wanting to have its cake and eat it. Moscow is careful, for example, to support the Iranian revolutionaries' anti-imperialist and specifically anti-American fervour, but falls short of openly backing the Ayatollah Khomeini in order to keep its options on Iran open and in order not to prejudice its relations with the conservative Sunni leaders in the Gulf. In fact this self-imposed restraint in part reflects the paramount weakness of Soviet projection of "progressive" elements in Islam. Moscow woodenly insists on Islam's secularisation at home and abroad, as it failed to accept the desire for autonomy of its Muslims shortly after the 1917 Revolution.

This is something which is intrinsically obnoxious to the Muslim

Brotherhood. Islam is *politics.* It is a religion of involvement, of engagement in all aspects of an individual's or a community's life. It is this theological insistence by Moscow on the need for "scientific socialism" *et al* on which the Kremlin's "official Islam" founders. A "good Muslim" cannot regard his faith simply as a private matter, to be kept aside from national or international affairs. Islamic revolutionaries are revolutionary precisely because they cannot and will not regard religious belief as a personal convenience. Islamic revolutionaries believe in exercising a world view, a complete and seamless system impinging on every single human activity. To that extent it is truly totalitarian and hence a major competitor for Marxism-Leninism. This is the essence of Soviet reservations over Islam.

Western commentators fall into a similar trap. There are basically two schools of thought: those who see the revival of Musim *culture* in the USSR as a challenge to the Soviet status quo, and secondly, those who regard Moscow's tolerance of and support for "official" or secular Islam as having successfully prevented or removed internal Muslim dissent. Both these arguments are faulty. They fail to take into account the essential nature of resurgent Islam as a religion of engagement. Whether the West, the Gulf or the Soviets have more to lose — or to gain — from this phenomenon is another matter.

This is not to imply that the Kremlin will not seek to harness Islam in seeking the overthrow of conservative regimes in the Gulf. Far from it. Moscow is adopting a "wait and see" attitude and can be expected to do what it can, possibly through allies like Libya, to provide material aid to movements capable of destabilising an area upon which the West depends for much of its energy resources. While the Soviets may see advantages simply in terms of a destabilising process in itself, this has to be measured against the implications for Soviet relations with other conservative Islamic leaderships and the long-term consequences of seeing a truly Islamic, revolutionary state emerging on its doorstep. Moscow once again has reverted to its characteristic "cautious opportunism." But the Muslim Brothers are similarly prodding away at the House of Islam across the Amu Darya.

The Economics of War

The war between the guerillas and the Soviet-backed PDPA regime has created two economies: the official, state system, and the largely rural, agrarian sector now largely in the hands of the resistance, for better or worse.

The state economy is being steadily integrated into the Soviet system. As the country's financial and trading position steadily deteriorates, so the process has accelerated. Official figures tell the story.

Seventy-one percent of Afghanistan's foreign trade is now conducted with Comecon countries compared with 39.5 percent in March, 1978, just before the communist coup. The Soviet Union's share has gone up over that period from 38 percent to nearly 56 percent and Soviet-Afghan trade is due to treble between 1981 and 1985. In 1982, 62 percent of Afghan exports and 67 percent of imports were conducted under barter arrangements with Soviet bloc countries, primarily the USSR itself.

Natural gas is the largest export commodity and according to official PDPA sources accounted for nearly half the government budget in 1981/82. The Soviet Union is the sole customer. Some 85 percent of production is piped direct to Soviet Central Asia.

The Soviets have consistently underpaid Afghanistan for the gas in terms of average world prices. Their price has recently been raised and on the basis of recent figures is believed to be about US$124 per thousand cubic metres. But this is still low by world standards and less than the price charged by Moscow for Siberian gas exported to Western Europe. The Soviets claim that Afghan gas is of lower calorific value, but this is disputed by former Afghan officials now in exile. In any case, earnings from gas are only notional and not paid in hard currency, since the value of the gas is offset against Afghanistan's debt for imports and loans from the USSR, estimated by December, 1982, to amount to about US$3 billion.

The Afghans are thus tied to the repayment of a constantly rising debt with a natural resource whose price is dictated, and deliberately undervalued, by the creditor. Moreover, Afghan officials are unable to verify the actual amount of gas pumped out, since the meters are on the Soviet side of the border, according to Dr. Abdul Latif Aurah, former head of the Gas and Petroleum Department of the Ministry of Mines and Industry.

According to official Afghan data, natural gas production in 1981/82 was 2.7 billion cubic metres. High priority is being given to expansion of the industry and further increasing exports to the USSR. Production is planned to rise in 1983/84 by a further — and staggering — three billion cubic metres.

Other developing countries have experienced a Soviet unwillingness to pay the world commercial rate for raw materials. Guinea has complained that the Soviet Union pays only two-thirds of the world price for its bauxite, for example. When in 1980 the Soviets offered Iran US$110 for 100 m^3 for its natural gas, the Iranians insisted on a price nearer the average world level. Moscow refused, and in April 1980 Iran stopped supplying gas to the Soviet Union. The Kabul regime, by contrast, is in no position to resist.

Most of the high-quality urea fertiliser produced at the Mazar-i-Sharif petrochemical plant is exported to the Soviet Union. In consequence the Afghans have had to import their own fertiliser from elsewhere, mainly the United States. Similarly, most of the output of the Czech-built cement factories in Afghanistan is exported to the USSR. The cement is of exceptionally high quality, because of the excellence of the local raw material. To meet their own needs the Afghan regime must import inferior cement from Moscow.

Afghanistan also loses under the arrangements governing the export of olives and citrus fruit from the Nangahar Valley Project in the Jalalabad area in the south-east of the country near the Pakistan border post of Torkham. Financed by the Soviets, the project remains under de facto Russian control. Nearly all the crop goes to the Soviet Union and the Afghans are obliged to meet the cost of transport to the Soviet border. Were the Afghans free to export to the most favourable market, the Afghans would no doubt sell to Pakistani companies which have already made clear their willingness to pay *twice* the price paid by the Soviets and to bear the transport costs as well, since even on these terms they could apparently make an attractive profit.

A group of former senior Afghan officials who defected to Pakistan in October 1981 have spoken of the resentment created by the manipulation to Soviet advantage of the barter system used now in Soviet-Afghan trade.

Afghan exports are priced below their real commercial value, while Soviet goods supplied in exchange are heavily over-valued. An economist who formerly worked in the Planning Ministry reported that in deals whereby Afghanistan bought sugar in return for cement, the Afghan authorities lost US$97 per tonne of sugar in terms of world prices.

The USSR also benefits from "switch-trading" in Afghan products. Fruit, olives, nuts, raisins and honey imported on favourable terms by Moscow are resold in Eastern Europe at a profit. Again, other developing countries have complained of this practice, saying it endangers Third World exports. Instances of the Soviets reselling Egyptian and Sudanese cotton were reported in the 1970s, and India has complained of switch-trading by Moscow in Indian machine-tools and cotton products.

Because so much Soviet-Afghan trade is based on barter, the regime is short of foreign exchange needed to buy goods on the world market which the Soviet bloc cannot supply. Although according to official Afghan figures Afghanistan achieved a surplus of about US$50 million on its foreign trade in 1981/82, the country's foreign exchange reserves are actually falling fast — from US$375 million in March, 1980, to US$238 million at the end of 1981.

Kabul is therefore forced to ask the USSR to buy goods from third countries on its behalf, the value of the convertible currency involved being debited against Afghan natural gas exports. Recent examples are the purchase of soap from South Korea and cooking oil from Malaysia. A surplus of several hundred million rupees which Moscow has accumulated in its trade with India is being used to buy a wide range of consumer goods for the Afghan regime.

Because of Afghanistan's dependence on Soviet aid, the presence of numerous Soviet advisers in the administration, and the Babrak Karmal regime's reliance on the Soviets for its survival, the Soviet Union has a preponderant role in Afghan economic planning. The emphasis is on energy, transport and minerals — all areas of benefit to the USSR.

Reports prepared in the 1970s by the World Bank and the UN Development Programme show that Afghanistan has a range of minerals which are of considerable value and strategic importance to Moscow. The Russians' own mining output is falling increasingly behind its needs. The Soviet mining industry faces problems of declining ore quality, obsolete technology and a shortage of labour.

The iron ore deposits at Hajigak in Baymiyan Province in

northern Afghanistan are estimated at 1.7 billion tons of high quality ore, with 52 to 62 percent iron content. The Soviet reserves of 10 billion tons have an average content of only 38 percent and need expensive upgrading. The huge copper deposits at Ainak, south of Kabul, are of a similarly high grade (0.7 to 1.2 percent).

A protocol signed on June 1, 1981, provides for the construction by the Soviets of an extraction smelting plant at Ainak which is due to start production in 1985. At US$600 million, this will be the largest single Soviet project in the country.

Moscow is also interested in Afghanistan's deposits of high-grade chrome ore, estimated at 500,000 tons, since the quality of their own rapidly diminishing reserves is declining. Other minerals identified by the numerous Soviet geologists working in Afghanistan include beryl, barite, fluorspar, lead, zinc, bauxite, lithium, tantalum, emeralds and uranium.

With the virtual termination of aid from the West and the Islamic world following the Soviet invasion, Afghanistan has become heavily dependent on Moscow for aid. Soviet non-military aid rose sharply from US$34 million in 1979 to US$284 million in 1981. Babrak Karmal said on November 14, 1980 that 80 percent of Afghanistan's foreign aid now came from the USSR.

Some 86 percent of Soviet economic aid to developing countries is now committed to four socialist allies: Cuba, Vietnam, Mongolia and Afghanistan. Available figures for the past three years are, in millions of US dollars:

	1979	1980	1981
Afghanistan	34	276	284
Cuba	3,450	3,000	3,200
Vietnam	890	1,050	1,000 (approx.)
Mongolia	n.a.	up to 775	n.a.

With the cessation of aid from other sources, and taking into account the considerable economic disruption caused by the fighting, a large proportion of Soviet aid has had to be in the form of essential commodity assistance (US$188 million in 1981). This covers such items as wheat, rice, sugar, edible oils and textiles. Some of these, such as wheat, have had to be paid for in hard currency. As the war continues this commitment is likely to increase.

Other Soviet aid continues to be concentrated in sectors which increase Afghanistan's dependence on the Soviet bloc and specifically on projects which are either directly related to the Soviet military occupation or are of potential benefit to the Soviet economy, for example maintenance and extension of the trunk road system, construction of a major road and rail bridge across the Amu Darya, plans for building the country's first extensive railway, expansion of airports and building of new runways, enlargement of the river ports of Hairatan, Sher Khan and Torghundi on the Amu Darya and an increase in production of the natural gas industry. Prospecting and exploitation of minerals and the construction of a 220 kv. electricity transmission line from the Soviet border to Kabul — on which Afghanistan will depend for its electrical power needs — are two other examples.

According to Tass on August 17, 1982, 170 major projects have been built or are in progress with Soviet technical assistance. They account for 60 percent of Afghanistan's total industrial output and for 70 percent of the production of the state sector. They cover all production of natural gas and of prefabricated housing and 55 percent of electrical power. Although the Afghan economy is predominantly agricultural, Soviet aid in this area is much less in evidence.

The Soviets maintain firm control of all types of aid through the joint Soviet-Afghan Economic Commission and the presence of numerous Soviet advisers in key posts in the Afghan bureaucracy. A protocol signed on February 6, 1982 provided for Moscow to engage "in all-round cooperation in promoting Afghanistan's development plans and assist in regulating Afghanistan's planning affairs."

Afghanistan is now dependent on Moscow for 84 percent of its imports of machinery and transport equipment, 65 percent of cotton fabric, 96 percent of refined petroleum products and all sugar imports. According to official figures, more than 400,000 tons of goods passed through the river ports of Hairatan, Sher Khan and Torghundi on the Amu Darya in 1981/82, an increase of 25 percent over 1980/81.

Although agriculture employs over 70 percent of the working population, the 1982/83 development plan gives priority to mining, industry and power (37.6 percent) and transport (27.4 percent) and allocates only 10.4 percent of resources to agriculture.

Food imports have sharply increased since 1978 and agricultural production has fallen primarily because crops are deliberately destroyed by Soviet and Afghan security forces to deny them to the *Mujehadeen* and force the civilians into dependence on the Kabul regime. Large numbers of farm workers have either joined the resistance, been conscripted into the Afghan armed forces, migrated to the relative safety of the cities or fled to Iran and Pakistan as refugees, often taking their livestock with them. As early as June, 1980, refugees were reported to have taken an estimated 1.25 million head of cattle out of the country. In areas dominated by the resistance, *Mujehadeen* in some circumstances keep food crops back from the local market for their own consumption. Guerillas have on innumerable occasions disrupted or intercepted military and civil supply convoys. Large numbers of official and privately-owned trucks have been destroyed by one side or the other. Distribution has been heavily hit by the war.

A former senior official of the Agricultural Development Bank (BDB), Syed Abdul Rahman Hashimi, who defected to Pakistan in October, 1982 said that less than half the country's arable land was now under cultivation. Earlier that year the ADB had announced loans of only US$10 million, "but there was no one to receive them" and only US$30,000 had been distributed.

In a paper written a few weeks after his defection, Hashimi described in detail the collapse of agricultural development projects since the Soviet invasion. Within a year of the April 1978 coup, the PDPA regime announced the registration of almost 1,200 farmers' cooperatives. "Almost all the registered cooperative societies collapsed in a short period of time," he wrote. By mid-1982 official figures showed just over 100 active cooperatives remained — but this was very much a paper exercise as the regime was no longer able to identify the farmers concerned, or their precise whereabouts. "The Soviets and the Soviet-backed Afghan Government have brought the country's agricultural system to the point of collapse," said the former official.

Food shortages are increasing and the distribution of available supplies poses an almost insuperable problem for the regime. In Kabul at a time when the harvest had been completed and supplies should have been plentiful — in September, 1982 — flour was selling at twice the official price and in some places it cost US$12 for 15 lbs, four times the official price.

In a statement on October 15, 1982 Babrak Karmal admitted that the people faced food shortages and malnutrition. He said large food imports were necessary "at a cost of massive amounts of foreign currency. If attention is not paid to this soon, the figure will soon reach a stage where it will get out of hand and exceed the country's economic ability."

He said current annual imports were 150,000 to 200,000 tons of wheat, 30,000 tons of rice, 17,000 tons of edible oils and thousands of tons of dairy products. Actual figures may be much higher, according to foreign observers: wheat imports are believed to have risen from 100,000 tons in 1978/79 to 240,000 tons in 1980/81.

According to the official news agency, Bakhtar, on May 18, 1982 sugar imports for that year would be 158,000 tons, up by 61 per cent over 1981. Afghan sugar beet production for 1981 was planned for only 34,000 tons compared with a pre-1979 figure of 100,000.

In the first 10 months of 1981 consumer prices rose by 37 percent. According to another senior Afghan government official who fled to Pakistan in May, 1982, prices had registered increases of up to 250 percent since the Soviet invasion. Tourism, worth about US$30 million before 1979, has ceased entirely.

The PDPA regime has been able to keep certain key industries — such as natural gas — going because they are concentrated and can be easily defended. Others are scattered, their supplies of raw material easily disrupted and their operations hamstrung by the exodus of skilled workers and managers to Pakistan and Iran and further afield as refugees. Technical advisers are reluctant to leave Kabul because of the general insecurity and obvious risk they run of being killed by *Mujehadeen.*

Electricity supplies are inadequate and unreliable, because of damage to plant and transmission lines and delays in repairing breakdowns. In Kabul during the autumn of 1982 load-shedding was general and some areas were without current for 12 hours a day; in Herat power was available only between 1800 and 2200 hours each day, while in Kandahar the supply was almost non-existent. The power failures in the capital reached a peak in mid-winter following successful resistance raids on power lines and the hydro-electrical station at Mahipur to mark the third anniversary of the Soviet intervention. For weeks at a time Kabul was in darkness. The shortages of firewood and heating oil compounded the city's misery and the authorities were obliged both to acknowledge the incidents officially in the media and to promise help in the form of relief supplies brought in under heavy military escort from the north.

Textile factories — such as those at Gulbohar and Jabal-ur-Seraj — as well as the nation's cement works are either closed down altogether or working well under capacity. The huge bakery in Kabul has been repeatedly damaged in guerilla attacks. The Kabul regime has given figures only for schools destroyed: 1,713 since the insurgency may be said to have started in earnest in 1978 — and 106 health clinics. The cost has been put officially at the equivalent of US$200 million, but may be several times that figure in reality. In a speech in Herat on October 22, 1982 Babrak Karmal claimed a modest increase in gross production of "about two to three percent," but he admitted that the work of the "counter-revolution" had stopped or disrupted some industrial enterprises, power lines and transport links. Progress on new enterprises was slow, he said.

Afghanistan has for a generation or more been a conduit for illicit dealing in Soviet roubles. Aeroflot crews have been known to carry caches of banknotes out of the USSR. But since the Soviet invasion — there are 105,000 soldiers' wages to be paid in the Soviet currency — the black market has expanded rapidly, so much so that duing the course of 1982 Soviet Secretary Yuri Andropov's anti-corruption drive has been extended to Kabul and provincial cities.

Western diplomatic sources reported over a series of months that the Soviets have initiated two major investigations into corruption in the country, at least one of which involved the KGB.

Cash finds its way out of the USSR illegally and is sold at a fraction of its official value on the Kabul money market, presumably in an effort to buy foreign exchange. These transactions have been large: resistance sources say the value of the Afghani against leading foreign currencies has fluctuated wildly — something they attribute to the purchase of large quantities of US dollars locally. The roubles are then reportedly resold at a higher rate of exchange and find their way back into the USSR where they are used to buy goods on the black market.

The diplomatic sources said in March 1983 that prior to the official investigation, Kabul money lenders did a brisk business in roubles, with even small stallholders around the Mikrorayon residential enclave doing a brisk trade, offering roubles at attractive rates. Roubles have also found their way to Singapore and Hong Kong in Southeast Asia, while there have been reports too that roubles have been used to finance gold smuggling to the Gulf, using Karachi as an outlet.

The scandal broke in January when a prominent money merchant, Surjet Singh, was taken off a departing airliner with two suitcases stuffed with more than a million roubles. Joint Soviet and Afghan teams raided the bazaar in Kabul and arrested over a dozen of Singh's associates and customers. Shortly afterwards, the upper ranks of the PDPA's Customs Ministry were purged of people allegedly involved in the racket. Rumours were rife that high-level PDPA leaders were involved. Mohammad Baralai, the President's brother and the man generally believed to be in de facto control of the regime's foreign policy, was persistently named as someone who carried large quantities of roubles back into the Soviet Union on his frequent visits there. The deputy head of the Supreme Court, Abdul Raouf Safi, is believed to have been removed from his post as a result of the investigation.

The Minister of Finance was rumoured to be under suspicion, although it has to be said that the rivalries within the PDPA are such that a scandal of this nature will be employed to good effect in discrediting leaders of one faction or another.

The diplomatic sources said that reports had been received that a Soviet Embassy official and a Soviet civilian adviser were leading lights in the mysterious currency dealings. First Secretary Saifullah Saidov, who worked at a new Soviet cultural centre in Kabul, returned to Moscow and the adviser, known only as Rajebov, was believed to be under investigation for his alleged links with Raoud Safi.

An investigation was also launched in the summer of 1982 into the activities of a Soviet official in Kabul known as Ivanosov, who held an important commercial post of several years in the Afghan capital. He is said to have played the role of *tolkach* — fixer — for local businessmen in Kabul seeking trade deals with Moscow. Ivanosov and his associates are said to have received kickbacks totalling 300 million Afghanis — valued at the time at around US$4.5 million — over several years. In return for a commission, Ivanosov allegedly would arrange for a local entrepreneur to import a large quantity of desirable items, such as rubber boots, and reduce the number of less negotiable commodities such as refrigerators his client would normally have been obliged to accept in the transaction.

Two of the commercial official's Afghan drivers were picked up and tortured. Their evidence seems to have led to the arrest of several leading merchants who were briefly held for questioning about irregular payments made to Ivanosov. The Soviet official subsequently returned to the USSR.

On a minor but pervasive level, Soviet officers and advisers frequently accept gifts from their Afghan comrades who seek to curry favour, often in their unceasing struggle for pre-eminence against their rivals in the regime. One Afghan Army officer who defected to Pakistan in late 1982 reported that the canteen on the second floor of the Defence Ministry in Kabul was a "front" for a brisk business in luxury foodstuffs. Soviet troops have been frequently reported to have sold their equipment in return for hashish and opium. The general air of despondency in the city among the Soviets was confirmed by two Soviet correspondents in Kabul in February, 1983 during a discussion with diplomats. The power blackouts, rumours of high Soviet casualties and reports flooding in of fighting around the country are all demoralising — and the gossip about those who are making their fortunes on the side rubs salt in already sensitive wounds.

If Kabul feels the economic pinch, the same goes for the guerillas — only more so. Reports reaching Peshawar from the *Mujehadeen* during the winter of 1982/83 suggested that civilians and resistance fighters alike faced considerable hardship. In a sense, their own success in disrupting the normal life of the country is at least partly responsible.

Another important factor is the failure of the resistance as a whole to unify, either in Peshawar or on the battlefield itself. The inability to coordinate an effective logistics programme, even on a regional basis, emphasised local shortages of food.

Kabul, Baghis, Ghor, Parwan, Maidan and Ghazni were among the names of areas which frequently cropped up in guerilla despatches as facing economic pressure. Not only was food hard to come by in local bazaars, but prices were largely out of reach of ordinary people.

The Soviet practice of buying up local grain in the northern cities of Kunduz, Mazar-i-Sharif and Faisabad fuelled inflation and exacerbated seasonal scarcity. It is not clear why the Soviets employed Afghan merchants well supplied with cash to travel about buying up foodstuffs — it may have been an exercise designed to replenish military reserves, to deny guerillas access to food or simply a freelance initiative in which the food is shipped back across the border into Soviet Central Asia and sold at a profit. The Afghan middlemen were either ignorant of, or indifferent to, local prices; they paid exorbitant rates and when guerillas captured some of these collaborators in Mazar-i-Sharif in 1982 they recovered well over a million Afghanis in their possession.

Random, frequent bombing of the Panjsher severely curtailed farming activity, with many families forced to spend their daylight hours hidden in caves, with the men emerging at night to try to collect the harvest. Rivalries among guerilla groups aggravated the problem. For many months a recalcitrant group of Hekmatyar's Hezb-i-Islami fighters at Andarab effectively isolated Jamiat-i-Islami guerillas in the valley until the latter broke the siege by force.

Kwashiokor was reported north of Faisabad during the winter of 1982/83, while anaemia, rickets, tuberculosis, thyroid diseases and other ailments caused or reinforced by an inadequate diet were widespread, especially in areas where a significant proportion of the populace had fled the countryside for the cities or across the borders to refugee camps.

The use of incendiaries to destroy standing crops and the burning of harvested grain have been reported on innumerable occasions by the resistance. What was initially regarded during the first two years of Soviet occupation to be the accidental spin-off from major counter-insurgency operations is now widely believed by both resistance sources and some diplomatic observers to be a deliberate policy aimed at the roots of guerilla activity: the civilians.

Rival guerilla groups each enforcing Islamic taxes on local people have helped alienate civilians in some areas. Where guerillas have failed to cooperate even in a passive sense, the imposition of *zakat* and *ushr* has simply added to the desire to leave and settle in refugee camps away from the front line. Guerilla commanders have complained that the Kabul regime's ability to use cash in large quantities to recruit collaborators has made life difficult for the resistance. Militiamen, for example, are normally paid an initial wage of 3,000 Afghanis a month — more than a Kabul University professor's salary. Those who do go over to the Government know at least that their families will not starve, whatever other fate may befall them.

Economic pressure on the resistance and civilians they need to provide them with support is not uniform. Variations in altitude, weather, soil conditions and proximity to major communications differ greatly, even within a single province. Evidence of genuine, visible hardship is hard to come by. Western diplomats say there is no evidence of serious hardship inside Afghanistan. What they do not say is that they have simply not looked very hard. Pressure is building up at least among some of the 17 Pakistani and foreign refugee relief agencies in the refugee camps for an accurate survey to be made of economic conditions in rural areas, although the mandates of several refugee organisations and the day-to-day political constraints imposed upon them by the donor countries and the local Pakistani authorities are such that a "land bridge" to bring relief to what are commonly referred to as the "internal refugees" may simply not be possible. But prevention is better than cure.

The first — and so far the only — serious investigation into the food problem was carried out independently by an Afghan refugee, Azam Gul, an American-trained agronomist at Kabul University before he too fled to Pakistan in 1982.

Azam Gul found several former agricultural students he knew and set about a scientific survey of food shortages in the autumn of 1982. The survey was designed to collect and analyse objective data to confirm or deny reports of food shortages, and to obtain an accurate description of the present agricultural situation in the country. The work avoided dealing with the conflict, and it was done independently of the resistance. Despite considerable difficulties faced by the researchers in terms of the political situation and the lack of support from the local Pakistani authorities, the final report was by any standards fair and dispassionate. Its findings were startling.

Using 1978 as the base figure, wheat prices per seer or seven kilos rose from an average of 62.2 Afghanis to 99 in 1981, and leapt to 153.4 by 1982 — an increase of 145 percent. The biggest increase was in Parwan Province, in which the price of wheat increased over four years by 200 percent. Over the same period, the average increase in the price of fertiliser grew by 67.9 percent.

Similarly disturbing results were obtained in terms of the decline in wheat production. Again using 1978 as the base, in four years the national average production fell by 79.6 percent. In a single year, from 1981 to 1982, production fell 53.4 percent. For a country in which 71.6 percent of the total labour force is directly or indirectly engaged in agriculture, this was a very serious development. Some 52 percent of the farm labour force was found to be absent. In 1978 an average farm had only 46 percent of its land cultivated, but by 1982 this proportion had fallen to only 16 percent.

The average yield per acre had also fallen substantially. By 1982, the wheat yield had fallen to 54 percent of the 1978 figure. Rice yield had fallen to 35 percent, barley 60 percent, corn to 63 percent and cotton to 70 percent. While the report studiously avoided involving itself with the contentious issue of the war, nevertheless forced conscription, military operations and the flight of some four million Afghans abroad were said to be the main reasons for the collapse of the country's agriculture.

There was no doubt about food shortages.

While the International Committee of the Red Cross (ICRC) delegation in Peshawar was reluctant to concede that a major problem existed, nevertheless it did collect information on food prices, although the method used was rough and ready. The "basket price" of food rose in Baghlan Province from 210 Afghanis in February, 1982 to 445 the following year; in Logar it went up from 235 Afghanis to 405 over the same period and Kabul's food prices jumped from 300 to 525 Afghanis. In Takhar Province the February 1982 price was 190 Afghanis and 12 months later it had risen to 433. In Kunar the price more than doubled. The "basket" consisted of figures for wheat, corn, potatoes and meat.

It can be argued that from the Soviet point of view, the huge international refugee relief effort mounted by donors to the UN and by the Pakistani authorities has in fact been of substantial benefit to the PDPA regime in Kabul.

The presence of three million Afghans in Pakistan's two poorest provinces is a major burden not only in financial terms but socially and politically. It is a spur to bring Pakistan to terms with Kabul. The knowledge that they will be fed, clothed and housed and even paid a nominal cash allowance is obviously an inducement to Afghans to quit when the going gets tough in Afghanistan; that is precisely what the security forces appear to want. Kunar Province probably has lost 70 percent of its rural population. Anything that moves, therefore, can safely be considered hostile which makes counter-insurgency much easier to conduct.

By March, 1983, there were 2,152,400 registered Afghan refugees in the North West Frontier Province alone, organised into 284 tented villages. Forty percent are settled in the tribal agencies stretching along the border. Here the local Pushtun tribes are fiercely independent and the only political representation takes the form of a single political agent and his staff to maintain Islamabad's writ. Indeed, in one area, the Afridi Tirah, no official, Pakistani or British, has been allowed to pay a visit since the last major British colonial military operation there in 1897. Water and grazing are scarce and in some areas the presence of refugees threatens to undermine social stability.

In Kurram Agency, for example, the indigenous population is dominated by the Shia community — in the majority locally but a minority in Pakistan as a whole. The arrival of more than 300,000 Sunni Afghan refugees in the agency has upset the demography of the area and it is aggravated by traditional enmity between the Touri and Mangal tribes who spill across the border into Afghanistan. It is no coincidence that the trouble between Sunnis and Shias — involving skirmishes lasting weeks and causing considerable damage to property — has disrupted a major guerilla supply route into Paktya and Logar provinces and points further north and west.

The Pakistani authorities are conscious of the need to keep a grip on the refugee relief operation, to avoid "inviting" Afghans to leave their homeland unnecessarily, and to ensure that the standard of living enjoyed by the refugees does not exceed that of the indigenous Pushtuns. It is a difficult task and it is to Pakistan's credit that neither a serious epidemic nor a large-scale uprising of locals against the newcomers has occurred, despite attempts by Kabul's agents to infiltrate the refugee camps to stir up disaffection. The Pakistanis are trying to move newly-arrived refugees — at a rate of 8-10,000 a month on average in NWFP — further inland, away from the border and even into Punjab Province. The danger here is the growth of a large "squatter" population of refugees unwilling to move away from the frontier; the further away they are, the more difficult it will be for males to return for the seasonal fighting. The presence of unregistered "squatters" would certainly, in large numbers, cause major political and social problems for Pakistan's military government.

Economics is certainly an essential part of the political capital which local banned opposition parties in Pakistan have tried to make by manipulating the refugee issue. Local figures such as Walli Khan, the National Democratic Party's *eminence grise*, make great play with the feeling that refugees are a symptom of superpower rivalry in South Asia, and that Pushtuns are paying the price — in blood in terms of Pushtuns living in Afghanistan and in political liberty and welfare in the frontier province. The NWFP is dominated by the NDP which has long sought provincial autonomy and which by tradition looks to Kabul and New Delhi in political, historical and cultural terms. A close second comes the banned Pakistan People's Party (PPP) with the "fundamentalist" Jamaat Islami Pakistan trailing far behind in popularity.

This may help explain why Jamaat — and to some extent the provincial authorities — champions the "fundamentalist" Afghan organisations such as Hekmatyar's Hezb-i-Islami over and above others. The weakness of Jamaat Islami Pakistan is ironically the reason why the best in terms of refugee aid and resistance material support is channelled to the former second-year engineering student from Kunduz.

It is a vicious circle: the worse the Afghan economy becomes, the more refugees are likely to stream across the border at a rate of up to 10,000 a month. The more this happens, the more sensitive relations between the refugees and their Pakistani fellow Muslims are likely to be. Finally, the more people who flee Afghanistan the more difficult it will be for the guerilla movement to operate effectively in-country without relying on Peshawar — with a commensurate increase in Soviet pressure on Islamabad to make concessions to the PDPA regime in Kabul.

Economic deterioration bears more heavily on the resistance than it does on Kabul. The worse the situation becomes for Babrak Karmal, the more reliant he is on Moscow. For the Russians the costs may be rising and they may be painful, but they are not unmanageable and in the long term the USSR will benefit from Afghanistan's considerable resources. That is far from being the case for the rag-tag army of resistance fighters. Time is not on their side.

Peace Talks

In June, 1982 the first indirect or proximity talks took place in Geneva between ministers of the Pakistan military government and the PDPA regime in Kabul. They did not meet each other, but chose to hold their discussions with a go-between, in the form of a Uruguayan diplomat, the UN's special representative on Afghanistan, Diego Cordovez.

Iran firmly declined to participate. It had declared its solidarity with the resistance forces in Afghanistan and made it clear that it would only be a party to negotiations if the guerillas were also present at the talks. Instead, an official from Tehran was on hand and was kept informed of progress.

Initially at least, the USSR tried to maintain as low a profile as possible and attempted to present the talks as primarily a bilateral, Pakistani-Afghan issue. But a senior official of the Afghanistan section of the Soviet Ministry of Foreign Affairs, Stanislav Gavrilov, was in Geneva throughout the talks. He was later posted to Kabul as an adviser to the Afghan Foreign Ministry.

Pakistan's approach was based firmly on the principles established in successive UN resolutions: withdrawal of foreign troops, self-determination for the Afghan people, restoration of Afghanistan's independent, non-aligned status and the creation of conditions in which refugees could return home in peace, and with dignity.

President Zia repeatedly mentioned these points in public. On occasions he would emphasize the right of Afghans to choose their own form of government and the need for a return not only to a non-aligned but also Islamic status for the country.

Kabul's position differed not so much in terms of principles (which can always be interpreted several different ways), as in priorities. The issue of guarantees of "non-interference" in Afghanistan's internal affairs came first, and the return of the refugees a close second. It has been the UN's task to draft both procedures and matters of substance in such a way as to find a degree of common ground.

Kabul has always insisted that the presence of "limited contingents" of Soviet troops have been requested in order to deal with "bands of counter-revolutionaries" led on the battlefield by American, Chinese and other foreign advisers. Its spokesmen have dismissed the refugees as either seasonal migrations of the country's estimated two million nomads or *kuchis* or else as "gangsters" based in military training camps in Pakistan.

At Geneva the Afghans — at Soviet behest — hinted at a willingness to discuss a possible framework linking these elements of a settlement together, in particular providing for the withdrawal of troops to start in advance of the return of refugees.

This appears to have been the source of much public speculation over the "flexibility" which President Zia spoke of after the round of talks. The Soviets had for the first time certainly signalled an apparent willingness to be flexible: Soviet spokesmen took great pains for the first time to encourage a favourable impression of the Geneva talks and the prospects for further progress. But in the UN General Assembly debate in November, 1982 the Soviet representative said that Afghanistan's "internal affairs" should not be discussed in the negotiations and that progress made in the Cordovez initiative — albeit largely on procedural matters — should be allowed to continue. Neither Afghan nor Soviet sources were willing to explain how guarantees of non-interference could be placed on the agenda if the country's internal affairs would not be permitted to come up for discussion.

It was not evident until a further round of "shuttle diplomacy" by Cordovez to the region's three capitals the following March that there was any substance in this so-called "flexibility." The Afghans, on behalf of Moscow, made no tangible concessions and in both public and private statements the position remained deadlocked: Soviet troops would only withdraw when the situation within Afghanistan stabilised and "external interference" had ceased, with guarantees against its revival. In other words, when armed opposition to the communist regime in Kabul had been crushed. More important, Moscow gave no practical sign of a readiness to pull out its forces. On the contrary, their numbers had been increased during the previous year from 85,000 to 100,000 and later to 105,000. Their supply lines were reinforced, with pipelines and storage depots under construction, airfields expanded, roads widened and their operations against the guerillas continued at as high a level as ever.

It was obvious to everyone — except possibly to Babrak Karmal's PDPA comrades — that the regime in Kabul would collapse very rapidly indeed were Soviet forces to withdraw. Moscow's motives in encouraging the continuation of the UN process by making a display of "flexibility" were seen by Pakistani and other foreign officials as having the following aims:

● To divert attention from their own central and primary role in the crisis.

● To soften international criticism of their actions. This was marked in the run-up to the November 1982 General Assembly debate.

● To secure at least tacit recognition of the PDPA regime as a legitimate government, by drawing Pakistan into direct talks at some future stage.

Moscow plainly hoped to capitalise on the attraction a political solution would hold for Pakistan, a developing country bearing the burden of 2.8 million Afghan refugees in areas ill-suited to accommodate them. The Soviets had at all times sought to take the opportunity to threaten Pakistani officials in contacts with them. The Soviets threatened in no uncertain terms in 1981 to close down the Soviet-built Gudda power station, the Soviet-run Karachi steel mill and so on. Moscow apparently encouraged Kabul to finance, train and equip Pakistani dissidents to despatch them over the country's long borders to carry out acts of sabotage and assassination. For a military administration obsessed with provincial movements pressing for autonomy and with law-and-order generally, the activities of small numbers of armed militants received attention out of all proportion to their effectiveness — as the Soviets no doubt hoped they would.

Prior to the first round of Geneva talks there were several hundred minor incursions by both Afghan aircraft and ground forces into Pakistan's airspace and territory. In some cases sheer incompetence in map reading may have been to blame. But the implied threat of "hot pursuit" raids was there, and it was remarkable that following the Israeli intervention into Lebanon, banned political parties in Pakistan made great play of fears of another "Lebanon" occurring in Pakistan as a result of Zia's robust support for the refugees and resistance.

During the latter half of 1982 these incursions abruptly ceased. Or at least they appeared to cease, if only in terms of Pakistan's publicity efforts in the country's censored press. The Soviets and their Kabul clients were apparently using the carrot and stick effectively if crudely to press Islamabad down a conciliatory path leading eventually to recognition of the Kabul regime.

The UN, somewhat naively, found room for optimism in the June talks — the fact that both sides pledged themselves willing to continue was reason enough for optimism. Cordovez continued to make trips to Tehran, Kabul and Islamabad and later to Moscow to ensure that at the very least the appearance of progress was maintained. There was no *real* room for optimism other than what appeared to be the emergence of a Soviet policy which had hitherto remained hidden. Cordovez found Pakistan's stand one of intransigence: he grabbed one Western ambassador by the arm and urged the envoy to use his influence to "modify" Islamabad's position.

Movement did become discernible following Cordovez's round of visits to South Asia in February, 1983. With Soviet prodding, Kabul seemed willing to soften its insistence on priority being given to the question of "non-interference." A senior Soviet foreign service official confided to a neutral country's representative in Islamabad that Moscow was eager to persuade Pakistan to allow the UN to establish and then monitor a "pilot project" involving the return of a sample number of refugees to Afghanistan. Earlier, the same official had been busy behind the scenes, especially among Third World embassies, by saying, yes, the Soviets would indeed withdraw — but the status quo in Kabul could not under any circumstances be a matter for negotiation. He hinted that Babrak Karmal's future was not seen by Moscow as a precondition for preservation of the PDPA regime.

President Zia attended the funeral of Leonid Brezhnev in Moscow. He was selected by the new Soviet leader and former KGB boss, Yuri Andropov, for a tête-à-tête. This clearly impressed the stout cavalryman, for he spoke on his return home from the Soviet capital of a "new freshness" in the Soviet attitude.

On closer inspection, his meeting with Andropov differed in style and presentation, not content. Gone were the implied threats, the rough language and crude intimidation he and his ministers had come to expect from overbearing Soviets in the past. Instead, Andropov was studiously courteous. "You want our troops out of Afghanistan. We want our troops out of Afghanistan. We both want the same thing . . ." was how one close observer described Andropov's approach. It was the red carpet treatment literally and metaphorically, and the little general was not immune.

Asked for their impression of the state of the negotiations, American diplomats were less than forthcoming, spectacularly so. But they made it clear that they had every faith in Pakistan's willingness to maintain its principled stand. Faith was about the right word to use, too, for other foreign observers were not so confident.

"Zia's state visit to Washington may have gone too well," said

179

one ambassador. "The Pakistanis seem to be saying: well, in December we convinced the Americans of our good intentions. Now let's get on with the job ourselves." Was Pakistan's Foreign Ministry overconfident? There seemed to be differences between the Foreign Ministry in Islamabad and Zia's closest advisers, that much was clear. And the foreign service officer directly involved in the talks seemed to place considerable weight on the nuances of drafting settlement clauses.

Cordovez certainly had drafted several substantive proposals. They took the form of issues raised by both sides, but linked together loosely. The aim was to introduce steps towards a comprehensive settlement by means of limited, phased stages. "It's full of blank spaces," said one observer in Islamabad in February, "and Cordovez is here again to try and fill them in."

At the root of the principles, communiqués and closely-held proposals lay a number of very real obstacles which no neat drafting or phrasing could overcome:

● The Soviets were not prepared to compromise over the nature of the future regime in Kabul. It would have to be Marxist-Leninist. Soviet troops would therefore have to remain, as no communist authority in Afghanistan could survive the day without them. The resistance had steadily increased its military challenge, while the PDPA was still deeply divided.

● The resistance, despite its ideological and regional differences, would not recognise the results of the talks until its own people were represented. The guerillas expressed the determination not to deal with the PDPA, but with the Soviets. The guerillas insisted there were only two issues to be discussed with the Soviets should such negotiations ever materialise: the manner and timing of an unconditional Soviet withdrawal. For their part, the Russians refused to accept the existence of a resistance movement.

● No one group or individual among either refugees or resistance fighters seemed capable of representing the Afghan people as a whole. On the face of it, the traditionalist elements appeared to be the most likely leadership to be willing to negotiate a compromise solution. Yet Pakistan clearly backed the most militant and "fundamentalist" trend which superficially at least took a hard line on the UN peace talks. The Islamic revolutionaries insisted on establishing a truly Islamic state in Kabul — and that would be something Moscow would not contemplate other than in a cosmetic sense of the word "Islamic."

● Iran held observer status at the talks, but refused to support the negotiations until such time as the *Mujehadeen* it supported were present. Iran meanwhile was stepping up its support for pro-Tehran Shia guerillas in central and western Afghanistan. No agreement would be worth the paper on which it was written without at least Iran's tacit acceptance of its contents.

Geneva negotiations resumed on April 11, 1983. The Pakistani and Afghan foreign ministers adjourned after two weeks to consult their respective governments. Mr. Cordovez declared himself "very satisfied" with the talks. A communiqué said the objectives had been drawn up, the "inter-relationship between the component elements of the settlement" had been agreed, and a timetable produced for implementation of the plan. The two delegations were due back in Switzerland on June 16 for what was supposed to be a brief meeting to finalise an agreement.

A considerable amount of last-minute delaying tactics were expected, because the basic positions of the two governments seemed to be far apart, at least on the ground. But the Afghan resistance leaders were worried. They had good cause to be.

The NWFP Refugee Commission imposed travel restrictions on Afghan refugees and resistance spokesmen seeking air tickets out of the country. A second move was made in the first week of April, a few days before the second round of talks in Geneva began. Officials from the Pakistan Refugee Commission's intelligence unit approached the two main resistance alliance headquarters in Peshawar and verbally ordered them to stop publishing their newspapers, or at least to submit a written application to Sheikh Abdullah, the Commissioner, for approval to continue publication. Five major newspapers were affected, and one English-language monthly bulletin, the editor of which was told over the telephone to discourage foreigners from visiting his office. The order emanated from the federal authorities in Islamabad, and it was followed by a further set of verbal instructions to move the resistance groups' political offices out of Peshawar city to the outskirts.

The Afghans involved took little notice, insisting that until these instructions were put down on paper they would continue. They did not fail to notice, however, that on April 16 Tehran Radio broadcast an Interior Ministry announcement that all Afghans in Iran should apply for new identity papers, and that travel between Iranian towns was prohibited with immediate effect without residence papers and the appropriate travel documents. Ostensibly both the Pakistani and Iranian moves had nothing directly to do with the UN talks, but were the result of official concern over deteriorating border security.

Resistance and refugee spokesmen privately feared that what Pakistan was doing was preparing the way for a political compromise involving the return of the refugees, or at least some of them. By moving the resistance offices into tribal territory, for instance, the Pakistanis could severely curtail access by foreign journalists to the resistance. That would mean that Pakistan would in large measure be able not only to control the individual resistance groups once they had been split up and dispersed further afield, but would be able to control the news output from Afghanistan to a considerable degree.

The next logical step, the Afghans feared, would be that Pakistan would promote one of its protégés in the resistance, such as Gulbaddin Hekmatyar or Rasul Saiaf, into the limelight where they would announce formally that they were prepared to abide by the agreement and return to Afghanistan. Tame Pakistani television crews and newsmen would then report a symbolic progress of carefully-selected refugees back into Afghanistan under the supervision of UN field teams. It would, in other words, amount to a sellout. That was how many Afghans saw the progress made in Geneva. A third round of talks in June failed to make substantial progress. The Soviets demanded international guarantees for Afghanistan, but refused to provide a timetable for a withdrawal. Once again, Iran did not participate.

"We can deal with the Russians," said one guerilla commander. "And we can deal with Babrak Karmal. It may take us 50 years, but we will. But can we trust our friends in Pakistan? We may well succeed on the battlefield, but our concern is now whether we will lose the war in Islamabad and Geneva."

Options

By April, 1983, a debate had surfaced on the fourth floor of the US Department of State over American policy on Afghanistan. This is where policy is implemented and discussed on a daily basis — it is the shop floor of foreign policy, the business end. It would not take a great deal to change the existing thrust of Afghan policy. Afghanistan is an esoteric subject. It has no place of its own in domestic American politics — it does not compare with the Cuban, Polish or Palestinian issues which, quite apart from their relative proximity and strategic importance, have large immigrant communities in North America. There are few Afghan "specialists" in government; the issue is an appendage tucked onto the end of memoranda and proposals put up by the numerous Soviet desk officers, China-watchers and officials hungry for reliable information on what is really going on inside Iran today.

There is enough going on in the world, anyway. Washington is trying to breathe life into its Middle East peace initiative, it must respond to Moscow's moves on nuclear arms control, it seeks Congressional approval to aid El Salvador's soldiers against rebels so American troops won't have to go there, it has to speed up arms deliveries to Thailand in the face of renewed threats from Vietnam. The diffuse nature of American foreign policy formulation does not help either. The Department of Defense, for example, will publicly cite Afghanistan and Pakistan in its public presentations on the Soviet threat, as it sees it, to the Persian Gulf. Afghanistan will come up in speeches on arms control and the alleged use of chemical and biological agents in Asia. The main problem is that the Afghan issue is a vacuum in Washington because there is no effective, well-informed lobby which can provoke or reject new ideas. There is no sounding board. Afghanistan is like the Baluch question; it is an area no one knows very much about, and ambitious academics, diplomats and pundits searching for opportunities to make their mark can seize upon it and come up with something which an equally ambitious but more influential assistant secretary up on the seventh floor has been waiting to hear. The whole process is tediously slow; an evolutionary turn in policy can take a year or two to work its way through.

Afghanistan has provided the Reagan administration with a useful stick with which to beat the Soviets, verbally at least. "It has been a knee-jerk issue for the Republican administration," said one Washington *aficionado.* "But there is a tendency to talk very loudly and do very little. That's a characteristic of this government. Politicians always want foreign policy to be 'consistent' and that means over-simplified. To be effective, foreign policy must be anything but. It should mean being able to carry out apparently contradictory policies towards different and often opposing powers without being seen to do so." But Afghanistan is merely regarded in Washington as a far-off, unimportant place which has been violated by Soviet force of arms — no more, no less.

The debate is of considerable importance. It comes at a decisive stage of UN negotiations which must either result in substantial progress in the form of a draft treaty, or face deferment for a further year or more. The debate coincides with questions over America's role in Sino-Soviet talks and the controversy over whether America should seek normalisation with Vietnam or actively support the Cambodian coalition. In South Asia Pakistan's dependence on the US for economic and military assistance will undoubtedly increase. The drop in world oil prices will reduce the Gulf market for Pakistani labour which has accounted for more than half Pakistan's total foreign exchange earnings — in 1982 a record US$2.2 billion. It is Pakistan which has so far kept the "window" open to resistance and refugee leaders and which may be coming round to consider direct talks with the Soviet-backed PDPA regime in Kabul. And if policy is changed, it will have an impact which will survive the 1984 presidential elections to some extent, and set the basis for the incoming administration.

The debators can be roughly divided into two. There are those who argue that the Soviets have no intention of withdrawing, that they will prevail eventually over the guerillas. The US should accept the Soviet presence in Afghanistan as a *fait accompli.* On the other side are individuals who believe a small-scale, arm's length programme of military aid to the resistance would have a decisive impact on the conflict. Both views share a common problem: the paucity of accurate, reliable assessments of what is likely to occur in the key neighbouring states of Iran and Pakistan.

A degree of wishful thinking pervades US State Department thinking. In an interview conducted with the Urdu-language newspaper *Nawa-i-Waqt*, Ronald Spiers, the American Ambassador to Pakistan, was frank on several issues. More than he intended to be, in fact, because he had been assured that the interview was for background use. But his words were recorded and printed verbatim.

Asked about the efforts to seek a political solution, he said: "I don't see such a possibility in the near future; Pakistan will not recognise Babrak Karmal's Government or withdraw support from the *Mujehadeen.* To withdraw its forces from Afghanistan, the Soviet conditions will be recognition of the Babrak Karmal Government and abandonment of the *Mujehadeen.* But it would be impossible for Pakistan to accept these conditions, as it is not in a position to seal the Durand Line. We fully agree with Pakistan that a government has been imposed on the Afghan people, with the help of a foreign power, which they are not prepared to recognise. So they will continue their struggle which is becoming very effective. But still, this struggle has been ineffective in forcing the evacuation of Soviet troops from Afghanistan's soil. Because of these factors, the need for a political solution attains basic importance. Some Indians have said to me that the United States wishes to prolong the Afghan issue. It is an incorrect charge. This issue is a constant source of vexation for the peoples of Pakistan and Afghanistan. America would like to solve the Afghanistan issue because it wants to develop its relations with the Soviet Union in the right direction — and it is not possible when 100,000 Soviet troops are present in Afghanistan."

Asked if the US would be prepared to join in an international guarantee of non-interference in Afghanistan, Spiers said: "If the Soviet Union fears that Pakistan, the US or any other country will set up an anti-Soviet front by making any hostile Afghan government an ally, a guarantee can be given to the Soviet Union on the pattern of Austria and Finland that such will not be the case. In my opinion, Afghanistan is not a threat to the Soviet Union and if the Soviet Union wants a guarantee of it — an Afghan government, chosen by the people — Pakistan and the US can collectively provide such a guarantee. If the Soviet Union withdraws its troops from Afghanistan, the confrontation will come to an end automatically, since the Afghan people will have no need to fight against anyone."

Pakistan's aim to "seal" the Durand Line may be physically impossible, but its inviolability in terms of bilateral and multilateral agreements is probably *the* major Pakistani aim in the UN talks and it is precisely this which matches Kabul's insistence on non-interference and brings the two regimes to the negotiating table. The spectre of Pushtunistan is never far from the Punjabi military government's mind in Islamabad. Pakistan supports some *Mujehadeen* and not others. The idea that a rugged, sparsely populated and landlocked Asian country with porous borders and a Muslim patchwork of inhabitants can be "Finlandised" is clearly impracticable. The suggestion that the confrontation would end "automatically" if the Soviets withdrew and Afghans were allowed to "choose" their "own government" flies in the face of everything that is known about the place and its history. The war would not end, particularly if a radical resistance group such as Hekmatyar's Hezb-i-Islami was lifted into the driving seat in Kabul with Pakistani, Iranian and Soviet help. How would the United States provide a "guarantee" to the Soviets over a future regime's neutrality in the face of the war of influence fought by all neighbouring states in the region?

At the root of the debate over US policy in Washington lies a moral dilemma facing American policy-makers generally. To what extent is the US justified in using military, diplomatic and covert means to protect what it has traditionally regarded as basic social values and a democratic way of life? To what extent may policy-makers justify to the electorate a programme designed to pre-empt a perceived threat to US interests? Is interference in the internal affairs of a foreign state acceptable if it deters the development of a hostile, totalitarian regime, whether it be in the Western Hemisphere, the Pacific or in South Asia? American experience of managing power in, say, Vietnam and Iran has considerably chastened those who regard America as the "good guy" standing up for the underdog, with a responsibility for protecting people abroad from their own worst instincts.

The furore over the West European allies' decision to proceed with the Soviet oil pipeline was a case in point. European misgivings over America's firm stance on nuclear arms and public demonstrations against the decision to install Pershing II and Cruise missiles in Europe to redress the growing imbalance in nuclear theatre forces have jolted American resolve. Differences of emphasis between Washington and its NATO allies over policy towards Israel's continued settlement of Palestinian territory is another example.

What is the limit to which the American taxpayer is prepared to underwrite the security of allies unwilling to take their share of the economic and political risks of preserving freedom? For example, can the US administration be justified in using its US$3.2 billion military assistance and economic aid programme for Pakistan as "leverage" over Islamabad in its treatment of the Afghan resistance and its role in the UN talks?

Knowledge of what is happening, and what is possible, on the ground is affected by a self-imposed passivity on the one hand and American public perceptions on the other. Before the Soviet invasion of Afghanistan, President Zia of Pakistan was portrayed in American media as the country's strongman, and he was usually shown in his general's uniform, dripping with medals and gold braid, an image of militarism most Americans find contemptible and amusing. During Zia's 1982 visit to Washington, the public impression had altered. Zia was shown in national, civil dress, a modest father-figure deftly and quietly parrying loaded questions from newsmen. He was cast as a bastion of the free world, a buffer against Soviet expansionism. Zia had benefited from Washington's need to "sell" Pakistan to Congress as a worthwhile recipient of American largesse.

American diplomatic communities in New Delhi, Islamabad and Kabul are limited in their contacts and sources and the Afghan "vacuum" ensures that the evidence produced tends to be given equal weight with numbing effects. Restrictions are largely imposed on diplomatic access to people who matter; but it is also true to say that Washington's insistence on a low profile in countries which depend heavily on American help aggravates the peculiarly American trait of fraternising with a social elite which very often is of little if any political relevance. Americans the world over tend to keep to themselves; in Muslim states the sense of isolation and innate local hostility and suspicion reinforces the limits on American political reporting. Trivial — and not so trivial — slights by Pakistan directed towards the American diplomatic community are ignored, with the result that they increase and help instill a sense of rage, cynicism and helplessness on the part of those charged with making dispassionate assessments of the local body politic. Americans want to feel loved, and they feel hurt and bemused when they are not. Loss of mutual respect is the first casualty; accurate and balanced understanding is the second and more important loss.

The debate over Afghanistan in Washington takes place in this context.

Advocates of both arguments in Washington over Afghanistan accept the view — incidentally, one which is held in other NATO capitals — that there is no indication of a serious intent to withdraw Soviet troops on any significant scale until the PDPA regime in Afghanistan is consolidated, that is to say the threat from the resistance removed one way or another. Diplomatic sources point to reasons of prestige and the ideological imperative of the USSR in preserving its gains in the region.

187

It is at this point that the debate begins. The one argument presupposes that the weight of Soviet resources and the ability of the Red Army to adapt to unfavourable military conditions will eventually bring home to Moscow that it will in the long term prevail. The point at which Moscow realises this it automatically loses whatever interest it might have had previously in a political compromise. Proponents of this viewpoint point out the Soviet attempts to create a new national government in Kabul of reconciled elements of the rival Parcham and Khalq factions and the use of the Fatherland Front as a magnet for support outside the confines of the PDPA. They draw upon evidence of long-term Soviet infrastructure programmes in Afghanistan as an indication that Moscow takes a very long view of the problem at the end of which the Marxist-Leninist status quo in Kabul will not only be preserved but reinforced, even if it takes more resources to achieve that. *De jure* still an independent state, Afghanistan may well have in reality to be colonised, annexed or partitioned to achieve Soviet goals, but the "disengagement" lobby argues that the costs for the USSR will remain manageable.

In other words, during the period in which the new Soviet leader Yuri Andropov establishes himself in power, the US should do whatever it can bilaterally and multilaterally to encourage the Soviets to enter into the UN proximity talks through Kabul's involvement by formulating a workable compromise. Clearly, the argument runs, any regime in Kabul with any chance of survival must be friendly towards its northern neighbour; it is only natural to expect the USSR to exercise control of Afghanistan's foreign policy and external security. The war may linger on, but American concerns should be directed at stabilising the region in terms of a rapprochement between India and Pakistan and in terms of achieving Soviet and the Kabul regime's recognition of the territorial integrity of Pakistan's border provinces.

The argument implies that an upsurge in resistance activity would encourage a Soviet increase in pressure on Islamabad and Tehran, that a failure to accept the political "reality" of the Soviet occupation and its eventual success in legitimising the Kabul regime would widen the scope of the conflict to neighbouring states. Continued American support for the Afghan refugees (America supplies more than half the world's relief resources) and public assertions of backing for the resistance would, they say, encourage the Soviets to seize whatever opportunities might arise in Iran following the anticipated demise of the Ayatollah Khomeini.

Furthermore, the US would be perceived as drawing closer to the unpopular and inherently unstable military dictatorship in Pakistan. There are, these officials say, no conditions in which American bases would be established on Pakistani territory and certainly no scenarios in which American military advisers, let alone combat troops, could be committed to Pakistan in the event of an external or internal conflict threatening Zia or his military successors. The United States therefore could not afford to mislead Pakistan into thinking that it could rely on Washington for its security and a continued impasse in Geneva would inevitably push Pakistan into an untenable position of potential embarrassment to Washington.

The central weakness in this argument, its critics claim, is that it overlooks the fact that the Soviets entered Afghanistan to shore up the PDPA, not to engage the guerillas which Moscow clearly underrated. Instead, rather than "prevailing" at the outset, which the Soviet leadership obviously thought it would, it found itself embroiled in an ever-increasing counter-insurgency role. The prospects of "prevailing" dwindled as time went by. The PDPA remained as unpopular as ever, the indigenous communist forces as unreliable as ever if not more so, and the Red Army's inability to understand let alone deal with a populist guerilla opposition all added up to a singularly remote chance of "prevailing" — at any stage. Hence the uncharacteristically friendly chat with General Zia.

The "contras" in Washington argue that while the USSR finds its present commitment to the continued military occupation of Afghanistan manageable in terms of lives and cost, they say this is because the resistance has failed to inflict decisive defeats on the communists. It is the lack of sufficient weapons of the appropriate effectiveness — in other words, a shortage of basic military skills and the air defence equipment to go with them — which accounts for the failure to raise the level of warfare to pressure Moscow to take peace talks seriously.

The advocates of *greater* US involvement suggest that for guerillas to increase their military assets in the overall equation, direct aid is needed from external sources in the form of training and specialised arms to mobilise not only more manpower, but to increase the guerillas' organisational abilities. Such aid need not be directly associated with Washington, much in the way that small quantities of Egyptian and Chinese arms are not directly related to the West now. A modest programme of military assistance should be channelled to the new generation of regional guerilla *commanders*, bypassing the official resistance-in-exile. Above all, it would help produce a degree of self-sufficiency among guerillas fighting in-country and relieve some of the pressure on Pakistan and Iran. Moscow would receive a "signal" that the war would not be allowed to wither away into a forgotten sideshow, and that the costs would rise substantially.

Both camps in the debate are unable to assess accurately the full impact of the war on the USSR itself. There is a view that in its need to justify its own defence spending the West has exaggerated the strengths of the Red Army. Another is that the lack of a free press in Russia does not necessarily give Moscow a free hand in the war; gossip, rumour and recollections of some 250,000 conscripts who have served there may have marked public opinion.

It is also suggested that while the USSR may have some 4.7 million people in uniform, the presence of 105,000 troops in Afghanistan and a further 30,000 on the border is more than half the strength of the Soviet forces in East Germany. The continued deployment of divisions at a high state of readiness in the southern theatre may in fact detract from Soviet military preparedness elsewhere and aggravate a growing manpower shortage in the armed forces. No one really knows the answers to these issues.

The argument that the US should help the guerillas with military assistance is also based on what appears to be growing Soviet concern over the future political reliability of its Muslim population groups along its southern border. A viable Muslim resistance in Afghanistan capable of seriously threatening the Soviets' grip on the country would not encourage Moscow to actively interfere in revolutionary Iran — rather the reverse, in fact. Furthermore, a coherent and self-contained guerilla movement would complicate Sino-Soviet talks aimed at resolving the long-standing differences between the two communist superpowers.

A long-term assessment of the implications of a decisive war of resistance in Afghanistan is difficult to obtain, primarily because no one is able to predict with any certainty the fate of Iran and its relations with Moscow when the Ayatollah Khomeini dies, other than to note a steady deterioration between the two states. Once again, although Afghanistan is the "hinge" tying in Central Asia with Iran, with the Indian sub-continent and China, it begs questions on issues which the few available "Afghan experts" inside and outside government are plainly unable to answer without recourse to lobbies and interest groups with far greater influence on policy formulation than they are able to command in their own right.

All indications are that Moscow will maintain its presence in Afghanistan. The Kabul regime's status quo will be preserved. The costs of continued military occupation are so far acceptable and likely to remain so for at least the short term. Nevertheless, while the UN peace talks continue, Moscow has shown greater moderation in its dealings with Pakistan in the hope of drawing concessions from Islamabad. Moscow's attitude towards Pakistan is restrained by the fear that overt hostility would push the military dictatorship closer to the US.

Iran remains an observer at the UN peace talks, but on the ground it appears to be hardening its attitude towards Moscow and towards its own Communist Party, the Tudeh. It also appears to be stepping up training and equipping Afghan resistance groups of a revolutionary nature and particularly those operating in central and western areas. Iranian sources suggest that an end to the Iran-Iraq conflict in the Gulf would mean a considerable increase in Iranian involvement in the Afghan war. Iran is probably the most important single factor in determining the final outcome in Afghanistan, yet remains the least accessible issue for Western decision-making.

President Zia has attempted to legitimise and consolidate what appears to be a permanent military role in government very largely through championing the plight of some three million Afghan refugees on Pakistani territory and by giving tacit or unofficial support to those resistance groups seen as useful assets in the country's domestic and foreign policy concerns, particularly over the Pushtunistan question. Domestically, there seems no alternative to Zia — but of course he is largely responsible for the disintegration of the political opposition.

Zia's Islamisation policies are aimed at preserving the military's hold on government, but little progress has been made because of competing Islamic interests: Jamaat Islami Pakistan, the radical and revolutionary party; the *pirs* or traditional saints; the *ulema* or religious scholars; the *mullahs* or parish priests and finally the executive itself — the army, police and civil service — which is Islamic in a secular, 19th-century sense. Zia has used periodic mass arrests and restrictions on leading political figures to retard his political opposition. The military has not developed institutions capable of absorbing or focusing the aspirations of a nation which consists of three strongly-nationalist provinces dominated by the military power of the fourth. At the same time the country has undergone considerable economic and social change, mainly in the form of rapid urbanisation. Law and order is deteriorating, while Zia's Government is not unnaturally preoccupied by concern for the security of its long frontiers.

While Pakistan's military rulers have achieved considerable

prominence internationally and reinforced its non-aligned position in the wake of the Soviet invasion, nevertheless the risks in security and economic terms of a continued crisis in Afghanistan are mounting. Zia may well feel compelled to make concessions to Kabul — possibly in the form of direct talks — in return for a treaty securing its Baluch and Pushtun borderlands. Pakistan would have considerable difficulty in forcing the refugees and resistance-in-exile to return and could not in a physical sense seal the border. But it could do a great deal to hamper the guerillas' ability to prosecute the war inside Afghanistan.

In Kabul the PDPA "rules" in name only, and with the support of a Soviet military and civil effort which is inexorably increasing as the divisions within the regime isolate it still further. These divisions between irrevocably divided factions have severely constrained the indigenous security forces in their attempts to deal with the resistance. The prospect of the PDPA "requesting" further Soviet military support, especially if the UN negotiations fail or are deferred, is a very real one although the performance of the Afghan armed forces is slowly improving.

Guerillas opposing the PDPA regime and Soviet occupation forces have succeeded in maintaining the level of military activity, although two distinct trends emerged during the course of 1982/83. First, there were signs of greater coordination and cooperation among some commanders in northern areas, with indications the conflict could be entering a stage Mao called a "war of movement." Success was dependent on whether or not these commanders could enhance their prestige and influence sufficiently to free themselves from the resistance-in-exile and the impact of Iranian and Pakistani policies on the conduct of guerilla operations. This would in turn depend on their ability to acquire and organise the means to wage war and to provide sufficient infrastructure to hold on to the civilian support base in their respective areas. The second trend was the growth in the "war of influence" among the guerillas, largely the result of Iranian and Pakistani policies of *divide et empira*. This has led to gains being made by the PDPA regime in its psychological warfare effort and intelligence operations.

No, Afghanistan is not Russia's Vietnam or Moscow's Algeria. Yet what observers have failed to recognise so far is that just as Americans suffer from a "moral dilemma" over their international role, so too the Soviets are blinkered by their own ideological contradiction.

Forced in 1980 to take on a steadily increasing burden of the conflict, Moscow finds itself in the unenviable position where it must contemplate a substantial increase in its economic and military commitment if the PDPA is to survive. An intensification of military operations would, however, not only aggravate international opinion and jeopardise the UN peace initiative, but it would further isolate the PDPA from the Afghan population at large and deepen hostility within one faction towards the Babrak Karmal minority. In short, the Soviets cannot "win" politically. The Soviet effort has been largely focused on a campaign of physical attrition aimed at eradicating a few "reactionaries." Ironically, the more efforts are made to enforce the status quo in Kabul, the less viable the alien ideology of socialism will become in the country.

Afghanistan is a test of the very basis of Soviet foreign policy; it threatens the basic assumption of superpower prestige, the ideological imperative of Marxism-Leninism and the drive to secure territorial gains. A sense of failure would undoubtedly have a lasting impact on the way in which the Soviet leadership sees its future role on the international stage. It may in time be forced to face the unappetising and so far inconceivable notion that Marx is not on the side of the big battalions, that the Soviet system does not travel well. There may be some brief consolation in the lessons drawn from guerilla campaigns elsewhere in history; irregular warfare has seldom succeeded on its own — external factors are usually decisive in the end. But if Washington hesitates to aid the guerillas for fear of prejudicing its delicate relations with other states in the region, the same cannot be said of Iran. Tehran's revolutionaries have a momentum all of their own and a deeply-held belief in their mission to export resurgent Islam. The war in Afghanistan may turn out to be merely a precursor of a drama in which Islam and the USSR edge towards confrontation.

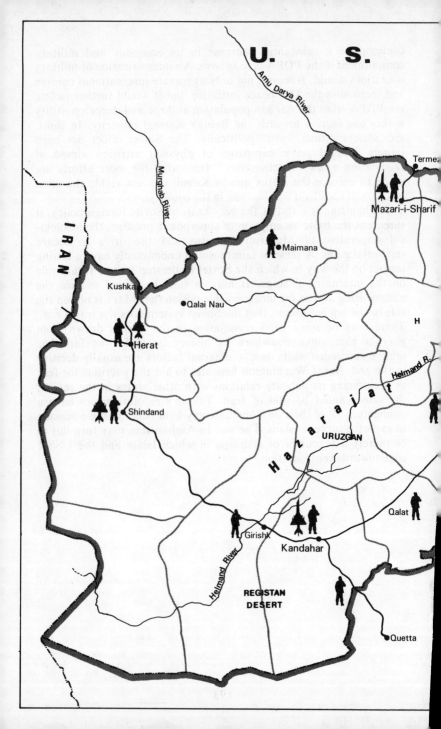

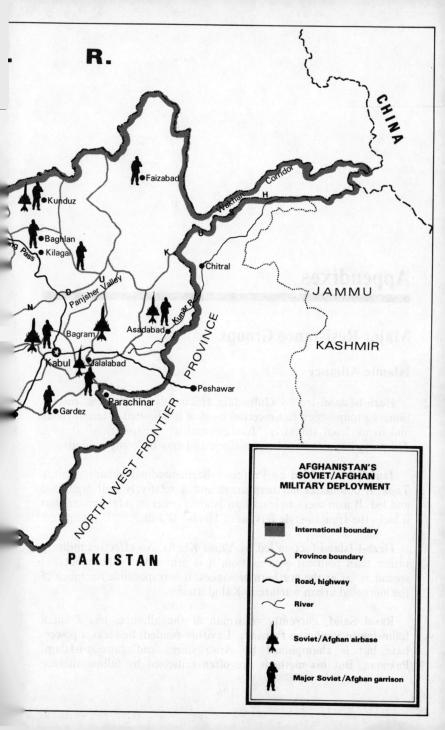

AFGHANISTAN'S SOVIET/AFGHAN MILITARY DEPLOYMENT

International boundary

Province boundary

Road, highway

River

Soviet/Afghan airbase

Major Soviet/Afghan garrison

Appendixes

Major Resistance Groups

Islamic Alliance

Hezb-i-Islami led by Gulbaddin Hekmatyar. A radical, revolutionary group which has received most of the limited external funds and arms from similarly "fundamentalist" organisations abroad. The party has a controversial history, and may be losing ground.

Jamiat-i-Islami led by Professor Barhanuddin Rabbani. Mainly Tajik, it dominates northern areas and is relatively well organised and led. It also seeks to install an Islamic order in Afghanistan, but it lacks the Iranian-style fervour of Hezb-i-Islami.

Hezb-i-Islami faction led by Yunis Khalis. An effective military rather than political organisation, it is primarily Pushtun but has spread as far as the northern provinces. It is responsible for much of the increased urban warfare in Kabul itself.

Rasul Saiaf, currently chairman of the alliance, has a small following in Paghman Province. Lavishly-funded, he lacks a power-base but is championed by Arab states and Jamaat-i-Islami Pakistan. But his methods are often criticised by fellow alliance

196

members.

There are three small factions in the Islamic alliance, two of which broke away from the rival Islamic Unity's Harakat Inquilab-i-Islami and one from Sibghatullah Mojaddedi's ANLF.

The Islamic Alliance is considered to be more effective than its rivals inside Afghanistan, largely because it receives better external support. However, the alliance is very much a paper exercise and has limited relevance on the battlefield itself.

Islamic Unity

Harakat Inquilab-i-Islami led by Maulavi Nabi Mohammadi is probably the largest single resistance organisation in Afghanistan, combining traditional elements with urban intelligentsia, but is poorly equipped and badly organised. It straddles the middle ground between extreme "fundamentalism" on the one hand and nationalist and leftist groups on the other.

National Islamic Front for the Liberation of Afghanistan led by Pir Syed Ahmad al-Gailani is a traditional, hereditary and largely family following, mainly Pushtun. While Gailani still has support for his democratic, nationalist views in the West, NIFA has failed to achieve effective organisation and is very poorly equipped. It is now limited to half a dozen provinces in the south and south-east and appears to be shrinking in size.

Afghan National Liberation Front led by Sibghatullah Mojaddedi is traditional, Pushtun and badly-organised with few external sources of military and financial support. Mojaddedi has considerable political influence personally.

In addition to the above two alliances, there are several smaller resistance organisations in exile, as well as independent guerilla groups operating inside Afghanistan without official representation either in Pakistan or Iran. Many groups are self-proclaimed royalists and nationalists. Others have a history of Marxist-Leninist support among the urban classes and are pro-Peking in some cases.

The differences among all Afghan resistance groups are primarily ones of personality and ethnic or tribal origin. Those groups trained by, or based in, Iran appear to be growing in importance, especially in the Shia minority.

Index

Bibliography

Books

Abdalati, Hammadah, *Islam in Focus*, Riyadh, 1975.

Akbar S. Ahmed, *Social and Economic Change in the Tribal Areas*, Oxford University Press, Karachi, 1977.

Arnold, Anthony, *Afghanistan: The Soviet Invasion in Perspective*, Hoover Institute Press, 1981.

Bennigsen, Alexandre and Broxup, Marie, *The Islamic Threat to the Soviet State*, Croom Helm, 1983.

Chaliand, Gerard, *Rapport sur la Resistance Afghane*, Berger-Levrault, Paris, 1981.

Dietl, Wilhelm, *Heiliger Krieg fur Allah*, Kindler-Verlag, 1983.

Griffiths, John C., *Afghanistan: Key to a Continent*, Andre Deutsch, 1981.

Gunston, Bill, *An Illustrated Guide to the Modern Soviet Air Force*, Salamander Books, London.

Harrison, Selig S., *In Afghanistan's Shadow: Baluch Nationalism and Soviet Temptations*, Carnegie Endowment for International Peace, 1981.

Hyman, Anthony, *Afghanistan Under Soviet Domination: 1964-81*, Macmillan 1982.

Isby, David C., *Weapons and Tactics of the Soviet Army*, Janes, 1981.

Jansen, Godfrey, *Militant Islam*, Pan Books, 1979.

Marwat, Fazal-Ur-Rahim Khan, *The Basmachi Movement in Soviet Central Asia*, Area Study Centre (Central Asia), Peshawar University, 1981.

Maududi, Syed Abdul, *Fundamentals of Islam*, Islamic Publications, Lahore, 1975.

Maududi, Syed Abdul, *Towards Understanding Islam*, Lahore, 1978.

203

Nayar, Kuldip, *Report on Afghanistan*, Allied Publishers, New Delhi, 1981.

Newell, Richard S. and Peabody, Nancy, *The Struggle for Afghanistan*, Cornell University, 1973.

Wiener, F., *The Armies of the Warsaw Pact Nations*, Carl Ueberreuter Publishers, 3rd ed., 1981.

Yodfat, Aryeh Y., *The Soviet Union and the Arabian Peninsula*, Croom Helm, 1983.

Periodicals, articles

Adamec, Ludwig W., *Who's Who of Afghanistan*, first supplement, Akademische Druk, Graz, 1979.

Barry, Michael, *Afghanistan: A Human Disaster Area*, Commentary, August 1982.

Beck, Denis and Fitzpatrick, Manalo, Sanders and Williams, *Afghanistan: What Impact on Soviet Tactics?* Military Review, March, 1982.

Bordewich, Fergus M., *The Pakistan Army: Sword of Islam*, Asia, Sept/Oct., 1982.

Deriabin, and Bagley, *Fedorchuk, the KGB, and the Soviet Succession*, Orbis, autumn 1982.

Broun, Janice A., *The Muslim Challenge Within the Soviet Union*, America, Feb, 12, 1983.

Broxup, Marie, *The Soviets in Afghanistan: The Anatomy of a Takeover*, Central Asian Survey.

Cockburn, Andrew, *Ivan The Terrible Soldier*, Harper's, March, 1983.

Davis, Tony, *Who is Winning?* Asiaweek, January 29, 1982.

Davis, Tony, *The Russians: Outcasts in a Hostile Land*, Bangkok Post, Dec. 27, 1981.

Donnelly, Christopher, *Soviet Operations and Tactics in Mountainous and Hilly Areas*, Soviet Studies, RMAS.

Donnelly, Christopher, *The Soviet Operation Maneuver Group: A Challenge for Nato*, Military Review, March, 1983.

Epstein, Edward J., *The Andropov File*, The New Republic, February 7, 1983.

Erickson, Professor J., *A Controversial Report on Afghanistan*, Pakistan Defence Journal, December 1981.

Feshbach, Murray, *A Different Crisis*, The Wilson Quarterly, Winter 1981.

Fink, Donald E., *Afghan Invasion Likened to 1968 Action*, Aviation Week and Space Technology, July 14, 1980.

Fullerton, J., *A Question of Firepower*, Far Eastern Economic Review (FEER), December 25, 1981; *Poisoned Earth Policy*, FEER, October 30, 1981; *The Patchwork Plan*, FEER, January 26, 1982; *The Blood Feud Goes On*, FEER, March 26, 1982; *Symptoms* of Change, FEER, July 23 1982; Shooting For The Top, FEER, October 8, 1982; A Rift Among Rebels, FEER, October 29, 1982; "1,000 Killed" In Afghan Tunnel Holocaust, Daily Telegraph, October 10, 1982; Many Soviet Deserters, Captives, Live Among Afghans, Philadelphia Inquirer, October 10, 1982; Afghan War Cost Russia £1 billion, Daily Telegraph, December 20, 1982; An Embattled Economy, FEER, December 24, 1982; Rouble Spells Trouble, FEER, March 31, 1983.

Gilette, Robert, Afghanistan: A Brutalizing War, International Herald Tribune, April 6, 1983.

Geraghty, Tony, The Secret Intelligence War Inside Afghanistan, Sunday Times, April 5, 1981.

Gray, Colin S., Reflections of Empire: The Soviet Connection, Military Review, January, 1982.

Griffith, William E., The USSR and Pakistan, Problems of Communism, Jan/Feb., 1982.

Harrison, Selig S., Fanning Flames in South Asia, Foreign Policy, Winter 1981/82.

Hart, Douglas M., Low-Intensity Conflict in Afganistan: The Soviet View, Survival, IISS, London Vol XXIV No. 2 March/April 1982.

Hutcheson, Major John M., Scorched-Earth Policy: Soviets in Afghanistan, Military Review, April, 1982.

Jacobsen, Philip, The Truth About Sasha's War, The Sunday Times, July 20, 1981; The Red Army Finally Gets a Chance To Test Its Stuff, Washington Post, February 13, 1983.

Kamrany, Nake M., Afghanistan Under Soviet Occupation, Current History, May, 1982.

Manning, Robert A., Overboard with General Zia, The New Republic.

Olcott, Martha Brill, Soviet Islam and World Revolution, World Politics, Vol. XXXIV No. 4 July, 1982.

Richter, William L., Pakistan: A New "Front-Line" State? Current History, May 1982.

Simons, Lewis M., Standoff in Afghanistan.

Stevens, Jenny and Marsh, Henry S., Surprise and Deception in Soviet Military Thought, Military Review, July 1982.

Rumer, Boris, Crushing The Afghans, The New Republic, April, 1982.

Wafadar, K., Afghanistan in 1981: The Struggle Intensifies, Asian Survey Vol. CC11 No. 2, February 1982.

Wimbush S. Enders and Broxup, Marie, The Central Asian Newsletter, Vol. 1 Nos 1-7, Vol 2 Nos. 1-2.

Van Hollen, Eliza, Afghanistan: A Year of Occupation, Feb. 1981; Afghanistan: 18 Months of Occupation; Afghanistan: Three Years of Occupation, December, 1982, US Dept. of State, Washington.